Immigration and Industrialization

JOHN E. BODNAR

Immigration and Industrialization

Ethnicity in an American Mill Town, 1870–1940

UNIVERSITY OF PITTSBURGH PRESS

This volume was published with the cooperation of the Pennsylvania Historical and Museum Commission in its continuing attempt to preserve the history of the people of the Commonwealth.

Published by the University of Pittsburgh Press, Pittsburgh, Pa. 15260
Copyright © 1977, University of Pittsburgh Press
All rights reserved
Feffer and Simons, Inc., London
Manufactured in the United States of America

Library of Congress Cataloging in Publication Data

Bodnar, John E.   1944–
  Immigration and industrialization.

  Bibliography: p. 199
  Includes index.
  1. Steelton, Pa.—Social conditions.   2.   Social classes—Pennsylvania—
Steelton—History.   3.   Alien labor—Pennsylvania—Steelton—
History.   4.   Iron and steel workers—Pennsylvania—Steelton—
History.   I.   Title.
HN80.S78B6   309.1'748'18   77–74549
ISBN 0-8229-3348-9

Grateful acknowledgment is made to Random House, Inc., for permission to reprint passages from *No Country for Old Men* by Warren Eyster.

For Eric and Brenna
so that they may know
their great-grandparents

Contents

Tables

Acknowledgments

The production of any book depends upon the assistance and encouragement of many individuals. Research for this study was aided repeatedly by staff at the Pennsylvania State Library, Harrisburg, the Pennsylvania Historical and Museum Commission, and the Immigration History Research Center of the University of Minnesota. Particularly appreciated is the kindness of John Badovinac of the Croatian Fraternal Union in allowing me to use its materials. Louis Rauco of the Pennsylvania State Library assisted me in securing local newspapers. My earliest efforts at obtaining data and oral interviews were enthusiastically assisted by Rev. Jerome Kucan, a Steelton Croatian. John Verbos of the Croatian community and Meter Dragovich of the Serbian community patiently provided information and valuable contacts for interviews. Important research assistance also came from Robert Plowman of the National Archives in Philadelphia, the Dauphin County Historical Society, the Eleutherian Mills Historical Library, Ronald Filipelli of the Pennsylvania State University Labor Archives, and Joseph DiSanto, United Steelworkers of America, Local 1688.

Individuals who offered critical remarks on various portions of the manuscript included Professors Robert Asher, Milton Cantor, Raymond Mohl, David Montgomery, and Bruce Stave. No person offered more generous advice, constructive criticism, and encouragement than A. William Hoglund, Professor of History, University of Connecticut. At the University of Pittsburgh Press, Frederick Hetzel retained an interest in the manuscript when my own wavered, and Catherine Marshall provided meticulous editorial work which improved the manuscript considerably. Finally, my wife Donna made the entire experience bearable. xi

Introduction

The mill towns and industrial districts which appeared in late-nineteenth-century America were obvious symbols of an emerging industrial society. Places such as Gary, Lackawanna, Homestead, Lorain, McKees Rocks, South Bethlehem, Sparrows Point, Youngstown, Weirton, Joliet, Whiting, Johnstown, and Braddock became both increasingly familiar and alike. Larger cities also acquired factories, mills, and districts populated exclusively by working people. The Cleveland "flats" or the south sides of Chicago and Pittsburgh were not unlike the smaller industrial towns with their sprawling mills, smoke-filled skies, and ethnic and racial diversity.

While historians have noted the highly visible changes effected by industrialization—such as the rise of cities, factories, immigration, and entrepreneurs—the deeper implications of this social process have received only preliminary treatment. Historical explanations have moved slowly beyond the artifacts of industrialization to probe the recesses of the social process itself. As a social process, industrialization altered social structures and social relationships at the national, regional, community, and familial levels. At the community level, the focus of this study, industrialization resembled the movement of a glacier. Vast surface changes were obvious to the naked eye. The smokestacks of an expanding steel mill, the multiplication of neighborhoods, and the creation of new wealth were emblematic of a new social order some felt would lead to progress and prosperity for all. Certainly, proponents of this new order abounded in industrial America.

Beneath a glacier, however, significant alterations in topography take place. Unnoticed from the surface, deep valleys and peaks are being carved. The full extent of these changes are not appreciated until the glacier recedes. Similarly, industrial America can be better understood only from the more distant perspective of history. Only now can the subtle alterations wrought by industrial expansion, immigration and migration, and urbanization be understood as the antecedents of modern urban America. For it was from this industrial glaciation that the ethnic, racial, and class features of our present urban landscape were carved.

Most general views of industrialization regard its impact upon community as essentially destructive. The oustanding feature of the new industrial society was its growing ethnic and class diversity. Industrialization was acknowledged to have accentuated this diversity and simultaneously eroded the apparent cohesiveness of the preindustrial community. What replaced this cohesiveness has never been made entirely clear. Especially lacking has been an understanding of the internal reaction of respective ethnic and socioeconomic groupings within the community. Within the community and community groups, the process of accommodation to the new industrial order has been obscured by a general acceptance of a purely destructive model.

Immigrants and migrants who were attracted to the new industrial districts have also fallen victim to the simplicity of the destruction model. Historians widely assumed that diverse groups eventually discarded their premigration behavior, prospered, and merged into the larger community. Native farmers, Italians, Irish, Germans, and Slavs, at varying rates, overcame initial difficulties and experienced integration and advancement. The low position of the Negro in this structure was acknowledged but attributed to his relatively recent arrival upon the industrial urban scene. It was thought that the process of social mobility would eventually bring about full participation in community power and prosperity for all groups, including Afro-Americans. To be sure, recent studies of immigration have emphasized the persistence rather than the destruction of premigration cultures. The emphasis on social mobility, however, has increased, and accounts abound of advancement and integration ranging from modest to dramatic in South Bend, Newburyport, Cleveland, New York, and Chicago.[1]

The stress on the destruction of preindustrial communities and the inevitability of social advancement in industrial society has oversimplified the complex process of industrialization and left an implication that mobility was a dominant societal value. Even defenders of cultural persistence have not adequately allowed for vast differences in orientations among newcomers based on demography rather than on culture. The examination of one American mill town in the late nineteenth and early twentieth centuries reveals a more intricate picture of the development of social structure and social relationships. The pattern of community development in Steelton, Pennsylvania, reduces the efficacy of the assumed leveling effects of mobility and suggests a different view. The social process of industrialization in Steelton was characterized not by destruction and subsequent integration but by reorganization and formalization. Ethnic and class alignments became more pronounced. But this development was not so much a sign of social disorder as it was a step in the transformation of the arena in which social relationships would occur. The interaction of people moved from an individual and familial level to one of larger organizations. During this process individuals seemed less interested in mobility than in security. And accommodation more nearly explained immigrant behavior than cultural persistence, destruction, or upward advancement.

This investigation of Steelton deals with the impact of industrialization upon social relationships at the turn of the century. The mill town was dominated by steel company officials and superintendents, professionals, and merchants. Ranking just below these leaders were the skilled workers who shared with the community elite a white, Anglo-Saxon, Protestant heritage. The mass of Steelton's lower class consisted of unskilled and semiskilled steelworkers who were predominantly Slavic, Italian, or black. Interaction between the various social strata as well as within social classes is the central problem examined in this study. An attempt is made to determine the extent to which industrialization affected social class and ethnic identity and influenced social relations. The effort of the dominant group to retain social control in the face of industrial change is described, as is the withdrawal of working-class groups into ethnic communities.

In the decades immediately following the founding of Steelton in 1866, professionals, merchants, and company officials acquired positions of influence in the mills and the community. Before 1890 Steelton had a relatively homogeneous population of under ten thousand. Residential segregation, with the exception of a small black community, was not pronounced. The old-stock elite was able to exercise its leadership during these years without serious interruption. A strike by skilled workers in 1891, which momentarily challenged the company's power, was quickly defeated. It was in the aftermath of this strike, however, that the company began to encourage massive immigration from southern Europe. The influx of foreign labor dramatically increased the social divisions in the town, chiefly because the policy that encouraged European immigration also segregated newcomers into certain departments in the mills. At the same time, segregation became more noticeable in the town's residential areas. Partially because of their orientation and demographic status, newcomers in Steelton found themselves in one of a number of communities: old stock, skilled workers, and merchants; southern European mill workers; or black laborers. These isolated groups formed their own institutions and seldom interacted with each other.

After illustrating the rise of ethnic segregation in the community, the study analyzes its implications. The extent to which ethnic divisions and working-class solidarity were incompatible is examined along with company labor policy which encouraged ethnic distinctiveness and resisted unionization. Social and geographic mobility rates are measured in order to understand the impact of social mobility upon community structure. Groups that experienced greater success and, consequently, more permanency, not only achieved more influential social positions but maintained them. Industrial mobility and traditional kinship in Steelton served to maintain rather than weaken the social structure. Finally, measures adopted by the old stock to retain their status and the growth of ethnic consciousness among newcomers are related to the process of social adjustment in Steelton before 1920.

The period after 1920 is assessed to gauge the extent to which polarization continued. Characteristics of Steelton's society prior to 1920 were traced to find possible alterations in social relationships, especially with the emergence of the second immigrant generation. Old-stock power remained unchanged if not unchallenged. Ethnic communities continued to flourish with immigrant children marrying partners of similar backgrounds. Social mobility rates revealed the lack of widespread southern European occupational achievement. Significant, however, was the overcoming of ethnic and racial divisions between southern Europeans and blacks in the mill and the strengthening of working-class solidarity. This phenomenon, heightened by the depression of the 1930s, led to the establishment of the steelworkers' union by the early 1940s and the weakening of company control.

A study of social relationships and change in an industrial community provides an opportunity to explore neglected aspects of American social history. David Brody has suggested the possibility of examining relationships among workingmen at the local level.[2] In Steelton the extent to which ethnic and racial diversity splintered the American working class can be studied. Such an inquiry also suggests how ethnicity served as a basis of social organization and adjustment for the newly arrived immigrant worker in an industrial society.[3]

Equally important are the differing rates of occupational and geographic mobility among various ethnic and class groups. While historians have been measuring the extent of mobility in America, they have seldom compared mobility rates among divergent ethnic groups or investigated the implications of limited occupational achievement.[4] They have been handicapped by the lack of statistical material after 1880. Until recently, manuscript census material for 1880–1900, the period that includes the bulk of Slavic and Italian immigration, was not available. Consequently, no studies have been done on "new immigrants." In Steelton, however, special surveys of the foreign population by the local tax assessors in 1903 and 1905 identified the majority of the town's foreign-born residents. Although the Annual Enumeration of All Persons, Places and Things did not provide a listing of jobs, the immigrants' occupations were readily identifiable in local city directories. When this information was supplemented with the recently opened federal census of 1900 and information on nativity and occupation from the Dauphin County Marriage License Dockets, an interesting picture of mobility for Steelton's immigrants began to emerge. One of the most significant phenomena clarified by these statistics was the devastating impact of the company recruitment of Slavs and Italians upon the mobility patterns of the community's blacks.[5]

In addition to an assessment of mobility, the mill town offered an opportunity to view the consequences of modest rates of upward social mobility. American historians and sociologists have detected a rising ethnic consciousness on the part of immigrants in America which surpassed the parochial identities they brought from Europe. Thus *paesano,* which to Italians meant another person from one's native village in Italy, came to mean any other person of Italian descent in America.[6] Steelton's immigrants turned inward and formed ethnic communities as did most other newcomers to urban America in the early decades of this century. The most obvious reasons were the resentment they encountered among the old-stock residents, their need for social contact with individuals of similar cultural backgrounds, friction within the work force, and outright prejudice. Seymour Lipset and Reinhard Bendix have argued that when immigrants felt aggrieved about their positions in the New World their natural form of accommodation was identification with, and organization as, an ethnic group rather than as an economic group.[7] The Steelton story demonstrates the validity of this theory. But frequently overlooked is the effect of limited economic achievement. Remaining largely in unskilled and semiskilled positions for two generations, Slavs could not easily move out of their low occupational status nor their ethnic community. Even if they left Steelton, they usually returned to Europe or moved to ethnic settlements in other steel towns. Newcomers, therefore, accommodated themselves to working-class status by fabricating ethnic communities which enabled them to define a place for themselves in the industrial town. In short, limited occupational advancement helped to nurture the growth of ethnic communities.

Finally, Steelton offered an opportunity to depict the experience of Slavic immigrants, perhaps the least studied of all American immigrant groups. Few monographs exist on the history of Slavic immigrants in urban America.[8] Slavs in Pennsylvania, a state which received about one-half of all Slavic immigrants between 1880 and 1920, have been treated in only two modern accounts.[9]

Steelton, then, serves as a laboratory to scrutinize the intercourse among various groups in an industrial community. Social relations in the mill town exhibited a definite pattern. Anglo-Saxons from northern Europe and rural America arrived first. Many of these old-stock residents obtained positions of influence and skilled and supervisory jobs, and sought ways to preserve their higher social status, including the encouragement of ethnic diversity within the working class. Southern Europeans and blacks arrived afterward, toiled in lower-level occupations for several generations, and created separate cultural enclaves whose persistence was assured by a relatively static social structure. This situation did not begin to change until after 1940 when the Negroes, Slavs, and Italians cooperated in supporting the steelworkers' union which broke the community control of the old stock. The Steelton experience suggests a model for explaining the evolution of social relationships in numerous American industrial towns since the late nineteenth century.

Immigration and Industrialization

1 Early Steelton

Steelton emerged as a steel-producing center in Pennsylvania after the Civil War. Situated just south of Harrisburg on the east bank of the Susquehanna River, the community consisted of only eight families in 1866. Stimulated by the expansion of the Pennsylvania Steel Company, however, the town soon attracted workers from rural Pennsylvania, Ireland, Great Britain, and Germany. With an additional increase in productive capacity in the 1880s, thousands of steelworkers were drawn to Steelton from the southern United States and southern Europe. By the end of the nineteenth century, industrialization transformed this Pennsylvania farm land into a bustling mix of production mills, row homes, and cultural and economic arrangements.

Steelton was certainly not unique. The expansion of the American steel industry at the turn of the century generated a proliferation of mill towns around the large steel manufacturing plants; Lackawanna, Gary, South Chicago, and Bethlehem and Homestead were only a few. In these communities the problems of immigration and industrialization were as intense as in much larger urban areas.[1] Indeed, the socioeconomic evolution of Steelton was a microcosm of the urban-industrial development of the larger American society.

These industrial towns were often established initially to furnish iron products for railroad companies. By the early 1860s practically every mile of track in America had rails of wrought iron. The weight and speed of trains, however, had gradually increased, with the result that wrought iron rails could no longer withstand the added stress. Consequently the stronger steel rails which had been perfected through the Bessemer process in England were in demand. To take advantage of this emerging market in steel rails and to eliminate any future dependence upon foreign manufacturers, the Pennsylvania Railroad organized a subsidiary—the Pennsylvania Steel Company.[2] In 1865 the new company began erecting its works in Steelton.

The company, under Samuel M. Felton, its first president, selected for its town site an elongated plot on the Susquehanna River south of Harrisburg. The Pennsylvania Canal and the main line of the Pennsylvania Railroad ran parallel to the river, and the value of the site was further enhanced by the proximity of the ore banks at Cornwall, Pennsylvania.[3] The company built its steel plant on flat land adjoining the river. But other town activities were located on higher ground beyond the canal, which separated the plant from the main part of the community. In 1866, with the erection of the steel plant, a town was laid out and named Baldwin, after the distinguished locomotive builder, philanthropist, and founder of the Baldwin Locomotive works at Philadelphia. In 1871 the name was changed to Steel-Works. Nine years later Steelton was incorporated as a borough.[4]

In 1867 the company imported an English mechanical engineer, Alexander Halley, who was familiar with the Bessemer steelmaking process. Halley did much of the early planning and supervised the construction of the first two Bessemer converters. When the first steel ingots were poured in 1867, Steelton's rail mill was not yet completed, and the steel was sent to Johnstown to be rolled. By 1869, the rolling mill was in operation. Soon the works included a forging department and a blooming mill, making Steelton the first plant in America for the production of steel.[5] By 1872 the company had begun to build blast furnaces to produce pig iron. Its first furnace was finished in 1873, with others completed in 1875 and 1883. The frog and switch department for fabricating railroad track switches was installed in 1872. A merchant mill was built in 1882 for the production of merchant bars, billets, and slabs.[6]

With the construction of the steel plant, a work force began to enter the emerging industrial town. It was recruited gradually, during the years of construction, and from many sources. A considerable number of highly skilled steelworkers, who were born in Ireland, like Cornelius Dailey, were brought from England. Irish laborers also came, along with a large force of men of Pennsylvania German extraction in the early 1870s.[7] A steady trickle of Negroes arrived from nearby Maryland and Virginia after 1871. But the white settlers from rural Pennsylvania, England, Ireland, and Germany formed the bulk of Steelton's society before 1890 and provided leaders for its power structure for the next half century.

In 1880 Steelton residents numbered less than twenty-five hundred. The population was relatively homogeneous, and it remained so until the onset of heavy Slavic and Italian immigration after 1890. Over 80 percent of the town's citizens were native-born whites. Only 9 percent were foreign born. Blacks numbered only 202. Areas which later became distinct immigrant sectors such as the "lower end" and the West Side were not even inhabited in the early 1880s. Steelton residents first lived mainly on six streets: Front, Second, Third, Adams, Lincoln, and "Steel Company Row."[8]

By 1890 American-born whites still constituted 72 percent of the population. The proportion of blacks and immigrants increased slightly, by about 4.5 percent each. Three-fourths of all immigrants were still English, Irish, or German. Only a few southern Europeans such as Croats and Slovenes were in the borough, and along with a small contingent of Poles, they did not amount to more than 4 percent of the population.[9]

Front Street, the community's main thoroughfare, ran the entire length of the borough from north to south and housed over six hundred persons. All of them were native born, with the exception of twenty blacks, twenty-two Irish immigrants, fourteen arrivals from England, seven German newcomers, and five Welshmen.[10] Other immigrants were likewise widely distributed. The Irish, English, and Germans were scattered throughout the town. Besides Front Street, Irish families were found on Second Street and in company houses on Steel Company Row. Pine Street, which later became a location for the fine homes of company officials, did not yet exist. Luther Bent, superintendent of the steelworks, lived on Front Street with his family and two Irish servant girls; his neighbors were common laborers, puddlers, carpenters, and bricklayers. This is not to suggest a complete absence of any social stratification in Steelton prior to large-scale immigration. The town possessed a wide range of occupational and economic levels. But residential segregation was not as acute in the early 1880s as it was after the arrival of thousands of southern Europeans. Blacks were, however, the exception in this case. Out of 145 people living on Adams Street, 138 were Negro, or approximately seven out of every ten blacks in the entire borough.[11]

Germans were among the earliest immigrants to arrive in the borough. In 1867 they helped form the United Brethren church. By 1875 the St. John Evangelical Lutheran congregation was organized. Members of the "Zwinglian community" organized a congregation and secured a minister in 1889. In the late 1890s, Steelton began to receive an influx of German Catholics from that part of Austria-Hungary known as the Banat. For a while these German Catholics worshiped in St. James parish, which was largely Irish, but by 1900 they decided to form their own distinctively ethnic church and began holding services in a rented hall.[12]

Irish settlers first celebrated mass at the residence of Cornelius Dailey on South Front Street in 1874. The cornerstone of the first Catholic church in Steelton was laid by the Irish in 1878. Until then they had held services at a public school. A parochial school was begun at St. James in 1887. The local press contained no evidence of nativistic sentiments toward the Irish. The *Item* even called St. James Church the neatest and most tastefully finished edifice in the town.[13]

Entering Steelton at a time of rapid expansion and with no entrenched ethnic group to oppose them, the Irish rapidly acquired influential positions in the community. Cornelius Dailey, a superintendent at the mill, later became mayor; Thomas

Nelley became the leading political figure in the community.[14] Irish community life also expanded. St. James School numbered over two hundred fifty pupils by 1892, and numerous Irish organizations such as the Ancient Order of Hibernians began to flourish. Irish picnics at Hess Island in the Susquehanna River became one of the town's most popular social events. When the Irish pastor, Gilbert Benton, was honored for his elevation to the rank of monsignor, the *Reporter* observed that it was a "most impressive ceremony." When blacks and Slavic immigrants were criticized for their "excessive" drinking, the Irish formed the St. James Total Abstinence Society. The Irish were clearly an "acceptable" part of the community by the last decade of the nineteenth century.[15]

The dominant force in Steelton at this time was the company itself. Pennsylvania Steel employed over one-half of all residents in the town. Probably no more than 10 percent of the male work force found employment outside the mills. Indeed, the United States Immigration Commission later concluded that the company had always been in a position to influence to a large degree the affairs of the town. Throughout the fifty years after 1870 a high company official usually served as president of the town council. Company superintendents presided over the council from 1887 to 1895. Luther Bent himself headed the school board for a decade after 1886. The attitude of the company toward candidates for local political office, moreover, represented the most important influence in local politics.[16]

Leading company personnel invariably assumed strategic positions in local politics. Adam Gardner, who was a descendant of German immigrants, came from adjacent Lancaster County in 1875. He took a position in the general office of the steel company and served as borough treasurer for fifteen years. Gardner was "an ardent Republican."[17] Jonah Diffenderfer, a superintendent at the plant, was burgess of Steelton in the early 1890s. Harry Campbell, general plant superintendent, was also president of the borough council. Luther Bent not only served on the school board but also hosted the meetings at his home. John J. Newbecker, a master mechanic at the mill, was also on the board of directors of the Steelton Water Company. The company's control was not only pervasive but unmatched by any other sector of the community.

A register of Steelton's prominent citizens in 1896 further revealed the pervasive influence of the company. Among the leading residents cited was the chief official of the Pennsylvania Steel Company, Luther Bent. After marrying the daughter of one of the company's founders, Samuel Felton, Bent became superintendent of the company in 1874. His activities, particularly his trips to other parts of the country and abroad, were continually reported in the local press. Bent was succeeded in 1896 by Edgar C. Felton, Samuel Felton's son.

Many company employees who were influential in the community also shared similar political and religious affiliations. A certain J. Reynders was in charge of the bridge and construction department for the company. Like Bent he was both Protestant and Republican and was active in the local YMCA. Harry Campbell, another Protestant Republican, was the general manager of the entire plant. One account described him as a "power in social circles." Other key positions in the mills were filled by men with similar views. Jonah G. Diffenderfer was the superintendent of the company's finishing and shipping department. Born in Lancaster County in 1859, he was a member of the United Brethren church. Milton Morris, master mechanic at the steelworks, was a member of the Presbyterian church and belonged to numerous societies such as the Knights of Pythias and the Knights of Malta. Born in Chester County in 1842, he worked for the Pennsylvania Railroad before he came to Steelton in 1870 and entered the machine shop. The foreman of the boiler department, Jacob Good, was born in Cumberland County. He learned boiler making in the shops of the Pennsylvania Railroad Company where he worked for nine years. He was affiliated with the local YMCA and was a member of the Baptist church. The superintendent of the rail and blooming mills, John Down, was an immigrant from Leeds, England, and attended the Episcopal church in Harrisburg.

The Irish were another group well represented in the ranks

of the company's supervisors. John W. Dougherty, superintendent of the blast furnace, came to Steelton from Pittsburgh in 1875. He had studied engineering at Lehigh University, was an independent in politics, and attended the Catholic church. Thomas T. McEntee, superintendent of the open hearth, was the son of an Irish immigrant to Lancaster County. Unlike most of Steelton's early leaders, he was a Democrat in politics and a member of St. James Catholic Church. A machinist foreman at the local mill, Michael Gallagher, was born in Ireland in 1846. He worked in steel plants in England until 1869 when he moved to Steelton. He was also a Catholic.

Other community leaders usually had both northwest European ancestry and a direct connection with the steel firm. Josiah Dunkle, who became Steelton's first burgess in 1880 and who was a director of the Steelton Light, Heat and Power Company, served as president of the Lutheran Church Council in Steelton. Dr. A. Shope was the grandson of a German immigrant who came to Dauphin County and became city treasurer. He was also "an active Republican" and a member of the United Brethren church.[18] Frank B. Wickersham, a prominent Steelton attorney, was from York County. Wickersham attended Shippensburg Normal School and was admitted to the bar in 1888. The following year he became a solicitor for the borough and later an attorney for the Steelton Home Water Company and director and solicitor for the People's Building and Loan Association. Wickersham was also a member of the school board and a director of the YMCA. Needless to say he was a Republican and a member of St. John's Lutheran Church. Dr. David Traver and C. H. Mumma, both leaders of the YMCA during the 1880s, came from rural Pennsylvania. Traver was a Republican and a Methodist. Mumma was also a Republican but attended the Lutheran church.

The influential editor of the *Steelton Reporter*, William Sieg, also had an Anglo-Saxon, Protestant background. Born near Millersburg, Dauphin County, in 1837, he was on the borough council from 1883 to 1885 and then became postmaster. In addition to being an ardent Republican, he was a member of the Presbyterian church. His paper consistently supported Republican candidates and the policies of the steel company. Sieg himself always attended the annual meetings of the company and was a stockholder. By 1890, his chief rival, the *Steelton Item*, had gone out of business and his paper became the only journalistic voice in the borough for several decades.

The influence of the company in the borough was frequently defended by the press and community leaders. In 1881 the *Item* remarked that the town was so closely tied to the success of the steel works that public interest required the company to "secure triumph" in its efforts.[19] When the Steelton Citizens' Railway Company failed to purchase rails from the local company in 1893, it was severely criticized by the town council. The councilmen reiterated the necessity of supporting the local mill and declared that the steel works were operated not for the purpose of profit but to supply work for their employees.[20] In 1887 several individuals wanted to form a Law and Order Society in Steelton. The *Reporter* was quick to note, however, that any criminal employees of the Pennsylvania Steel Company were discharged from their work upon conviction. Because of the influence of the company, the paper argued, no borough in the state with so mixed a population as Steelton was "so well contented." The *Reporter* concluded: "At least five thousand of the inhabitants of Steelton are governed, morally by the Pennsylvania Steel Company, and we need no better society for the protection of the other two thousand than this institution officered as it is by men who spend their money here for the improvement of the town and for strict law and order enforcement."[21]

But confidence in the steel firm was momentarily challenged when differences arose between Steelton's local leaders and the steel firm. During the summer of 1885, Steelton businessmen invited citizens to a meeting to "form a monopoly to control the business of Steelton." The Front Street merchants were annoyed that the company did not pay a greater share of each worker's wages in cash. Because the company deducted a portion of the steelworkers' earnings from their accounts at the company store, the workers had less money to spend in local business establishments.[22] After a series of meetings, local merchants forwarded a petition to the company requesting the firm to pay all wages in cash and allow men to purchase goods where they pleased. The company's initial response was a series of large advertisements in the *Steelton Reporter* claiming that the company store sold goods only at cost and thus provided an advantage to the workingman which was the equivalent of an "immense raise in wages."[23]

Although the *Reporter* supported the company's claims and published figures indicating that, of the 70 percent of the labor force which patronized the Steelton company store, only 9 percent had accounts in excess of wages, the firm relented. A greater proportion of goods at the company store was made available for cash. The *Reporter* launched a series of detailed articles describing the goods and services of local business establishments. The series emphasized that local merchants were considerably "lower in price" than those in Harrisburg. In effect, the *Reporter* was soothing local merchants' feelings with a substantial amount of free advertising.[24]

In 1894 the company tried to insure the election of town councilmen who were sympathetic to the needs of the firm's East Harrisburg Railway System. In attempting to establish a monopoly on local streetcars and, therefore, to raise fares, the steel firm used "bribery, terrorism, and intimidation" to secure favorable candidates and destroy the rival Citizens' Railway. The *Harrisburg Call* chided the steel firm: "Once honored and respected name now bedraggled in the filth of a miserable struggle to prevent competition with a wretched steel railway monopoly! Ye frogs and fishplates, if your iron lung could have blushed, ye would have become redder for very shame than if ye had burned in the crucible."[25]

Disputes of this type were infrequent. Company officials and town officials usually worked together. A prime illustration of such cooperation was the Literary Institute headed by L. E. McGinnes, the school superintendent, Luther Bent, Dr. D. B. Traver, Edgar C. Felton, and William L. Ziegler, who also served on the school board. The institute was formed in the late 1880s to minister to the intellectual life of the borough and to furnish amusements for its leading citizens. At monthly meetings topics of current interest were discussed and musical recitals were heard. In 1891 at one particular discussion on the "qualities that win," the members of the institute agreed that success was gained only by concentrating on one's goals. The institute's membership was totally native born, Irish, German, or English.[26]

The company worked closely with the community on local educational matters. In 1881 Pennsylvania Steel donated a $100,000 school building to the town, and the local press hailed the action as a "departure from the usual policy of a soulless corporation." Luther Bent was credited with bringing the project to fruition. Besides donating the building and gaining a seat on the board for Bent, the company helped pay the salary of the school superintendent, L. E. McGinnes.[27] The school was intended not only to provide a normal education but also to give mechanical and vocational instruction, preparing Steelton's youth for work in the mill. The *Steelton Item* thought such instruction "imparted to our boys" would make them superior workingmen whose labor would be beyond competition from European immigrants.[28] In addition, the company promised not to employ any student during the school term. In fact, if a man failed to send his children to the school regularly, he could be discharged from the steel firm.[29]

Company officials also gave the annual commencement addresses at the local high school, whose students were old stock. Edgar Felton told the ten graduates at the 1885 ceremony that they had received the best education that their "native place" afforded. Felton claimed that these students were now the "most enlightened persons in this community" and would inevitably occupy important and highly responsible positions in the borough. On the eve of mass immigration into Steelton, Felton encouraged the old stock when he concluded his oration: "Whatever of advancement there is to be in our borough in the years to come, whether it be in increased refinement and culture of the home circle or the higher standards in public morality, it is from among you . . . that this good is to come. You are the germ from which the future of this town is to spring; it is you who are going to lead it in the years that are not very far off."[30]

The company even sponsored annual picnics for steelworkers which attracted not only most employees but company officials as well.[31] No mention of such picnics for the entire work force was found after 1890. And, before the onset of heavy southern European immigration, the entire town usually turned out for the annual United Brethren picnic, the community's largest. Indeed, when the United Brethren Sunday School celebrated its anniversary in 1885, almost all of Steelton's officials, clergymen, and merchants attended, as well as nearly one-fourth of the town's population.[32]

When Dauphin County celebrated its centennial in 1885, the company demonstrated its widespread influence by organizing a contingent for a parade planned in Harrisburg. Under the direction of the superintendent, Edgar Felton, a huge procession was organized of over one thousand steelworkers, more than half the entire work force. The Steelton men were arranged in a sequence which portrayed the steel-making process and showed to the rest of the county the ostensible "unity" of the borough.[33] Each department in the plant marched separately, and the men, neatly attired in uniforms, marched "with the precision of veterans." The Bessemer department, for instance, was represented by 250 men from the first shift and 150 from the second shift, each group headed by its respective foreman. All were dressed in white caps, blue shirts, white ties, dark pants, with a clean white towel around the neck. Black workers were represented by the Negro Cornet Band. The plant was closed for three days for the occasion. In these festivities the steel town displayed a unity which would not be repeated, except briefly during World War I, for the next fifty years.[34]

The company's prominent role in organizing the centennial parade was symptomatic of the dominant position the firm held in the entire community. Writing on Steelton in 1955, Warren

Eyster, a novelist, correctly perceived the inordinate influence exercised by the steel company over local affairs and the workers in its mills. Eyster wrote of one union organizer who "exposed the illegal influence of the company and the local police. He gathered exact evidence about rows of company houses and about profiteering in the company store. One of the things which he was striving to obtain was further testimony in regard to the bonus which had been promised to workers at the end of the war, and a practice of forcing workers to buy bonds. On the inadequate safety precautions he had a sound case."[35] Indeed the local company exerted significant control over the educational, social, and industrial sectors of Steelton.

Prior to 1890 Steelton's social order was dominated by men who held important positions at the Pennsylvania Steel Company or who came from Steelton's business and professional classes. In the brief dispute between local business interests and the company over the influence of the company store, it was the local editor who appeased Steelton merchants by offering free advertising. While the informal alliance between the company and the community's professional and business class was established and unchallenged,[36] however, the task of maintaining social dominance became increasingly difficult as the relative homogeneity of the population declined.

If Steelton's two initial decades witnessed the growth of a relatively cohesive population, the quarter century after 1885 saw the rise of a pronounced ethnic diversity. A myriad separate communities formed within the borough, each with an institutional life of its own. The source of this diversification was a tremendous increase in black migration in the late 1880s and an influx of immigrants from southern Europe in the late 1890s. The inflow of blacks continued, and the in-migration of Italians and southern Slavs intensified between 1890 and World War I.

The federal census returns, summarized in table 1, clearly illustrated the changing character of the town's population. In

TABLE 1: *The Population of Steelton, 1880–1940*

	Total Population	Native Born of Native Parents	Native Born of Foreign Parents	Foreign Born	Negro
1880	2,447	1,714	300	231	202
1890	9,250	5,784	902	1,201	1,273
1900	12,086	7,039	1,244	2,992	1,244
1910	14,246	6,417	1,927	4,667	1,234
1920	13,428	5,676	2,475	2,896	1,973
1930	13,291	—	—	2,122	2,533
1940	13,115	—	—	1,651	2,514

Sources: "Tenth Census, 1880"; *Eleventh Census, 1890,* p. 553; *Thirteenth Census, 1910,* p. 679; *Fourteenth Census, 1920,* p. 872; *Sixteenth Census, 1940,* p. 161. (Complete citations of census manuscripts and published volumes are given in the Bibliographical Essay.)

1890, out of a population of 9,250, over 2,300 were foreign born and 1,508 were Negro. By 1910 the population had leaped to 14,246, one-third of whom were foreign born. Moreover, 1,927 individuals were classified as the native-born children of foreign-born parents. While no Steelton resident in 1880 was born in southern or eastern Europe, by 1910 the newcomers from Italy, Slovenia, and Croatia, and their children, accounted for one-third of the town's population. The United States Immigration Commission found that the largest racial and national groups were Serbian, Croatian, Negro, and German. The Serbian community alone numbered just over 2,000, while the Croatian total was just under 2,000. Blacks numbered over 1,200, and Germans totaled around 1,000. Other groups included 650 Bulgarians, 600 Slovenes, 525 Italians, 400 Irish, 250 Jews, and 400 Slovaks, Poles, and Roumanians.[37] Of 4,595 workers surveyed by the Immigration Commission in 1910, 2,000 men were foreign born. Some 200 were Negroes and about 280 were American-born children of immigrants. Less than half the work force was native born.[38] Of the foreign-born employees at the Pennsylvania Steel Company, nearly one-third were Croatian. Slavic immigrants constituted

70 percent of all foreign-born workers in the mills just prior to World War I.[39]

Steelton experienced the greatest rise in its foreign-born population between 1890 and 1910. The 1890s witnessed an influx consisting mainly of Croatians and Slovenians and some Poles. A considerable number of German Catholics also came. After 1900 the Serbs, Bulgarians, and Italians constituted the bulk of the new arrivals. The black population, however, remained relatively stable between 1890 and 1910. It did not begin to increase again until the period after World War I when European immigration was curtailed.[40]

As early as 1896 the *Steelton Reporter* noted the changing character of the town's population. In commenting on the difficulties encountered by local teachers at the Fothergill School, the *Reporter* claimed that instructors had their "hands full trying to teach English." The journal described one classroom of sixty-two pupils which included thirty-three "Americans," two Germans, three "Polanders," six Hungarians, five Bohemians, three "Slavonics," four "Colored" and one "Arab." The newspaper also noted that the entire West Side was becoming a "foreign section."[41]

Recognizing the diversity of the population, local officials frequently gathered information on the town's ethnic communities. In 1898 a canvass was made to ascertain the number of nationalities represented. The final count revealed thirty-three different nationalities within the borough limits including "one Japanese, two Turks, four Arabians, one Frenchman, and two Syrians."[42] Tax assessors also completed a number of surveys on the town. In 1903 they made a complete list of foreigners. Their list graphically pointed up not only the extent of the foreign population but also the pattern of settlement. It showed that immigrants were concentrated in the first ward, known as the West Side. Nearly one-third of Steelton's population was classified as foreign. Indeed, the report complained that many foreigners had moved from the community to boardinghouses just outside the city limits to escape taxation by local officials.[43]

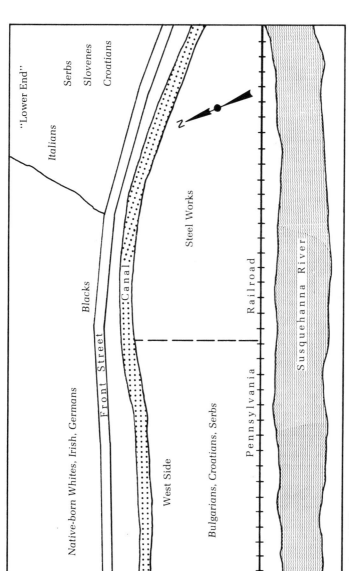

Steelton, 1910

U.S. Immigration Commission, *Reports of the United States Immigration Commission, Immigrants in Industries, Part 2: Iron and Steel*, 2 vols., S. Doc. 633, 61st Cong., 2nd sess., serial 5669 (1911), I, 659.

With the arrival of blacks and southern Europeans in significant numbers after the late 1880s, Steelton's residential patterns, for the first time, acquired a strongly segregated character. Whereas the Irish, German, and native-white stock were mixed together, the newcomers after 1890 occupied ethnic neighborhoods of their own.[44] No better indication of the growing ethnic diversification exists than the rise of a variegated residential pattern.

The pattern of immigrant settlement was strongly influenced by the activities of the Pennsylvania Steel Company in constructing workers' housing. Many of the row houses which still stand in Steelton were erected by the company, especially on the West Side near the river. At one time in the 1880s, for instance, the firm built 500 houses.[45] Tenements, usually with about five rooms and renting for about eight dollars a month, were constructed on low land near the mill to house both blacks and immigrant newcomers. The units were built not only to keep employees near their work but also to allow the company to engage in land speculation. Such dwellings were continually cited by the state for their unsanitary conditions and overcrowding.[46]

The boardinghouses on the West Side were often ravaged by floods. The inundation of January 1886, caused by a sudden winter thaw, forced the "Hungarians and Polanders" to move their meager furniture to the second stories of buildings. The *Reporter* wryly observed that many lives were lost in the West Side flood—"bugs and rats."[47] The flood of 1902 also brought huge chunks of ice which crumbled entire rows of boardinghouses. Three days after this particular inundation, cold weather froze the water which had been in basements and on first floors. Most of the immigrants lacked food and fuel, and damp conditions caused widespread sickness.[48]

Near the boardinghouses on the banks of the canal, the company also built "shanties." Occupied wholly by Negroes and Slavs, the shanties were arranged in blocks of five to ten. Each shanty had but one room, about seven feet by twelve feet. One-half of a window at the rear of each unit provided the only means of light and ventilation. Each shanty rented for $2.50

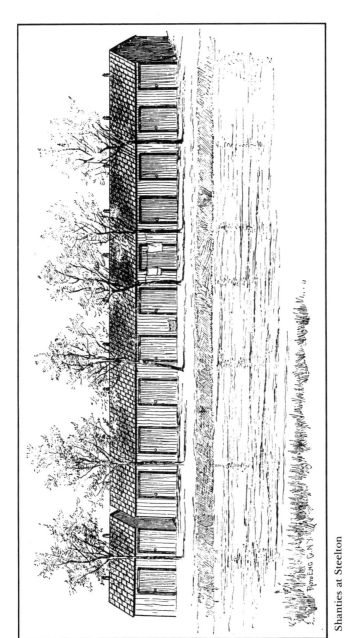

Shanties at Steelton

Commonwealth of Pennsylvania, *Annual Report of the Secretary of Internal Affairs, Part III: Industrial Statistics, 1886* (Harrisburg, 1887), p. 26.

per month, "or enough rent to pay in one year the original cost of the entire row." One observer commented that the filth in and about the place was intolerable.[49]

Since company housing was built in sections to accommodate the influx of immigrants, laborers tended to settle in the same area. This is not to say that newcomers did not choose to congregate around the individuals who spoke the same language. They invariably did. But the pattern of housing construction by the company insured the emergence of such a housing arrangement.

The rising ethnic diversity heightened residential differences. Italians and Slavs especially were concentrated in the West Side and in the "lower end." As late as the 1930s Slavs were still clustered in such areas.[50] Until about 1890 lower-class native whites formed a significant part of the population of the West Side. The area was known as a totally "American section." With the arrival of numerous immigrants the complexion of the West Side began to change until, by 1910, usually only Slavic peoples were found there. In this area were Croatians and nearly the entire Bulgarian community. The bulk of the Serbs and Croats lived in the lower or southern end. Italians were concentrated to the north.[51]

The social fragmentation is caught in Warren Eyster's fictional portrayal of Steelton. His novel is structured around two different narratives which eventually, for a brief moment, come together. One narrative concerns a family, the Langs, who were officials of the local steel company—wealthy, influential, and white, Anglo-Saxon, Protestant. The other narrative traces the family of Bart Mijack. The Mijacks worked hard, were poor, led lives that were grim in contrast to the gaiety often experienced by the Langs, and were distinctively "foreigners." Eyster's plot suggests that after 1890 deep and irreconcilable social divisions separated Steelton's foreign and native population. When Bart Mijack's son marries Dorothy Lang, the marriage is quickly annulled. All hope for bridging the social chasm between the old stock and the foreign poor is lost and Steelton remains a divided town.[52]

If the varied influx which began in the 1890s splintered Steelton's social order, the responsibility could not be placed on the newcomers themselves but on the forces which brought them to Pennsylvania. The steel company in particular implemented systematic steps which practically insured a fractured society. In an effort to maintain a source of inexpensive labor, Slavs were recruited directly, for instance, or funneled into the Pennsylvania Steel plant through a cooperative system with certain boardinghouse keepers. Blacks were periodically recruited in groups. Such procedures established a beachhead which led to a chain migration into the ethnic community for several decades. In building cheap row houses for workers, moreover, the company implicitly facilitated and determined the future pattern of ethnic residential dispersion.

The difficulty of maintaining social dominance in the industrial community increased with the diversification of the population. Steelton acquired a cultural mixture which was reflected in the town's residential patterns. The native-German-Irish old stock, which formed the basis of leadership in Steelton, was securely entrenched. Irish Catholics and German Protestants, while retaining aspects of their own heritage, placed class above culture and cooperated effectively. The company's recruitment policies, however, forced the old stock to implement various measures to control the course of local events. In both the community and the mill the early leadership would attempt not to alter the social order Steelton acquired by the end of the nineteenth century but to preserve it.

By the early 1900s the elements of Steelton's diverse social order were present if not stabilized. The community attracted a diverse population. It would be a mistake to assume, however, that everyone who came to the borough arrived with similar intentions. Migrants came at different times in their lives, under varying circumstances, for dissimilar reasons. This notion is crucial in understanding the subsequent pattern of social relationships in Steelton and the desire of the old stock to keep the social order intact.

2 Strategies

The peopling of an industrial community was not a random process. The mechanisms which brought specific persons and groups to Steelton included numerous familial and individual decisions and plans. Examination of this complex process is crucial if we are to understand the groups that settled in the borough and their intentions. Blacks, Slavs, Germans, and even native whites were not lured only by promises of opportunity in industrial America. There were dreamers to be sure, but most migrants were pragmatic individuals arriving at realistic decisions about their present and future survival. Steelton held specific solutions to the varying problems of widely differing individuals. Steelton, and for that matter America, was not viewed as a panacea. This was clearly evident to newcomers not only after several months of settlement but prior to emigration as well.

Both blacks and southern Europeans were attracted, of course, by the industrial wages offered by the Pennsylvania Steel Company in its desire to attract unskilled, rural migrants from Virginia, North Carolina, Italy, Croatia, Slovenia, and Serbia. An unskilled worker was paid about twelve cents an hour in 1908, just under the average of thirteen cents an hour for unskilled workers in the eastern United States. He could work, however, a twelve-hour day which enabled him to earn $1.44 per day. Steelton also had a large cigar factory which employed over eight hundred women. In both the plant and factory, wages were more than one could earn in the agricultural areas.[1]

Slavic immigration into Steelton consisted primarily of South

Slavs: Croats, Serbs, Slovenes, and Bulgarians from Macedonia. They arrived from the southern areas of the old Austro-Hungarian Empire which today constitute the northern regions of Yugoslavia.[2] Croatians from the coastal regions of Dalmatia had sailed regularly to the United States since the beginning of the nineteenth century. The federal census of 1870 listed hundreds of "Slavonian" or South Slav names. The bulk of the South Slav immigration, however, did not begin until after 1890. Beyond the attraction of American industry and the desire to avoid military service for Austria-Hungary, other causes stirred South Slavs to move. In the 1870s an infestation of grape phylloxera ravaged the vineyards of Dalmatia and the inland regions south of Zagreb. With no aid forthcoming from the Austrian government, some two hundred thousand people were deprived of their only source of income. Moreover, the gradual extinction of the Croatian *zadruga,* or communal household, led to a shortage of land. Many land-hungry peasants emigrated in search of wages which would allow them to extend their holdings at home.[3] The distribution of both Croats and Serbs was influenced by immigrant correspondence between Europe and America. Serbs from Lika, for instance, settled around Chicago and throughout the Midwest. Those from Herzegovina went in large numbers to the Pacific coast. The Serbs who constituted the heavy settlements around Pittsburgh and in Steelton, especially after 1900, were largely from Croatia.[4]

Italians first came to Steelton in 1897. The flow increased noticeably in the spring of 1889 when Italian laborers were brought to the borough to work on the construction of a large sewage treatment plant. By the early 1900s, the Pennsylvania Steel Company was actively recruiting Italian labor for its mills. Indeed, when an inspector with the Italian consulate in New York came to Steelton in 1906 to inspect the living conditions of the Italian immigrants, he expressed pleasure with the arrangements made by the company for housing his countrymen. They were much better, the inspector observed, than the poorly ventilated and unsanitary shanties he had found in the South.[5]

The last group of newcomers to find their way into Steelton

were Macedonian Bulgarians from the area around Prilep, especially the village of San Sinot. The first Bulgarians arrived about 1901 and a second wave came after the Illenden Insurrection against the Turks in August 1903. By 1904 the immigrants, most of whom were males, decided to send representatives to bring their wives and children from Macedonia.[6] They had left not only because of impoverishment but because of political oppression by the Turkish government.

In addition to newcomers from southern Europe, Negroes from Maryland, Virginia, and North Carolina had been coming to Steelton since the inception of the borough. Steelton's black population numbered only slightly more than two hundred in 1880. The vast majority of Negroes arrived between 1884 and 1895, swelling the number to over twelve hundred. During the late 1880s blacks were the largest group brought to the steel plant. Weekly lists of new employees at the plant revealed Negroes coming often in groups of fifteen or twenty. In one week in 1889, for instance, fifty new mill employees included twenty-five Negroes. In other weeks no blacks were listed.[7]

Blacks were usually recruited when the company was short of unskilled labor, especially before 1890 and during World War I. In fact, the *Steelton Press,* a Negro publication, mentioned a Liberian Migration Society which arranged for Negroes who were seeking employment in the North to settle in Steelton.[8] During the hightide of immigration from Europe, the Negro population of Steelton had declined, but by 1912 the *Reporter* warned, "If a number of foreigners cannot be secured immediately more Negroes will be taken." When labor became scarce during World War I, nearly six hundred blacks were recruited by the company's general labor department, brought to Steelton, and housed in barracks in a labor camp at Locust Grove just outside the borough.[9] Steel men saw labor as an item of cost that had to be narrowed to an irreducible minimum. With this belief in mind the owners of the company, particularly Samuel Felton, deliberately imported blacks and immigrants in order to keep wages low.[10]

As the company prospered and expanded its capacity, the

demand for unskilled labor rose significantly. Periods of prosperity always brought more trains carrying foreign laborers to the Harrisburg and Steelton stations. During the spring of 1902, for instance, several hundred immigrants were arriving every week.[11] When enough workingmen could not be secured through "natural" means, the company sent foremen to New York and Boston to obtain alien labor through employment agencies.[12] In 1898 nine Croatian immigrants were detained in New York after asserting that they had received contracts to join Pennsylvania Steel for $1.20 per day. The steel company did not deny the assertions by the immigrants but refused to pay the transportation of the nine to Steelton. Frank Zotti, publisher of the Croatian newspaper, *Narodni List,* eventually brought the men to Steelton, and they started work at the plant.[13]

The initial migrants, nearly always recruited to Steelton, established ethnic beachheads in the community. Although most of the Slovene and Croat pioneers recruited in the late 1880s and early 1890s returned to Europe, the minority who remained behind invariably brought their wives to the mill town. They often operated a boardinghouse which served as a center for the Slavs who followed. Even if the early pioneer returned to Europe, he informed his particular locality about Steelton. Thus Thomas Benkovic arrived in the mill town from Croatia in 1903 because his father had worked there in 1887.[14]

Information in the federal census of 1900 suggested a typical pattern for Croats and Slovenes who arrived before 1895. The mean age of these migrants by 1900 was forty. Since they had been in America an average of ten years, most arrived around age thirty. Of this group only 13 percent were single and 57 percent were heads of households. In *all* cases these household heads were married and kept boarders. Thus the pioneers who remained in Steelton were essential in bringing additional newcomers. This fact explains why Steelton received large numbers of Croats, Slovenes, Serbs, and Bulgarians from specific regions but almost no Slovaks, Ukrainians, Rusins, or Poles. Furthermore, boarders offered the pioneers in each ethnic community an added source of income. All adult Croat and Slovene women in Steelton in 1900 were married to these pioneer boardinghouse keepers and worked continuously packing lunches and caring for their families and boarders.[15]

The recruitment of unskilled workers never had to be extensive. Once a small number of them were obtained the mechanics of kinship and chain migration operated to insure a subsequent supply of labor when work was available. The pioneers who established themselves in Steelton acted as labor agents or intermediaries between foremen in the mill and the newcomer. They usually were aware of job prospects. Some pioneers received a fee from the company for persuading their countrymen to work in certain departments. During slow periods in the summer, labor agents often secured jobs for "foreigners" outside of Steelton. In this manner, hundreds of Steelton Bulgarians and Italians engaged in railroad construction in the South.[16]

In some cases the agent was the proprietor of a coffeehouse or small store within the immigrant community. Through him, letters were sent to Europe encouraging fellow countrymen to leave for Steelton. Often his store or coffeehouse was the sole destination of the incoming alien. Upon his arrival he was cared for by the agent, taken to his friends, and work was secured for him.[17] Interviews with immigrants revealed the sense of relief which many newcomers felt when they met this fellow countryman and heard him speak in their own language after a journey filled with strangers and uncertainties. When the head of a boardinghouse secured a job for the newcomer, he might receive a fee from both the company and the immigrant. In nearly all cases, kin, or more likely a fellow countryman, provided the necessary contact with the mill for securing a job.[18] Kinship and ethnic connections were helping to determine the origins of immigrants, their settlement patterns in Steelton, and the distribution of the work force in the plant. When some immigrants failed to establish such a link to the old country, their local enclaves remained small, and were outnumbered by other groups. All of the Croatian immigrants, for example, came from just three regions in Croatia: Karlovac, Bjelovar, and Voyvodina.[19] But the small Polish settlement in Steelton before 1890 was overwhelmed by the sweep of southern Europeans after 1900 and drifted away to Reading, where their countrymen formed a more significant element of the population.[20]

The use of ethnic contacts is illustrated by looking at the records of an immigrant ship arriving at Philadelphia from Bremen in 1915. All of the Croats on the *Brandenberg* listed themselves as laborers or farm laborers with less than thirty dollars (most had about thirteen). All listed friends or relatives with whom they were going to live in Steelton. Nikola Malobacic intended to seek the house of a friend, Milan Crevar, in the borough. Gjuro Novakovic, coming to America for the first time at the age of eighteen, was headed for the home of his cousin, Yanko Malcovic. Yuro Levocic was going to see his friend Milos Petrovic. Mile Majkovic, who had been here before, was traveling to his brother's residence.[21]

Slovenes exhibited a similar pattern of migration. Among the early Slovenes in Steelton were George Vuksinic and Marko Petrasic, who came from the village of Metlika. Arriving in New York in 1882, they heard of the expanding mill at Steelton. Petrasic soon began to write friends in Metlika advising them to follow him. One who did, Martin Krasovic, found Petrasic living with "colored people" on the West Side. The Slovenes were not, however, so numerous as the Croatian residents.[22]

Since Slavic chain migration went beyond kinship and relied on wider contacts among fellow countrymen, it nurtured a reliance on ethnic ties rather than on kin ties alone. Survival in Croatia and Slovenia had required the collective efforts of joint, communal families.[23] Migration to the industrial city was forcing Croats, Slovenes, and Serbs to rely for the first time on broader ethnic contacts. In this manner, the initial steps were taken to create a community in the industrial milieu which depended upon both kinship and ethnicity. Martin Matyasic followed a sister to Steelton from Croatia but was assisted by friends in securing a job shoveling ore. Louis Lescanec left his native village of Verskovic in Voyvodina, Croatia, in 1903 because he had more relatives in Steelton than at home. During his passage to America he met a fellow Croat who described a "good job opportunity" in Chicago. Lescanec decided to follow kin rather than opportunity, however, and came to Steelton where friends provided the contact with the mill foremen which enabled him to start work as a water boy.[24]

Unlike the old stock, who often possessed specific skills and training, the Slavs were almost entirely farmers or landless agricultural workers. Yugoslav statistics reveal that about 80 percent of emigrants from Croatia-Slovenia were agricultural workers of whom one-third were landless.[25] Even among those who possessed land, the need for additional acreage to sustain their family was crucial. The majority of Slavs came to Steelton to earn sufficient wages to enable them to purchase additional land in Europe. They were not young men in search of opportunity in the expanding industrial borough so much as they were older, married men seeking temporary solutions to their economic problems. A larger study of Croatian repatriation estimated that one-third of all Croats who emigrated to the United States returned to Croatia.[26] Even among those who stayed, many returned several times before deciding to settle in America and reconstruct their families.

The transiency of South Slavs can be illustrated by looking again at the passenger list of the steamship *Brandenberg*. Of the twenty-three Croatian men bound for Steelton, eight had been in the United States before. Nikola Malobacic, from Glina, had worked in Youngstown, Ohio, between 1911 and 1912. Mile Majkovic had lived in Brownsville, Pennsylvania, between 1906 and 1907. Adam Zlatovic and Marko Glisnac were the only ones in the group who had previously lived in Steelton. Zlatovic had worked at the mills between 1910 and 1912, while Glisnac had labored for Pennsylvania Steel between 1908 and 1911. Three other Croats bound for Steelton in 1913, Dmitar Lusio, Stojan Litak, and Ivan Cugalji, had all worked in Buffalo, New York, between 1906 and 1911.[27]

Such immigrants came to America with vague notions of first

earning wealth and later returning to their native land. Several Serbs from the village of Pjecanica knew only in 1899 that they were going to America. "Ja idem v Ameriku," they exclaimed. But their exact destination was not certain. Like Miles Bojanic, they came, hoping to accumulate funds and then return home. George Dragovich, who arrived in 1898 and returned to Pjecanica after a few years, came back to Steelton a second time, discouraged with the impoverished life in his homeland. His second trip to Steelton ended his dream of ever returning to Europe to acquire his *ral*—little better than an acre of land.[28] Others like Tom Benkovic would have returned at once if they had "had the money."[29]

To imply, however, that the characteristics of Slavic migration were representative of all migrants to the industrial town would be misleading. In comparing the Slavs with the old stock and the blacks, important differences emerge, especially in the intentions of the newcomers and in their reliance on ethnic and kinship contacts. Michael Anderson's pathbreaking study of nineteenth-century Lancashire particularly underscored the importance of kinship in the migration process. Anderson explained that kinship links provided migrants with essential information about housing, job prospects, and living conditions.[30] But not all migrants to Steelton relied on kin or friends to the same extent. Like the Rumanians, Slovaks, and Italians arriving in Cleveland, Steelton's newcomers displayed variegated and dissimilar patterns of migration.[31]

In Steelton, three types of migrants were discernible: skilled men arriving with a nuclear family and seeking a somewhat permanent home; highly transient single males arriving alone in search of industrial wages; and married, middle-aged men arriving alone in search of a temporary source of income. The first of the categories could be most clearly associated with the old-stock native whites and with Irish and German newcomers. Blacks belonged primarily to the second category of single males. The middle-aged men arriving alone for a temporary stay were most common among the southern Europeans. Clearly, not all migrants were the same age, came to Steelton under the same conditions, or had similar intentions. These differences were often subtle but must be understood if varying experiences in adaptation are to be explained.

The early old-stock settlers in Steelton were not single young men seeking their fortunes. Nearly seven out of ten native white males were middle-aged family men who already possessed a particular skill. In 1880, their mean age was forty, as shown in table 2. They were already practicing mechanics or blacksmiths when they came to Steelton, in their thirties, attracted by the opportunities of the newly formed mill town. The fact that they were able to bring both their families and a skill probably facilitated their adjustment to the community. The composite picture of the native white migrant to Steelton in 1880 as a middle-aged, skilled, family man is supported by the demographic information in the 1880 federal census for Steelton. Migration usually occurred in family units. Eight out of every ten native white males over the age of eighteen were married. Among native white heads of households, the average age in 1880 was forty-three. Sixty-eight percent of this population were listed as household heads in 1880, and only 32 percent were living as boarders. Since nearly all of this sample would have had to migrate to Steelton within the previous decade, the preponderance of household heads over boarders reinforced the stable image of the native white migrant.

TABLE 2: *Male Population Over Age Eighteen, 1880–1900*

	No.	Mean Age	House- hold Heads	Boarders	Living with Kin	Married
1880						
Native white	68	40	68%	32%	68%	79%
German, Irish	42	33	55	45	66	66
1900						
Black	164	31	36	64	44	46
Slavic	314	32	11	89	15	60

Sources: For native whites, Germans and Irish, "Tenth Census, 1880"; for blacks, Croatians, and Slovenes, "Twelfth Census, 1900." Few Italians, Serbs, or Bulgarians were in Steelton in 1900.

Like the native whites, the early German and Irish settlers usually had worked somewhere else in America before coming to Steelton. John Lehman, a blacksmith living with his wife and four children, was born in 1821. Since Steelton was founded only in 1867, Lehman must have been in his late forties, his occupation and family already established, when he arrived. John Dress, a baker from Bavaria, had children born in America in 1863, again prior to the founding of Steelton. And Thomas Gaffney, an Irishman, worked in West Virginia before coming to Steelton with his family and his familiarity with blast furnaces. This population was only slightly less organized into family units than the native whites. In the 1870s, most of Steelton's Irish and German newcomers were living with kin. Fifty-five percent of Irish and German adult males were heads of households. A full 66 percent, moreover, were living with kin. Since the average age of adult German and Irish males was thirty-three years, most had emigrated in their late twenties. While they were younger than the native white population, the typical old-stock newcomer was married (66 percent) and living in a nuclear household (69 percent). Only about one out of every five Irish and German households contained boarders. This was almost the same as the percentage of native white homes with boarders and indicated that these arrivals were not only migrating largely in family units but were coming to Steelton to seek more permanent roots. This interpretation is based on the assumption that single men were more transient, although many solitary migrants did later reconstruct family units.

While native whites, Germans, and Irish settlers characteristically migrated in family units, blacks and southern Europeans were likely to arrive alone. The preponderance of boarders in both groups was relatively high. Over six out of every ten southern-born adult black males in Steelton in 1900 were boarders, and only 17 percent of these boarders were living with kin. Among Croatian and Slovenian immigrants, nine of every ten in 1900 were boarders, and only 9 percent were residing with kin. While the large majority of native white and

Irish or German adult males were heads of households during their first years of settlement, only 36 percent of the black males and a remarkably low 11 percent of the Croatian-Slovenian males were household heads during their first decade in Steelton. By 1900, after a decade of Slavic emigration into Steelton, only 15 percent of all Slavic adult males were living with kin. This was considerably below the figure for Irish and German immigrants in 1880 (66 percent) and even the figure for blacks in 1900 (44 percent).

The common stereotype of a young, single male as representative of Slavic immigration, which was so characteristic of earlier histories, is not substantiated, however, by the Steelton data. A sample of Slavs who entered America after 1890 revealed that their average age was thirty-four. The mean age at the time of emigration was 32.6. Of this sample, moreover, 58 percent of recent arrivals were married, and they had been married an average of ten years.

The nature of later black and southern European migration can be further understood by focusing on the social condition of boarders (see tables 2 and 3). Even during their initial settlement periods, considerably fewer than one-half of the native white, Irish, and German male migrants in Steelton were living as boarders. The figures for blacks (64 percent) and Slavs (89 percent) in 1900 are much higher. What is even more interesting is the difference in marital status of boarders. The percentage of migrant boarders who were married and living apart

TABLE 3: *Boarders in Steelton, 1880–1900*

	No.	Mean Age	% Married	Mean Years Married
1880				
Native white	22	31	27	9
German, Irish	24	24	22	3
1900				
Black	106	27	20	9
Slavic	280	31	56	10

Sources: "Tenth Census, 1880"; "Twelfth Census, 1900."

from their families in Steelton was similar for native-born whites and Irish and German newcomers in 1880, and for blacks in 1900, usually between 20 and 27 percent. Among Croatian and Slovene boarders in 1900, however, 56 percent were married. Since the average age of Slavic boarders was thirty-one, and they had been married an average of ten years, these were not young men coming to Steelton with romanticized dreams of a new life. They were married men with families migrating in search of industrial wages which promised to alleviate the economic pressures of taxes and insufficient land at home. The data reinforced a fundamental aspect of Slavic migration: the intention of the early Croatian and Slovenian immigrant to earn a sum of money in America and return to Europe. Many later decided to stay in America and reconstructed their families in Steelton; this, however, was seldom their original intention.

In contrast to the old-stock or Slavic immigrants, black migrants were predominantly single males. They did tend to resemble the Slavic profile in age but were somewhat more likely to be living in nuclear families or with kin than were Slavs in 1900. The large component of younger single males made the black settlement in Steelton somewhat less permanent than that of the old stock. This factor may have also made the black male more likely to move on when Slavs began to reconstruct families after World War I and to sink roots of their own. As long as Slavs viewed Steelton as a temporary home, they did not seriously disrupt black status. Black males who came to Steelton were single and less likely to have a family to reconstruct.

The differences among Steelton's migrants are articulated by a comparison of household composition during the years of migration (see table 4). The Slavic reliance on kin and ethnic friends was evident. In 1880 only about one-fifth of native white and Irish and German households contained boarders. During 1900, however, when Slavs were migrating to Steelton, over 80 percent of Croatian households had boarders. Blacks more nearly resembled Slavs than the old stock but were still less likely than the Slavs to have boarders. A decade later Serbs and Croats still took in more boarders than any other group. While about 10 percent of Irish households were augmented in 1910, nearly 71 percent of the Croatian households and 94 percent of the Serbian contained boarders. At the other extreme, no one exceeded the old-stock tendancy to live alone in nuclear families.[32]

TABLE 4: *Household Composition, 1880–1900*

Household Type	Native White 1880 (N=200)	German, Irish 1880 (N=87)	Black 1900 (N=100)	Croatian 1900 (N=120)
Nuclear	70%	69%	24%	9%
Extended	8	8	13	10
Augmented	22	23	63	81

Sources: "Tenth Census, 1880"; "Twelfth Census, 1900."

Close examination of demographic and other data revealed important differences in the migration patterns of the old stock, blacks, and southern Europeans. Migrants came to the industrial town at different times in their lives for different reasons. These differences were influential in explaining subsequent patterns of adjustment—why, for example, the old stock would be preoccupied with preserving Steelton's social order. They came to the town with every intention of making it a permanent home and were less inclined to embrace significant alterations. Transient, single blacks came in search of wages and frequently a new home. Their tendency to arrive as unmarried, young men increased the likelihood that they would eventually move again. Slavs originally viewed Steelton as an expedient to survival in Europe. A strong desire to make Steelton home would not emerge until the maturation of the second generation whose aims would clash with those of the old stock.

3 Steelworkers

The alteration of Steelton through the migration of different groups with varied goals was reflected in the steel plant itself. Attracted by the wages and promises of the growing steel company, the work force acquired an ethnic diversity which threatened the potential for successful labor organization in the three decades after 1890. The company, rigidly opposed to any form of labor organization by its workers, reinforced this diversity by labor practices encouraging ethnic segregation in its various departments. Ethnic tensions between workers impeded labor solidarity.

Pennsylvania Steel grew rapidly after 1880. Between 1886 and 1906 the work force, despite a temporary decline during the depression of 1893–1894, grew from twenty-eight hundred to over nine thousand, with the bulk of the newcomers coming from southern Europe. Simultaneously the company completed a new shipbuilding plant at Sparrows Point, Maryland, acquired vast new ore properties in Cuba, and purchased two blast furnaces at Lebanon, Pennsylvania. By 1900 the local firm had added a new frog, switch, and signal department and, three years later, it modernized its open-hearth furnaces so as to diversify its product line. The result of continued expansion was a doubling of net profits between the late 1880s and 1910.[1]

Expansion at the Steelton facilities continued after Pennsylvania Steel was purchased by the Bethlehem Steel Corporation in 1916. Because the commodity clause of the Hepburn Act prohibited a railroad from owning shares in a company whose goods it transported in a commercial capacity, both the Pennsylvania Railroad and the Reading Railroad decided to dispose of their majority holdings in Pennsylvania Steel and sell the company to Charles Schwab and the Bethlehem Steel Corporation. Bethlehem immediately invested over $12 million in improvements at Steelton, including three new blast furnaces and new electric, hydraulic, and steam plants.[2]

As the local company expanded its productive capacity, it gradually developed a pattern for distributing the work force gathering in Steelton. For unskilled newcomers, the normal entry position at the plant was the labor pool in the brick department. Crews in the brick department had the responsibility of relining the open-hearth furnaces. Every two or three days, old brick lining was torn out of the furnaces and replaced. The crews, according to several steelworkers, engaged in "hot, dirty work." As openings for unskilled workers occurred in other areas, the employment office transferred men from the brick department. In requisition forms asking for men in other departments, Joseph DiSanto recalled the frequent notation, "whites only."[3] Croats were invariably sent to the open hearth, while Serbs found themselves in the blast furnace along with blacks. It was rare to find an open-hearth foreman who was not Irish. Some department superintendents even had definite views on the relative efficiency of different ethnic groups and thus denied work to foreigners in their departments. It was no accident that in 1910 the general labor department, which was composed largely of unskilled workers, was 85 percent Slavic, while the frog and switch department, which required skilled workers to fabricate railroad switches, was 87 percent American, German, English, and Irish.[4]

While no direct evidence was found to indicate a conscientious effort by the company to maintain any particular ethnic composition in its various departments, the employment office really determined the distribution of men initially. Afterward the pattern was maintained by ethnic and kin connections. By 1920 a pattern had emerged which remained for nearly half a century. Blacks were gaining a stronghold in the brick-lining department, the splice bar mill where they cut tie plates and spliced bars, and the rail mill where first they, and later "Spanish-speaking" workers, predominated. Croatians were invariably assigned to the open hearth; "on the floor" of the open hearth everyone was Croatian except the general foreman, who was either Irish or German. In the pit area of the open hearth, Croats were mixed with blacks and Serbs. The labor gang of the Steelton-Highspire Railroad, which operated wholly within the four-mile-long plant and transported slag and other material, was totally Bulgarian. White Anglo-Saxons dominated the car repair shop and the locomotive repair shop.[5]

In a department such as the blast furnace, where the production of steel began, immigrants predominated. Seven furnaces were operated in the Steelton mills prior to 1920. While the head blower who supervised all seven furnaces was invariably Irish, blacks and southern Europeans worked at the back of each furnace filling skips with ore, fuel, and limestone. The large ore shovels were, in fact, known as "Hunky banjos." Newcomers were seldom found in areas of the plant which required skilled workers to produce specialized products such as rails, magnets, and electric alarm signals.[6]

The degree of segregation of the various races and nationalities at the Steelton plant was revealed graphically in a 1910 survey by the United States Immigration Commission. In the departments where labor was the least skilled and working conditions the harshest, the men were mainly foreign born. Of 159 men surveyed in the blast furnace, 123 were either Slavic or black. Of 419 men studied in the open-hearth furnace, 325 were either foreign born or Negro. In departments requiring skilled or less physical labor, such as the machine shop, only 9 blacks and immigrants were among the nearly 250 surveyed. And these few were usually "helpers." The investigation also found that of 59 Slovenians surveyed in the mill, 36 were in the open hearth.[7]

The differences among native whites, blacks, and immigrants were also seen clearly in the distribution of wages. The United States Immigration Commission classified all workers earning under $1.50 a day as unskilled and all earning over that amount as skilled. Six groups had more than half of their workers in the "skilled" category. They included the Irish (75 percent), the German (60 percent) and the Negro (59 percent). In 1910 fewer than one-half of the Italians and Slavs were in this category. Only 30 percent of the Croatians earned over $1.50 per day. Groups like the Serbs and Bulgarians had fewer than 15 percent of their countrymen classified as skilled. Indeed, 92 percent of the Bulgarians were unskilled.[8]

The distribution of the blacks reflected the modest gains that they had made before the onset of heavy immigration from southern Europe. Both blacks and Slavs had not made any real encroachments, however, into supervisory positions. Of 136 foremen studied by the commission, 117 were either American, German, or Irish. Only 2 Negroes were among the foremen, who included 1 Serb, 3 Croats, and 1 Slovene.[9]

In real earnings the figures again tended to follow racial and ethnic lines. Native-born whites and western Europeans generally earned more than Croats, Serbs, Bulgarians, and other newcomers from southern Europe.[10] In 1910 the average unskilled immigrant in Steelton earned approximately eleven cents an hour. This rate remained fairly constant from 1890 to 1910. While the Steelton newspapers hailed the company when it granted a 10 percent increase in prosperous times, the raise only amounted to one cent an hour for the unskilled and was always rescinded when business slackened.[11]

News accounts in the Steelton press suggested the grimness of life in the mills. Men lost arms, legs, and "were burned to a cinder." In 1902 five "Austrians"—Jurovic, Marovoich, Gatis, Muza, and Radjanovic—were burned to death "in a horrible manner" when molten metal from the open hearth poured on them. In 1906 Anton Picjac, a boy of sixteen, fell through the top of a gas oven and was cremated. The story was repeated frequently and became a way of life. Immigrants, working in the most dangerous jobs, were continually killed. The list of victims in 1907 speaks for itself: Tesak, Pajolic, Stifko, Knukle, Termer, Petruti, Pierce, Oconicke, Ukelic, Krameric, Szep, Peffer, Gross, Susic, Restoff, Trajbarico, Polanec, Turnbaugh, and Pugar.[12]

Newcomers not only received the most menial occupations but also faced resentment from the native workingmen. Old-stock workers vented their dislike of foreigners repeatedly to investigators of the United States Immigration Commission, claiming immigrants were hired because they were willing to work for lower wages than were native residents. The American-born worker did not care to work with the "Hunkie," the report indicated, and in many cases transferred his own labor to an occupation such as a clerkship, often at a lower wage.[13]

In 1905 the Steelton branch of the Order of United American Mechanics, an organization of skilled workers consisting entirely of old-stock whites, passed a resolution to support immigration restriction. The branch declared:

> Whereas, the record of immigration shows that more than 800,000 foreign-born persons landed upon American soil during the past year—not the sturdy people who came before the sixties to find a place where they might worship God according to the dictates of their own conscience, to build homes for themselves . . . but from pauper districts of Southern Europe . . . the incubators of nihilism, anarchy, disease, and crime. . . .
>
> Therefore, be it resolved that we demand the enactment of such laws as will shield us from the depressing effects of unrestricted immigration, to the end that the American laborer may not only be protected against the product of the foreign pauper laborer, but that we may be protected against direct competition in our own country by the incoming of the COMPETITIVE ALIEN—the foreign pauper laborers themselves.[14]

The actions of native whites also tended to strain relations with the immigrant and black worker. The native workers insisted that Slavs and blacks march in their own parades on patriotic occasions rather than in the regular American parade. Native whites also avoided working with immigrants at the mill. During the depression of 1908, when the plant manager at

Steelton offered his skilled men jobs that were normally performed by immigrants, he found few willing to accept. They preferred to be laid off. Natives were also frequently guilty of exploiting foreign workers. In 1913 Charles Saul, a foreman at the frog and switch department, was arrested for charging immigrants fifty dollars to obtain a job. Such resentment and exploitation kept Steelton's labor force badly divided.[15]

While division within the ranks of Steelton's workers was pervasive, old-stock, skilled workers attempted to forge some form of organization in 1890 when they established a local chapter of the Amalgamated Association of Iron and Steel Workers. The company had already explained its views on labor organization through the *Reporter*. The paper noted that labor organizations were not needed in Steelton because the people in the mill town were "satisfied" and under no circumstances would the company allow extraneous interference with its business.[16] In its most extensive discussion of the drawbacks of labor organization the *Reporter* argued:

> Workingmen who enter into "combinations" usually interfere with the great laws of supply and demand . . . that combination in labor is the wrong way to attain any benefit for labor, for such combinations always provoke like conditions, the effects of which are antagonisms which destroy confidence on both sides. . . . But there is combination which every workingman can make for himself, from which he can derive lasting benefits. This combination everyman must make with himself, and its main feature is that of personal rectitude, sobriety, thrift, and the careful hoarding of wages. A man cannot be true to himself who consents to become a part of an organization which deprives him of free speech. . . . A workingman should try to please his employer since a worker's employer is his customer.[17]

Consequently, when the Amalgamated local prepared a set of demands for presentation to company officials in May 1891,

Steelton witnessed a great deal of "street talk" concerning the impending confrontation.[18]

A committee of the Amalgamated Association presented demands for increased wages and recognition of their union to Superintendent Felton at the steel works in July 1891. The company reacted immediately. Felton responded that he would have nothing to do with labor organizations and that if the men had any grievances, they would be given individual hearings. A notice was posted at the mill to the effect that no labor organization would be recognized in any way by the company.[19]

The Amalgamated announcement gave the company seven days to consider the various demands. Each department in the plant had its own union lodge, which preserved particular grievances in addition to the general demands of the union. The merchant mill, for one, had over thirty demands regarding working conditions, including a request for more help. Moreover, the Amalgamated presented a supplementary request for wage increases whenever a price rise was secured for steel rails by the Steelton plant. It offered to accept wage decreases when prices fell but not below the level of 1891. Finally, the union asked for the reinstatement of all men previously discharged by the company for union membership.[20]

On July 22, Felton issued orders to shut down the plant. For the first time in its history the Pennsylvania Steel Company's plant was closed and Pinkerton detectives were hired to guard the mills. A committee from the Amalgamated appeared at the company's offices to ask about their demands but was not given an audience. Town officials passed an edict closing all hotels and bars in order to keep liquor from the men, while sheriff's men and "coal and iron police" patrolled the streets. As several hundred union men began marching through the borough, F. L. Shunk, a leader of the Amalgamated lodges, claimed twenty-six hundred men sided with the union. His estimate was quite accurate and included a scattering of the relatively few Croatians and Slovenes who lived in Steelton at that time.[21]

Shunk asserted that the union was well prepared to withstand a long siege at Pennsylvania Steel. The company responded by bringing in several hundred black strikebreakers from the South. The issue was little in doubt, however, by late July when it became apparent that the national headquarters of the Amalgamated would not provide support to the Steelton lodge. At the outset of the strike Shunk announced that men from Steelton had already paid some $50,000 into the national treasury, and they would surely receive aid. But William Weihe, president of the Amalgamated, came from Pittsburgh on July 29 and declared the local strike to be unauthorized. Weihe claimed that the men in Steelton drew up a wage scale in March which had not been approved by the national headquarters as feasible at that time.[22]

With the announcement by the Amalgamated that it would not provide support, the strike at Steelton was weakened. Felton telegraphed *Iron Age* that the "trouble was practically over" and all old employees could return under the same conditions as before the strike.[23] Actually, Felton's statement covered up the real extent of the company's recriminations. Former jobs were denied to men identified with the Amalgamated on the grounds that they had made themselves "obnoxious" to the management. A "spotted list" was drawn up of those who would not be reinstated. All employees were required to sign an agreement that they would not join any labor organization.[24]

During the strike itself, the company stopped making deductions from wages for the Steelworkers Beneficial Society and consequently greatly weakened the organization and its resources. The society had been created in 1886 in order to pay sick and disability benefits and other forms of compensation for "white employees" of the steel plant.[25] The blatant discrimination with which the Beneficial Society treated Negroes caused a serious division in the ranks of Steelton's labor force during the strike. At the height of the walkout, blacks remembered their exclusion. "We were not wanted at the first, and we will not join under any circumstances," proclaimed a statement issued by a Committee of Colored Men.[26]

The community press also was a deterrent to the success of the strike. Generally, local support for management in many steel towns was a vital force in maintaining the labor status quo. Steelton proved to be no exception. The *Reporter* observed, after the strike ended, that the management was very lenient with its old employees. As to those who were expelled from their jobs, the paper felt that this was only the mill's way of getting rid of a large quantity of "dead wood." The Pennsylvania Steel Company was always so successfully managed that it provided steady work despite economic fluctuations. "It would cause great suffering to many of our people," the *Reporter* insisted whenever strike rumors were spread, "if the works closed for an indefinite period."[27]

In 1892 the Amalgamated experienced a much more devastating defeat at Homestead, near Pittsburgh. The union was never again a powerful force in the industry. Its demise doomed Steelton unionism. For the next twenty-five years Pennsylvania Steel completely defeated any semblance of unionism in its labor force. It was not surprising, therefore, that the United States Immigration Commission found that of 750 men surveyed in 1910 in Steelton not one was affiliated with a trade union.[28]

Pennsylvania Steel was relentless in its attack upon any form of labor protest. In the summer of 1894 over three hundred Negro steelworkers were sent by train from Steelton to the coke fields of Westmoreland County in western Pennsylvania to help break a strike. One of them had his Steelton home dynamited, apparently by a "person in sympathy with the strikers" in the coke fields.[29] In July 1904, fifteen "Slavonians" who initiated a brief strike at the billet mill of the plant were ousted from their jobs despite pleas for reinstatement. The mill had put the Slavs on piece work. When production became slow, however, the workers asked to be placed back on a regular hourly basis. The company refused and argued that they would not operate their works to suit the convenience of foreigners. The Slavs vented their disgust in "vigorous and excitable Slav lingo," purchased steamship tickets, and returned to their farms in Europe.[30]

The most blatant use of strikebreakers by the Pennsylvania

Steel Company occurred in 1906. In March of that year, Italian laborers who had been working the company's ore banks at nearby Cornwall struck for a ten-hour day and a wage increase. Pennsylvania Steel reacted by sending sixty Italian laborers from the Steelton plant's general labor department to work the ore mines in place of the strikers. When the Italians from Steelton arrived, the men at Cornwall encircled them and began to yell and jeer. At this moment armed state and local police "attacked the howling Italian strikers" and sent them fleeing and "cursing in their native tongue."[31]

After working the mines on March 7, the imported strikebreakers were taken to boardinghouses at Cornwall and guarded by state police. The *Lebanon Daily News* carried the headline, "Dago Miners in Ugly Mood." Italians marched through Cornwall waving red handkerchiefs and singing their national anthem. The Lebanon paper hastily added, however, that "Americans" took no part in the demonstration or marches and accused the Italians of using "threats of violence" to keep many miners from work. Within another day, Pennsylvania Steel, with further protection by the state police, sent a "carload of Hungarians" from its labor department at Steelton. The strike was now broken, and the few Italians who still resisted were clubbed by police. The *Lebanon Daily News* assured its readers that they deserved clubbing.[32]

In 1912 when cranemen and yard crews at the Steelton plant walked off the job and demanded more pay, many of them were promptly fired. This caused further walkouts among the other departments, and a committee was sent to meet with Pennsylvania Steel officials. Although the company heard the men's demands, it largely ignored them in the end. Moreover, the strike caused hundreds of foreign laborers to be idled. While the strikers waited for the company's response, many immigrants accepted jobs from steel firms in Pittsburgh and Williamsport. Most immigrants could not afford to go long without pay. Thus, the steel company's policy not only effectively resisted labor's demands but also caused many workers to be uprooted from time to time.[33]

Acquiring the Steelton plant on the eve of America's entry into World War I, Bethlehem Steel experienced minimal labor trouble during the conflict. In August 1918, a local branch of the American Federation of Labor was chartered in Steelton. Ignoring the local appeals of the Win the War Publicity Association of Central Pennsylvania to work together and maintain production, the new trade-union members walked off their jobs. About three hundred men, two-thirds of whom were native-born, old-stock machinists in skilled positions, demanded the same wage scale as their counterparts had at the plant in Bethlehem. Local union leaders claimed that they were taking advantage of a recent ruling by the National War Labor Board forbidding interference with organized labor. Due to the relatively small number of men involved, however, the walkout was short-lived. The calm did not last long. Once the demands of the war effort were lifted in 1919, steelworkers in Steelton and elsewhere did not remain quiescent.[34]

Tension between labor and industry had mounted during World War I. The total commitment which labor ostensibly had to make for the war effort certainly enhanced its standing and prestige. On the other hand, labor was unable to win any substantial economic gains. The National War Labor Board, however, did make certain decisions which benefited the workingman at Bethlehem Steel during the war. In July 1918, it ordered the company to conform with the minimum hourly rates of the war and navy departments, to pay time-and-a-half for work over eight hours and double time for Sundays and holidays, to desist in its antiunion activities, and to deal with shop committees elected by the employees under the supervision of a federal examiner.[35] It was this last decision which sparked the brief outburst by the embryonic AFL lodge in Steelton.[36]

Once the war ended, labor was more than ready to press its demands for union recognition by the steel industry. Management, on the other hand, had different ideas. Eugene Grace, president of Bethlehem Steel, bluntly told a War Labor Board examiner in November 1918 that since the war was over, his firm needed a free hand to meet peacetime conditions. Grace informed his listeners that his company no longer felt itself bound by the board's decisions. Such an implacable stance inevitably collided with the rise in unrest over increasing unemployment and the decline in real wages that followed the termination of the war. The result was the steel strike of 1919.[37]

Steelton's labor disturbances began in March 1919. Men who had been in great demand during the war were put on a reduced working schedule. One by one the blast furnaces, which had been in continuous operation for several years, were shut down. While seven blast furnaces had been kept busy during 1918, only two were operating by late March 1919. Bethlehem Steel, moreover, was actively resisting any possible incursion of the AFL into factory towns such as Steelton. Its tactics included the use of company-sponsored employee organizations. This policy, claimed Frank Morrison, secretary of the AFL, would sow the seeds of Bolshevism by denying employees the right to organize.[38]

By March 28, 6,000 men worked on a reduced hourly basis in Steelton, representing 60 percent of the wartime labor force. Persistent rumors circulated around the town suggesting that the plant would soon close. As workers grew more discontented, officials attempted to forestall any drift toward radical solutions. By April the local papers were filled with full-page advertisements speaking out against Bolshevism and the Industrial Workers of the World. They warned that the "Grasping Hand of the IWW" was antagonistic to the ideals of honest labor. "Bolshevism offers no possibility of advance for labor," according to the *Harrisburg Telegraph*. "It is an imported theory fomented by foreigners." One large drawing in the *Telegraph* depicted a wolf, who represented Bolshevism, on a hill overlooking an American industrial plant, while a caption warned that, if Bolshevism came to America, "Liberty will be destroyed and women and children will be the property of the state."[39]

Charles Schwab himself came to Steelton in May to assure the men that the plant would not be closed. Promising that millions of dollars would be spent in improving the Steelton plant, he predicted that an unusual period of prosperity would soon follow in the steel business. Labor, however, was impatient. Machinists at Steelton had already organized into a larger group with their counterparts in Reading and Pottstown. By July, petitions were being circulated at Steelton asking for a decided increase in wages. Frank Robbins, the plant's general manager, returned the petitions and argued that such increases were impossible.[40]

When the national strike began in September, officials at the Steelton plant indicated that a local strike was highly improbable, although local workers had formed six branches of the AFL within the past year. On September 22, however, union spokesmen in Bethlehem asked for a conference with company officials and indicated the possibility of a strike if demands were not met. After waiting five days, union leaders in Bethlehem recieved a note from Eugene Grace saying that he would neither grant a conference with the union nor abandon Bethlehem's program of company-sponsored employee organizations. The union immediately ordered a general strike against Bethlehem Steel. In response, Frank Robbins, the company superintendent, announced that "there will be work for all who do not desire to quit" and insisted that the Steelton plant would not close.[41]

On September 28 the AFL opened strike headquarters in Steelton and began to register sympathizers. Although the plant remained open, about one-half of the work force stayed away on the first day. The strike was most effective among skilled workers in the machine and bridge shop as well as among the electricians. Workers' groups, moreover, issued impassioned statements to the press:

> During the war we fabricated munition plants, small arm plants. . . . We did the work cheerfully, without strikes or trouble of any kind. We were so exhausted after a day's work that we fell asleep at the supper table. We pared to the bone in order to buy Liberty Bonds, to give to the Red Cross, and similar organizations. For what? To make the world safe for democracy. . . .

The whole industrial world is in chaos and it is up to the Industrial Kings of America to grant their employees industrial democracy.[42]

The mayor of Steelton, Thomas McEntee, who was also a superintendent at the plant, requested all citizens to keep order and refrain from congregating. He even deputized over one hundred of the steel company's special officers as borough policemen. While law and order were maintained by constant police patrols, pickets now appeared around the plant and several large rallies were held. The Steelton AFL Policy Committee, devoid of any Negro, Slavic, or Italian representation, issued a notice charging that "modern industrial autocrats" were more "arrogant, more brutal, and more tyrannous" in their methods than King George III. This statement insisted: "We want our economic rights defined as our political rights have been defined."[43]

The strike organizers faced a difficult situation. By the third day, strikers represented less than one-half of the labor force, and the plant was never completely shut down. Local police protection enabled men who wanted to work to do so without any interference from pickets. Company police made certain that pickets were kept as far away as possible from the plant. In fact, over one hundred policemen kept the peace at Steelton (and the pickets away), while in normal times only ten were needed.[44]

By October 5, the strike effort in Steelton was slowing down. Failures on the national level, of course, contributed to the waning of the effort locally. But more symptomatic of defeat was the decision on October 5, when the strike was nearly over, to try and save it by making special appeals to Steelton's foreign sections. James Brown, a local union official, called a meeting of "foreigners" at Croatian Hall. While the meeting was well attended, it was the first major effort the local made to attract Steelton's immigrant workers. The early strike initiative had come mostly from the highly organized, skilled departments at the plant, staffed predominantly by old-stock whites. The appeals made at the Croatian Hall came too late. They failed. Blacks were not approached at all. Ethnic differences proved a powerful deterrent to unity, hindering any chance of success for workers in Steelton. After the meeting at Croatian Hall, many foreigners simply returned to work.[45]

Just as blacks were left out of union activity in 1891, immigrants were excluded from the Steelton union in 1919. Since immigrants were lodged primarily in unskilled and semiskilled occupations, the local lodges of the AFL had little use for them. As a Croatian newspaper remarked several years after the strike, "It was not easy for Jugoslav workers to join unions, the more so because the American trade unions served the working aristrocracy of skilled tradesmen."[46] Furthermore, some foreigners had no clear idea of what was involved in the strike or who was behind it. John Verbos, a Croatian, stayed away from work out of fear and lost his job. Another Croat remained home for two days even though his superintendent had promised him "protection." Lewis Zuvic, a Croatian who had arrived in Steelton in 1913, was skeptical of the "union man" who tried to keep him from going to work and decided to stay home for a few days in order to avoid "radicals and trouble."[47] One Croat distrusted the union organizer's handling of dues. Thus, a badly divided work force had to wait nearly twenty years more for strong union representation.

The antagonism which limited the effectiveness of union activity in Steelton originated in the ethnic and racial pattern which the company had woven throughout the plant. The growth of ethnically diverse segments in the mills was assisted by the recruitment and distribution of various workers. Moreover, the gulf between skilled and unskilled workers was reinforced since old-stock elements predominated in higher-paid positions and began to regard the newcomers as competitors after 1890, although blacks and Slavs were not moving into skilled trades. The fruits of the company's actions were reaped in 1891 and 1919. Blacks were excluded from the local Amalgamated lodges in 1891, and Slavs were largely omitted from the AFL organizations in 1919, thus weakening both strike efforts.

If the unskilled immigrant and black were to abandon their lowly status and integrate themselves into skilled departments, upward occupationally mobility was needed. Faced with old-stock resentment, however, southern Europeans and blacks could not rise easily from their positions. In fact, their career mobility was limited with few moving only slightly from the unskilled jobs. Blacks fared even worse after 1900. And the old stock which had first established itself in the plant retained its dominant position.

4 Community and Mobility

If Slavs, Italians, and blacks were ever to establish permanent roots in the town and participate in the leadership of the plant and the community, they needed a degree of upward occupational mobility. But the company had placed them in the lowest positions. The careers of Slavs, Italians, and blacks were less successful and more transient than those of old stock workers. The unskilled southern Europeans and blacks had difficulties in climbing upward and were more susceptible to moving during hard times. They could not afford to remain out of work long and, therefore, sought employment elsewhere when jobs were scarce in Steelton. While all steelworkers were subject to transiency and limited mobility, the chances of being geographically mobile and occupationally stagnant were greater for unskilled blacks and southern Europeans than for the old-stock workers who dominated the skilled positions.[1] The process of mobility did not function as an integrative mechanism for unskilled, industrial newcomers. Statistical analysis of social and geographic mobility suggested that the industrial worker would have to seek alternatives such as ethnic groups and, later, unions, if security, equal power, and a measure of prosperity were to be obtained.

The notion that occupational success rewards diligent workers has pervaded American literature and life. Steelton was no exception. While it is difficult to measure precisely the extent to which industrial workers believed in the "American dream," steelworkers were certainly exposed to some discussion of the subject. In 1886 the *Steelton Reporter* cautioned readers not to believe demagogues who argued that poor men were at a disadvantage in America. The journal concluded that since Andrew Johnson, Ulysses S. Grant, and Jay Gould rose from humble origins, anyone could do so. The difficulty was that most men were simply not willing to live within their means. Consequently, the paper observed, the "survival of the fittest" operated continually to assure that only those who practiced self-denial and pursued self-improvement would elevate themselves.[2] Several years later the journal claimed that "there is always room at the top of the ladder of fame and fortune." The *Reporter* claimed that most prominent men in the country's history began their lives under difficult circumstances. No matter what a man's chosen occupation, however, he would not succeed if he did not work. "The aim of every young man," the paper said, "should be to climb to the top of the ladder and never to rest a moment."[3]

The ideology of mobility pervaded other areas of Steelton life as well. Each June much was made in the local press of the motto chosen by the graduating class of Steelton High School. In 1893, the twelve graduates (in a town of over ten thousand people) decided upon Onward and Upward. The following year the graduates picked Diligence Insures Success. And at graduation they heard such speeches as "The Possibilities of the American Boy," which promised that, although life was a struggle, success would come to all who were prepared.[4]

While immigrants may not have been as familiar with the concept of social mobility, the majority were seeking to maintain their precarious economic status through industrial wages. Most newcomers planned to return to Europe with their earnings. Several, such as Lewis Zuvic, had heard of the abundance of money in America and came to acquire their share.[5] In 1913 a survey of 43,500 Slovenes revealed that 87 percent said they were coming to America "to earn more."[6]

Most of the immigrant press reflected a middle-class bias and exposed the newcomer to preachings of the success ideology. One South Slavic organ which was read in Steelton, *Jugoslavia*, was quite explicit when it affirmed:

Here everybody is an immigrant or the child of an immigrant. . . . It is not true that life is harder than it was before. Do not believe him who will say to you that here is the bitter bread, the hard life. Do not trust him. Because here is open to you every road, every door, every career. Before you is that grandiose life, this powerful state, which will give you the possibility to live, to work, and to be happy.

All is yours, what you make by your work and thinking capacity.

Always be of good cheer. Here they do not like people who despair and worry continually. Here the only person is lost who is his own gravedigger.[7]

Not all immigrant publications, of course, reflected such faith in American society. *Zanje,* a Croatian socialist paper, claimed that America did not turn out to be the country "agents told us." It argued that there was no trace of opportunity or liberty for the workingman.[8]

Before achieveing any form of social mobility, the newcomers had to establish some sort of permanent status in the steel town. Frequent moves to Europe or other industrial areas might in some instances result in upward mobility, but transiency did little to enhance their status in Steelton or elsewhere and was more often a reflection of their failure to secure steady employment. The extensive geographic mobility among Steelton's work force was a manifestation of a trend that could be found in other industrial cities. The phenomenon was recognized by contemporary observers who talked of a "floating population," frequently moving in search of more money or another job.[9] The United States Immigration Commission's report in 1911 identified industrial mobility with the races of recent immigration, originating in southern and eastern Europe.[10] The floating labor supply was, indeed, composed chiefly of immigrant and Negro groups.

It was not uncommon to read accounts of the shifting of the industrial work force from time to time in Steelton. When employment was slack at the local mill, steelworkers often looked for jobs in the plants at Braddock or Homestead or other mills in the Pittsburgh region. After the failure of the 1891 strike in Steelton, most of the striking steelworkers who lost their jobs moved their families to steel districts in western Pennsylvania. A Harrisburg newspaper noted that an almost continuous stream of heavily laden wagons moved to the railroad stations as the steelworkers moved westward. In 1902 the anthracite coal strike likewise forced several hundred unemployed miners to seek work at the Pennsylvania Steel Company in Steelton.[11]

After the federal census of 1910 reported the borough's population as 14,246, the *Reporter* claimed that it was not disappointed by the small gain of only 2,000 in the past decade. "The population is largely a floating one," the journal observed, "and considering conditions in similar towns, Steelton's gain compares very favorably with any steel town in the state." The local paper felt that if the census had been taken before the panic of 1907, when economic conditions were better, the population count would have been much higher.[12]

Among immigrants the tendency to move about from one industrial job to another was particularly widespread. *Radnick,* a Croatian socialist paper, claimed that immigrants were slow in joining unions because they moved so much that they considered themselves transients. Shortly after their arrival in 1901, the "restless and more adventurous" Bulgarians decided to move from Steelton, "lured by the opportunities of the Middle West."[13] After Slovenian immigrants became skilled in the operations of manufacturing steel, they moved to western industrial centers such as Pittsburgh, Cleveland, and Lorain, in Ohio.[14] Each year a segment of Steelton's Italians spent the months between October and March harvesting in the wheat fields of Argentina, where they were given free passage by the Argentine government.[15]

The depression of 1907–1908 was especially devastating to any stability established by Steelton's immigrant workers. An undetermined number of Croatians withdrew their savings accounts from local bankers and either returned to Croatia or found jobs in the anthracite and bituminous coal fields.[16] Bulgarians, the most recent arrivals among immigrants, were hardest hit by the panic. Fifty-four percent were forced either to return to Macedonia or seek employment elsewhere. Many were hired to work on railroad gangs in the southern states. Over one-third of the Serbs, Croats, and Italians were also forced to leave the town. The United States Immigration Commission listed 2,300 Serbs in Steelton in 1907 and only 1,400 in 1908. Of 1,600 Croats in 1907, only 1,100 remained in 1908. Of 650 Bulgarians in 1907, 300 were present the following year. On the other hand, none of the 400 Irish immigrants sampled in Steelton in 1907 had left by the following year.[17]

Even minor fluctuations in the economic cycle magnified the incidence of geographic mobility. In the autumn of 1910, when the mills were slack, the *Reporter* noted that steamship agents in the borough reported three times as many Austrians and Hungarians returning to Europe as the year before. The following year a local official attributed the absence of arrests in the Serbian community during the January Christmas celebration to the outward flow of Serbs to Europe "during the present hard times."[18] Yet just as certainly as hard times forced immigrants to look elsewhere for employment, prosperity would bring them back to Steelton. Many of the aliens who left the borough in December 1907 came back two years later. Local observers even attempted to gauge the extent of prosperity by the flow of immigrants. In 1911 the *Reporter* concluded that the large number of foreigners returning to the borough was a sure sign of prosperous times, and that many immigrants could afford to bring friends and relatives to Steelton with prepaid tickets. This practice contributed to the immigrant tide during "good times."[19]

Finally, although the economic cycle stirred a good deal of migration, often an immigrant moved simply because he was tempted by higher wages. Every spring hundreds of immigrants left Steelton, lured by offers of "large" wages placed in Croat papers by employers of outdoor workers. When this seasonal employment finished, the Slavs and Italians returned to Steelton hoping to secure a position at the mill for the winter.

They claimed, upon their return from summer jobs, that they had just arrived from Europe and were new to this country. Pennsylvania Steel, in order to control this seasonal distribution in its work force, employed a system of fingerprinting to identify employers more effectively and thereby discourage them from leaving again.[20]

Further evidence of extensive geographic mobility in Steelton is provided by a quantitative measurement of the town's population turnover. Persistence, which is the proportion, usually expressed as a percentage, of a population remaining in a delimited area after a particular time interval,[21] was characteristic of only a minority of steelworkers between 1880 and 1925. Between one-third and one-half of the town's entire population usually left during each ten-year period.

The persistence rates for the entire population indicated that between 1880 and 1888 about one-half the population of Steelton either died or moved elsewhere. Since church records in Steelton showed only a few deaths each month, the vast majority of those whose names disappeared from the city directories were undoubtedly moving away. The longer that workingmen remained in the industrial city, however, the less was the likelihood of their seeking employment elsewhere. Between 1888 and 1896 and between 1896 and 1905, persistence rates increased for the population which remained in the town during the eight years after 1880. Although 50 percent of the population reported to be living in Steelton in 1880 was not in the borough in 1888, of the 50 percent who remained, 77 percent still resided there in 1896. Of those who remained until 1896, 73 percent could still be found in 1905 (see Appendix 1, table C).

Not surprisingly, persistence rates were lowest in the decade of the 1880s for the unskilled laborer who was most susceptible to changes and fluctuations in the economy. The unskilled formed the bulk of the transient laboring classes which wandered from one industrial job and from one city to another. Of 398 unskilled workers listed in Steelton in 1880, only 44 percent could be identified in 1888, 35 percent in 1896, and 23 percent in 1905.[22]

After 1900 the outward flow of the industrial work force increased even more. While the persistence rate had been 50 percent in the 1880s, it dropped gradually to 35 percent between 1915 and 1925. This decline coincided with the onset of southern European immigration. In the 1880 and 1905 groups, unskilled workers displayed the least inclination to remain in Steelton over a given period of time. By 1905 only about one in every five of the unskilled identified in 1880 were still there. An almost identical rate was found for the unskilled workers in 1925 who had been listed in the 1905 group.[23] As might be expected, the highest persistence rates were found in the nonmanual classifications which provided steadier employment.

Persistence was most prevalent among old immigrants such as the English, Irish, and Germans, as shown in table 5. Where only one-half of the entire population remained in Steelton from 1880 to 1888, nine out of every ten English, Irish, and German immigrants did so. Moreover, high rates for this group continued through the next seventeen years and ran over 20 percent above the persistence rate for the population as a whole. Among the semiskilled and skilled, all old immigrants remained in Steelton from 1888 to 1905. While the persistence rate was lower for the unskilled old immigrant, it was still considerably higher than the rates for the rest of the population.

New immigrants like the Slavs and Italians had a persistence pattern which differed significantly from that of Irish, English, and German arrivals from northern Europe. Whereas 90 percent of the old immigrants stayed in Steelton during the 1880s, only 32 percent of the Slavs and Italians remained from 1905 to 1915. As usual, the longer an immigrant lived in the town, the less were his chances of leaving. Yet, even among those newcomers who had lived in Steelton from 1905 to 1915, over one-half still decided to move in the decade after 1915.

The unskilled, newly arrived immigrant showed the greatest tendency to leave the borough from 1905 to 1915. Only 27 percent of the unskilled immigrants who were in Steelton in 1905 could be found there ten years later. This was considera-

TABLE 5: *Persistence Rates for Newcomers, 1880–1925*

	Unskilled	Semi-skilled	Skilled	Nonmanual	Total
1880 group (English, German, Irish)	(N=42)	(N=8)	(N=4)	(N=4)	(N=58)
1888	90%	90%	100%	100%	90%
1896	86	100	100	100	90
1905	100	100	100	75	96
1905 group (Slavic, Italian)	(N=303)	(N=30)	(N=0)	(N=70)	(N=403)
1915	27%	43%	0%	44%	32%
1925	40	46	0	45	47
1915 group (Slavic, Italian)	(N=479)	(N=61)	(N=20)	(N=76)	(N=636)
1925	37%	59%	30%	53%	42%

Note: Read "27 percent of 303 Slavic and Italian unskilled workers in 1905 were still in Steelton in 1915; of those who persisted between 1905 and 1915, 40 percent could be found in the community in 1925." To compare immigrant rates with the rest of the population see Appendix 1, table C. The difference in persistence rates for skilled and nonmanual immigrants between 1880 and 1888 is too small to be statistically significant.

bly less than the 44 percent of nonmanual immigrants from the 1905 group who persisted through the same period.

Interestingly enough, among immigrants who remained in Steelton for at least a decade after 1905, the persistence rates of the various skill categories among Slavs and Italians were nearly the same between 1915 and 1925. However, a turnover of more than one-half the immigrant population still took place each decade. The southern Europeans who appeared in the 1915 sample were slightly more stable in the subsequent decade than the Slavs and Italians from the 1905 group. Yet only four out of every ten could still be identified after a decade as compared with three in ten for the 1905 group. Again, persistence rates were considerably higher for nonmanual workers than for the unskilled.

While comparing poorly with the English, Irish, and Germans in Steelton during the 1880s, blacks had persistence rates only slightly lower than those for the population as a whole (see table 6).[24] Forty-seven percent of the Negroes appearing in 1880 could still be found in Steelton eight years later. Characteristically, of the blacks who remained in Steelton for most of the 1880s, the chances were more than eight in ten that they would remain throughout the 1890s. During the years of heavy Slavic immigration into Steelton, however, Negro rates fell to 23 percent between 1905 and 1915 and to 21 percent between 1915 and 1925. These rates are lower than the 32 percent (1905–1915) and 42 percent (1915–1925) shown by Slavs and Italians. The downward trend in black persistence rates contrasted with the slowly rising Slavic and Italian rates.[25]

TABLE 6: *Persistence Rates for Blacks, 1880–1925*

	Unskilled	Semi-skilled	Skilled	Nonmanual	Total
1880 group	(N=82)	(N=3)	(N=0)	(N=2)	(N=87)
1888	45%	33%	0%	100%	47%
1896	90	100	0	100	85
1905 group	(N=183)	(N=96)	(N=0)	(N=21)	(N=300)
1915	33%	10%	0%	10%	23%
1915 group	(N=220)	(N=84)	(N=0)	(N=19)	(N=323)
1925	28%	7%	0%	0%	21%

Note: Read "45 percent of 82 unskilled blacks in 1880 were still to be found in Steelton in 1888; of those persisting to 1888, 90 percent continued to persist in 1896."

While the turnover in Steelton's population was rapid, those who managed to stabilize their lives and remain in the borough sought to attach themselves permanently to the town. Wage earners who had acquired property displayed a marked tendency to persist longer.[26] The persistence rate for property owners was considerably higher than for the population as a whole (see table 7). Exactly one-half of Steelton's property owners who lived there in 1905 were still there in 1915. This compared with only 39 percent of the population as a whole. A sample of property owners in 1915 showed a persistence rate of 53 percent in 1925. This was some 18 percent higher than the rate for the entire population during the same decade.

TABLE 7: *Persistence Rates for Property Owners, 1905–1925*

	1905 Group		1915 Group	
	No.	% Remaining in 1915	No.	% Remaining in 1925
Value of assessed property				
Under $1,100	242	42	280	50
$1,100–3,000	249	57	314	57
Over $3,000	147	50	73	50
Total number	638	—	667	—
Average percent	—	50	—	53

Sources: Persistence rates were computed for individuals traced in the five ward books of the Annual Enumeration of All Persons, Places, and Things for 1905, 1915, and 1925.

In both the 1905 and 1915 groups the rate of persistence for those owning less than $1,100 worth of property was lower than for the middle range who owned between $1,100 and $1,300. In the 1915 sample, however, the persistence rate for those who owned over $3,000 worth of property was identical with that of the lower-value property owners. This might be partially explained by the fact that large property owners between 1905 and 1925 were dividing and selling their holdings to newcomers during these decades of expansion and moving into more "desirable" areas. For instance, the estate of George Cumbler owned $41,600 worth of real estate in Steelton's first ward in 1915, an area populated by Slavic immigrants. The only property owner whose holdings were larger than Cumbler's was the Pennsylvania Steel Company. By 1925, however, the Cumbler estate owned only $1,450 worth in the same ward. Real estate transactions revealed that the property was sold piecemeal. Moreover, despite the turnover among large property owners and those with lesser holdings, the persistence among small property owners was higher than for the population as a whole. And, since property owners' persistence rates raised the average for the entire population, the rates for propertyless immigrants alone would surely be even lower.

The newcomers to Steelton were unable to acquire property quickly. In 1910 the Immigration Commission's survey found that 47 percent of the Irish, who had been there longer, and nearly 40 percent of the Germans owned homes. But only 2 percent of the Serbs and 14 percent of the Croats, who had been in the town a shorter period, were homeowners. Local Croatians insisted that their countrymen did not buy property until World War I when their pastor, Anton Zuvic, urged them to do so because conditions in Croatia after the war would be unbearable.[27]

It would be wrong to infer, however, that southern Europeans purchased property suddenly. They made modest but steady gains before 1920, as shown in table 8. In the alien wards of Steelton in 1905, only 18 percent of all property owners were immigrants. This was certainly modest for wards whose population was entirely foreign born. By 1915 immigrants constituted 35 percent of the property owners in alien wards such as the West Side and the "lower end." Most Slavic and Italian newcomers, moreover, held under $1,100 worth of real estate. Of 153 immigrant property owners in the first and fifth wards in 1915, 45 percent held less than $1,100 worth of real estate. In 1905 and 1915 most immigrant-owned property was valued at less than $3,000. In 1905 while 23 percent of all property owners in the first and fifth wards held property valued at over $3,000, no immigrants held property valued above that amount. A decade later only 3 percent of all immigrant property holders reported more than $3,000.

TABLE 8: *Immigrant Property Owners, 1905–1915*

	1905		1915	
	All Owners	% Immigrant	All Owners	% Immigrant
Value of assessed property				
Under $1,100	151	20	186	45
$1,100–3,000	157	27	208	32
Over $3,000	90	0	48	3
Total number	398	—	442	—
Average percent	—	18	—	35

Sources: Immigrant property ownership was tabulated for immigrant wards one and five from the Annual Enumeration of All Persons, Places and Things for 1905 and 1915.

Even if an unskilled steelworker could ever purchase property and establish ties in the borough, however, he usually needed to advance occupationally. His failure to escape unskilled status would make it more difficult for him to remain in the town during periods of unemployment caused by economic fluctuations and strikes. Among the unskilled, social mobility was least characteristic of the careers of the Slavs, Italians, and blacks. While advancement was certainly not pervasive, the old-stock steelworkers could have higher expectations of climbing from unskilled status. They included semiskilled molders, melters, blacksmiths, electricians, labor foremen, and crane operators whose hourly rate was usually between sixteen and twenty-six cents. Skilled workers, such as machinists and patternmakers, were often placed on salary at three to four dollars a day.[28]

Between 1880 and 1905 the proportion of unskilled laborers in the work force declined some 30 percent (see table 9). Whereas 66 percent of all workers were unskilled in 1880, only 37 percent were unskilled in 1905. On the other hand, the percentage of Steelton's wage earners in semiskilled endeavors had doubled during the same period. The skilled sector of the labor force still comprised about 11 percent of the population, as it had a generation ago. In 1905, however, more than twice as many people held nonmanual jobs as in 1880.

TABLE 9: *Occupational Distribution of the Work Force, 1880–1915*

	1880 (N=606)	1905 (N=3338)	1915 (N=3586)
Unskilled	66%	37%	39%
Semiskilled	15	30	33
Skilled	11	12	9
Low nonmanual	6	14	12
High nonmanual	2	7	7

Sources: For 1880, "Tenth Census, 1880"; for 1905 and 1915, *Boyd's Directory of Harrisburgh and Steelton,* 1905, 1915.

While the alterations in the occupational distribution of Steelton's work force were considerable in the two and one-half decades after 1880, the period from 1905 to 1915 revealed little structural change. A slight drop occurred in the nonmanual segment of the work force, due largely to a decline in small Slavic and Italian business establishments. The ranks of lower-class, or unskilled and semiskilled wage earners, however, grew only by about 3 percent.

Throughout the period from 1880 to World War I, the proportion of native-born whites, mainly of German, English, and Irish ancestry, in the unskilled category was considerably lower than for the population as a whole (see table 10). While only 60 percent of the native whites were employed in menial, unskilled tasks in 1880, 66 percent of the entire labor force was unskilled. Furthermore, by 1915 only 28 percent of the native whites found themselves laboring in unskilled positions. On the other hand, the increase of native whites in the semiskilled positions was significant. Whereas only 18 percent were semiskilled in 1880, 37 percent were semiskilled in 1905 and 40 percent a decade later. Among the white-collar or nonmanual positions, native whites increased their share of positions such as clerks, merchants, and draftsmen. While only 8 percent of native whites worked in white-collar jobs in 1880, over one in five held such positions in 1905 and 1915.

TABLE 10: *Occupational Distribution of Native-born Whites, 1880–1915*

	1880 (N=461)	1905 (N=2,635)	1915 (N=2,617)
Unskilled	60%	25%	28%
Semiskilled	18	37	40
Skilled	14	15	12
Low nonmanual	5	14	14
High nonmanual	3	9	6

Sources: Native-born whites for 1880 were identified from the "Tenth Census, 1880." The 1905 total of native-born whites was a composite drawn from the "Twelfth Census, 1900," and the Annual Enumeration of All Persons, Places and Things, 1903 and 1905. The 1915 group consisted of native whites still residing in Steelton from the 1905 group as listed in *Boyd's Directory of Harrisburg and Steelton,* 1915, and the Annual Enumeration of All Persons, Places and Things, 1915.

An analysis of the steel town's occupational distribution suggested an improvement in the position of native-born whites between 1880 and 1915, especially in the rise of the American-born in white-collar positions. Being foreign born, however, often placed a greater burden on steelworkers. Because southern Europeans and blacks could not climb from their lowly positions, ethnic differences in labor organizations and residential patterns remained intact. The 1880 federal census listed fifty-eight immigrants in Steelton, all from either Germany, Ireland, or England. Seventy percent of them held unskilled jobs, compared with 60 percent of the native whites. Among the newcomers, 13 percent were in semiskilled positions, slightly less than the 18 percent for native whites.[29]

For the southern Europeans who arrived in Steelton after 1890 it was even more difficult to obtain jobs outside the unskilled category (see table 11). Of 403 Slavic and Italian immigrants identified in 1905, some 79 percent were in unskilled occupations. This was only slightly higher than the figure for old immigrants in 1880. Slavic and Italian newcomers in 1905 had fewer members in semiskilled ranks and skilled trades than the Germans, Irish, and English immigrants in 1880.[30] Exactly twice as many Slavs and Italians held low nonmanual positions in 1905 as did the Germans, Irish, and English in 1880. The higher proportion of Slavs and Italians in low nonmanual callings was due largely to the employment of clerks in the many business concerns such as bakeries, barber shops, and grocery stores operated by their countrymen. In 1905, 12 percent of the Slavs and Italians worked in nonmanual positions for an employer. But 4 percent, consisting only of immigrant businessmen, such as Marko Kofalt who ran a steamship ticket agency, were self-employed or in the high nonmanual category. The percentage of self-employed Slavs and Italians was slightly lower than the ratio for the Germans, Irish, and English newcomers in 1880.

By 1915, some two decades after the first Croatians and Slovenes had settled in Steelton, over three-fourths of the immigrants were still in unskilled jobs. This was still three times the

TABLE 11: *Occupational Distribution of Immigrants, 1880–1915*

	1880 German, English, Irish (N=58)	1905 Slavic, Italian (N=403)	1915 Slavic, Italian (N=616)
Unskilled	70%	79%	76%
Semiskilled	13	5	9
Skilled	9	0	3
Low nonmanual	0	12	11
High nonmanual	8	4	1

Sources: For German, English, and Irish immigrants, the "Tenth Census, 1880." For Slavic and Italian immigrants, 1905 and 1915, volumes of the Naturalization Service, Petition and Records, Prothononotary's Office, Dauphin County Court House; Records of Internment for St. Mary's Croatian Church and St. Nicholas Serbian Orthodox Church; *Golden Jubilee of St. Ann's Italian Catholic Church* (Steelton, 1953); *Consecration and Sixtieth Anniversary, Holy Annunciation Macedonian-Bulgarian Orthodox Church* (Steelton, 1970); *30th Anniversary of the Founding of St. Peter's Church* (Steelton, 1939).

ratio for native whites and a slight increase from 1905. While the number of Slavs and Italians moving into semiskilled and skilled positions increased, the rise was small. The 5 percent of immigrants who were classified as semiskilled in 1905 increased to 9 percent in 1915. Unrepresented in the skilled trades in 1905, 3 percent attained such positions a decade later. More important, however, was the dwindling number of nonmanually employed immigrants between 1905 and 1915. Due substantially to the tenuousness of immigrant business concerns and the efforts of the steel company's store to eliminate its competitors, the ranks of the self-employed, high nonmanual immigrants shrank from 4 percent in 1905 to 1 percent in 1925.[31]

If immigrants tended to congregate consistently in low, blue-collar positions before World War I, black migrants in Steelton fared no better (see table 12). In 1880, almost all, or 95 percent, of the eighty-seven blacks employed in Steelton were unskilled. This ratio was substantially larger than for any other group, comparing poorly with the 66 percent of the native whites who occupied unskilled positions. No Negroes held skilled positions in 1880, nor did Slavic immigrants in 1905. Only 3 percent were in semiskilled positions, and only 2 percent in nonmanual callings. The latter category consisted wholly of two self-employed Negro barbers.

TABLE 12: *Occupational Distribution of Blacks, 1880–1915*

	1880 (N=87)	1905 (N=300)	1915 (N=323)
Unskilled	95%	60%	70%
Semiskilled	3	33	26
Skilled	0	0	0
Low nonmanual	0	4	3
High nonmanual	2	3	1

Sources: For 1880, "Tenth Census, 1880." A list of all black males was then taken from Dauphin County Marriage License Dockets, 1880–1915 (microfilm, Pennsylvania Historical and Museum Commission, Harrisburg); "Twelfth Census, 1900," and the membership lists in the *AME Church Dedication, 1905*. This list was then traced through *Boyd's Directory of Harrisburg and Steelton* from 1903 to 1907 for the 1905 figures on black occupations and from 1913 to 1917 for the 1915 data. In this way more blacks could be found and a larger sample could be studied.

By 1905 blacks had considerably improved their lot in Steelton's work force. The proportion of Negroes employed in unskilled tasks had dropped to 60 percent while the percentage in semiskilled positions had increased tenfold since 1880. What is peculiar and perhaps crucial to the entire Negro experience, however, is that while the percentage of blacks in unskilled positions was at its lowest point in 1905, the ratio of Negroes in semiskilled and nonmanual positions reached its peak in 1905 and declined thereafter. Blacks were never able to become skilled workers such as machinists. The 33 percent of Negro workers in semiskilled jobs in 1905 declined to 26 percent by 1915 and remained at that level thereafter. In addition, the percentage of black workers categorized as unskilled had never been lower prior to 1905 and would not again be as low. These facts are even more striking in light of the fact that the Negro population of Steelton, which had increased to 1,273 by 1890, declined between 1900 and 1910 when Slavic and Italian immigration was heaviest.[32]

In reality the premigration experience of black workers was similar to that of the Croat, Serb, or Italian immigrant. Both the alien and the black were largely laborers coming from a rural environment into an industrial-urban milieu. They were in direct competition with each other for the low-level, blue-collar jobs provided by the Steelton plant.[33] Blacks had made modest advances in Steelton prior to 1900 and held a stronger occupational position than Slavs. They had established three churches and a newspaper, the *Steelton Press*. A black was elected to the town council in 1904 and several black constables were in office during the 1890s. Although laborers were moving only into semiskilled blue-collar jobs, they were advancing.

At the height of European immigration in 1905, blacks actually held a stronger position in the labor force than did Croats, Slovenes, and Serbs. Only six out of every ten Negroes were classified as unskilled in 1905. In comparison, 75 percent of all Slavic and Italian workers were in low-level occupations. Afro-Americans had a higher proportion of workers in semiskilled tasks (32 percent) than did the new immigrants (8 percent). The United States Immigration Commission even discovered in 1910 that the average earnings of Negro laborers were higher than those of any other ethnic group except native-born whites (see table 13).

TABLE 13: *Wages in the Steelton Plant, 1910*

	Number	% Earning Over $1.50 per day	% Earning Under $1.50 per day
Native white	1,450	79.4	20.6
Negro	149	59.1	40.9
Slovenian	57	47.4	52.6
Croatian	676	34.3	65.7
Serbian	273	14.3	85.7
Bulgarian	61	8.2	91.8

Source: U.S. Immigration Commission, *Reports of the United States Immigration Commission: Immigrants in Industries, Part 2: Iron and Steel*, 2 vols., S. Doc. 633, 61st Cong., 2nd sess., serial 5669 (1911), I, 653.

Note: In Homestead, blacks had a greater percentage of workers earning more than $12 per week than did Slavs. See Margaret Byington, *Homestead: The Households of a Mill Town* (New York: Russell Sage Foundation, 1910), pp. 14–15.

By 1915 the differences between immigrants and blacks had changed slightly. The gap between the proportion of Negroes and immigrants in unskilled endeavors had narrowed. The ratio of blacks in semiskilled jobs dropped from 33 percent in 1905 to 26 percent in 1915. The number of immigrants in semiskilled jobs rose by 4 percent in the same decade. The proportion of Negroes in unskilled positions had increased in the ten years after 1905 from 60 to 70 percent. The ratio for Slavs and Italians in this period remained the same. Immigrants held more nonmanual positions than blacks in 1905 and 1915. This was due primarily to a greater proliferation of neighborhood ethnic stores among Croats, Slovenes, and Bulgarians than among blacks. Neither Negroes nor immigrants made significant incursions into skilled trades. No Afro-American appeared in these trades in 1905 or in 1915. Immigrants finally made slight inroads into the ranks of the skilled by 1915, but only 3 percent were involved. This trend, which was discernable before 1915, accelerated afterward. Immigrants modestly improved their occupational standing, while blacks lost the gains they had made before the arrival of southern Europeans.[34]

The distinctive characteristic of Steelton's work force from 1880 to 1925 was career immobility. In 1888 nearly seven out of every ten workers held the same position as eight years earlier. The tendency to remain fixed at the same occupational level, moreover, increased the longer that one stayed in the borough. From 1888 to 1896 the ratio of immobility increased from 68 to 88 percent. Between 1896 and 1905 the ratio rose to 91 percent. The most common experience for an individual who remained in late nineteenth-century Steelton was to encounter little upward or downward mobility.[35]

During the 1880s 34 percent of the unskilled workers were able to climb to a higher rank. This was due partially to a sudden increase in the number of jobs available at the semiskilled and skilled levels. Indeed, during that decade the steel plant doubled its working force. In 1880 all of the town's immigrants were English, German, or Irish, many of them with previous experience in British mills. They encountered little prejudice when compared with blacks and Slavs after 1900. These immigrants left unskilled ranks in the 1880s at about the same rate (29 percent) as the population as a whole, a rate three times that of the black steelworkers.[36] Yet they rarely achieved any further advances. The upward mobility rate of those who had climbed between 1880 and 1888 was only 8 percent between 1888 and 1896 and 3 percent between 1896 and 1905. A small proportion, usually 5 to 7 percent, of those who did gain higher ranks after 1888 were not able to hold them.

Among the semiskilled who persisted, however, the chances for advancing appeared slightly stronger. While only one out of ten semiskilled laborers advanced into the skilled or non-manual ranks in the 1880s, two out of ten did so between 1896 and 1905. This amount was more than cancelled out by the 15 percent who skidded downward in the same period.

Despite these occasional gains of the lower, blue-collar levels, upward occupational mobility was anything but the rule in Steelton between 1880 and 1905. Only about one worker in five rose out of his place in the 1880s, usually to the next highest level. Upward rates in 1896 and 1905 for those who had experienced advancement in the 1880s averaged only between 5 and 9 percent, indicating that one modest move was all that anyone could expect if he stepped upward.[37]

Like their counterparts in the 1880s and 1890s, workers in the first two decades of the twentieth century experienced little upward mobility. The rates were very similar in the period from 1905 to 1925 to those of the previous twenty-five years. Between 1888 and 1896, for instance, 9 percent of the entire work force attained some form of upward mobility. In the ten-year period after 1905, 6 percent of the employed moved upward, while 10 percent rose between 1915 and 1925. Upward mobility rates varied little throughout the forty-year period.

In addition to the fact that upward mobility in Steelton was modest, a portion of the work force continually skidded into lower positions. Net mobility in Steelton, the difference between the gross number of people moving upward and those

skidding into lower levels, was consistently very modest between 1880 and 1925 (see table 14). While 9 percent of the
workers in 1880 encountered upward movement between 1888
and 1896, 6 percent slipped into less skilled occupations. Between 1905 and 1915 6 percent of the work force who remained in the borough moved upward, while 3 percent
dropped to lower levels. Thus, the net mobility rate was merely
3 percent, or three workers in every hundred, in the decade
after 1905.

TABLE 14: *Net Mobility Rates, 1880–1925*

	Number	% Moving Up	% Moving Down	Net Upward Mobility
1880 group				
1880–1888	300	22	6	16
1888–1896	230	9	6	3
1896–1905	169	5	4	1
1905 group				
1905–1915	1,302	6	3	3
1915–1925	664	6	2	4
1915 group				
1915–1925	1,288	10	4	6

In fact, the workingman of the early twentieth century revealed a marked tendency to remain at the same occupational
level if he continued to reside in the borough. Nearly eight out
of every ten men who stayed in Steelton from 1905 to 1925
remained in the same occupation for several decades. Like the
men who were traced from the 1880 federal census, 79 percent
of the 1,302 men who were traced between 1905 and 1915
remained at the same occupational level. Of over 600 men on
the 1905 list who were traced between 1915 and 1925, 76 percent did not alter their occupational status (see Appendix 1,
tables E, F, and G).

Upward mobility was always highest among the ranks of the
unskilled, especially since technology was replacing unskilled
with semiskilled labor. If mobility occurred, it was usually from
unskilled to semiskilled; few moves were made into skilled jobs.

Between 12 and 13 percent of the unskilled wage earners in the 1905 group moved upward in both the decades after 1905 and 1915, nearly always to semiskilled positions. Twenty percent of a group of 1,298 workers listed in 1915 moved upward in the next ten years, although eight out of every ten of the moves were only to semiskilled trades. The higher upward rates for the 1915 group as compared with the 1905 workers may be partially explained by the increased opportunities opened up by the expansion in production during World War I. The upward rate for semiskilled steelworkers in the 1915 group, however, differed little from that of the 1905 group. In fact, semiskilled status was the usual stopping place for the steelworkers who moved upward.

New immigrants who attained semiskilled status, however, did not usually do so through individual striving. Technological innovations in the early twentieth century transformed the American steel industry and reduced the need for unskilled workers while increasing the demand for semiskilled machine operators. One observer concluded that the semiskilled became a "new class of worker" created to operate machinery.[38] Steelton was no exception to this trend. Between 1910 and 1915, for instance, the number of unskilled workers required to produce gas for the ovens was reduced by one-third.[39] Even distinctions between skilled and semiskilled became increasingly blurred, a fact which may have encouraged old-stock workers to keep newcomers out of their union activity and shops as a means of preserving their own identity and distinctiveness.

While upward moves on the occupational ladder were certainly the exception in the industrial town, the incidence of success often varied according to ethnic grouping. English, German, and Irish immigrants enjoyed considerable upward mobility. Nearly one in three advanced between 1880 and 1888. Indeed, for the fifty-eight newcomers from northern and western Europe, who experienced an abnormally high degree of occupational advancement, there was virtually no downward mobility (see table 15). Between 1880 and 1888 the upward mobility rate of newcomers (29 percent) exceeded that of the population as a whole (22 percent). The rate dropped considerably as they became entrenched in their careers, however, and eventually leveled off at a rate that was similar to the population as a whole. The old immigrants were also much more upwardly mobile when compared with Negro workers in the 1880s. English and Irish workers moved upward nearly three times as fast as blacks between 1880 and 1888. After that time the mobility rates for both groups leveled off.

TABLE 15: *Mobility Rates of Immigrants and Blacks, 1880–1925*

	Number	% Moving Up	% Moving Down	% No Change
Germans, English, Irish				
1880 group	58	—	—	—
1888	44	29	1	70
1896	39	3	3	84
1905	39	4	7	89
Blacks				
1880 group	85	—	—	—
1888	38	10	4	86
1896	32	6	1	93
1905 group	300	—	—	—
1915	67	25	4	71
1925[a]	—	—	—	—
1915 group	323	—	—	—
1925	35	13	0	87
Slavs, Italians				
1905 group	403	—	—	—
1915	95	5	4	91
1925	46	29	0	71
1915 group	616	—	—	—
1925	214	22	2	76

Sources: "Tenth Census, 1880"; *Boyd's Directory of Harrisburg and Steelton,* 1888, 1896, 1905, 1915, 1925.
a. Figures are too small to compute.

English, German, and Irish newcomers not only entered Steelton with higher positions, but also displayed a greater tendency to move upward. Most old immigrants and blacks, however, tended to stay at the same levels. While seven out of ten immigrants remained in their occupations between 1880 and

1888, and eight out of ten did so between 1888 and 1896, the rate of immobility among blacks was even higher. The Afro-American immobility rate was 86 percent between 1880 and 1888 and 93 percent from 1888 to 1896. Slavic and Italian patterns of mobility were similar to those of the black migrants. Between 1905 and 1915 only 5 percent of the Slavic and Italian immigrants were able to rise occupationally. This was substantially less than the ratio of one in four blacks who advanced in the same period. In the next decade their rate of upward mobility increased to 29 percent. Yet the most common experience by far was immobility for Italians and Slavs. An average of eight out of ten new immigrants remained immobile between 1905 and 1915.

Although blacks showed considerably more upward mobility between 1905 and 1915 than did immigrants from southern Europe, all seventeen of them moved only from an unskilled to a semiskilled position. While the rate of Negro advancement was greater than that of the new immigrant before 1915, the pattern was reversed during the ensuing decade. Southern Europeans advanced more than twice as fast as blacks between 1915 and 1925. Whereas 25 percent of the unskilled and semiskilled blacks experienced some upward movement between 1905 and 1915, only 13 percent advanced between 1915 and 1925.[40]

While the limited jumps made by blacks and southern Europeans into semiskilled status may have slightly improved their earnings, it did not necessarily make working conditions any better. Most advancement to semiskilled positions by newcomers occurred in the open-hearth, blast furnace and general labor departments. Working in intense heat at the front of the blast furnace, for instance, were "hot blast men"[41] and keepers who regulated the blast and directed the work of making a cast. Upward movement for a Croat, Serb, or Negro meant leaving the ore shovel to become a keeper, which was hotter work but brought extra pay of three to four cents per hour and periods of rest while casts were being molded. At the open hearth, Croatian helpers or laborers threw lime into furnaces, readied stock, or wheeled in limestone. A higher paid melter was in charge of regulating the furnace. Again, any southern Europeans advancing from helper to melter received slightly higher pay. But the new job was nearer the source of the heat as he left the back loading areas for positions in front of the furnace. The most frequent promotional sequence for Croats in the open hearth was from third helper to first helper.

Of those steelworkers who remained in Steelton for a substantial length of time, few experienced extensive occupational mobility. English, German, and Irish arrivals, often possessing important skills, not only rose to a greater extent than did later immigrants but also tended to remain in the community for a longer period of time. Blacks experienced very modest gains prior to the onset of heavy Slavic and Italian immigration. By 1915 these immigrants seemed to be eroding black gains and rising somewhat faster into semiskilled occupations. But overall, Slavs and blacks experienced less upward mobility. Limited oral history data suggested that discrimination toward Slavs and blacks by the Masonic order kept newcomers out of skilled jobs, especially in the bridge department. Consequently in 1917 unskilled unloaders at Steelton's blast furnaces, a physically demanding occupation which exposed its practioners to choking dust, were all "negroes or foreigners." Most immigrants were immobile in their careers if they remained in Steelton at all.[42]

Such mobility patterns tended to keep the borough's social structure intact rather than to promote integration. Racial and ethnic division within the work force, within the various departments in the mills, and within the community continued. Newcomers, in the three decades after 1890, were making little incursion into the skilled and supervisory positions held by native whites, Irish, and Germans, and finding it more difficult to attach themselves to the borough. Assisted by the mechanics of kinship and ethnicity in securing jobs, and by the decisions of the company's employment office in distributing workers from entry levels, newcomers tended to group together in certain occupations and departments. Ironically, the continued reliance on ethnic contacts in obtaining work, a device which surfaced during the migration process, partially influenced the subsequent mobility pattern of Slavs in particular. Thus, Anglo-Saxons continued to fill the skilled sector of the plant, while southern Europeans occupied unskilled and semiskilled positions. Blacks, losing the minimal gains they had made prior to 1900 and lacking strong ethnic networks for securing jobs, toiled in unskilled pursuits and moved more frequently in search of work. It is not surprising that the most successful and permanent citizens, the old stock, actively dominated community affairs.

5 Maintaining the Social Order

Although holding influential positions in both the steel mill and the community, the old-stock elite felt challenged by elements of industrialization such as labor turmoil and the newcomers from eastern and southern Europe. They tried to protect their social dominance in spite of their minority status. Their frequent expressions of criticism toward newcomers were not designed to exclude workers who were needed in the mill. Instead, Steelton's political, civic, business, and religious leaders instructed the southern Europeans and defined the limits of immigrant behavior. Realizing the company's need for an inexpensive supply of labor, the local elite wanted to fuse immigrants into the larger community without granting them social equality. This fusion was to be accomplished without any sacrifice of social position by the upper classes.

After Steelton's incorporation in 1880, the city's leaders were delighted that their community was an industrial boom town. Expressions of satisfaction with its rapidly emerging status as a manufacturing center, and of faith in the town's future, were frequently made. In 1880 an observer, who noted that Steelton was booming and would continue to do so, wrote that with the largest steel works in the country, with two railroads, a river, and a canal, "why shouldn't Steelton boom?"[1] Indeed, a local newspaper thought that few places in the state could reasonably hope for a more rapid increase of industry. One resident was even moved to poetry:

> To a city shall this borough run
> Its rapid changes through

Before the child is twenty-one
This saying will come true.[2]

Along with this abundant faith in Steelton's future was the implicit assumption by the community boosters that all people, regardless of their origin, were welcome. In 1880 the *Steelton Item* boasted how rapidly the plant's work force was increasing and how workers had covered the nearby hill with their homes and churches. Interestingly, each religious group was thought to be a valuable contributor to the town's progress. "And above all, what crowns the whole with grace and glory, the churches of Steelton keep their lights burning, the intense Methodist, the cheerful Lutheran, the blue Presbyterian, and the dim religious light of Catholicism are bright as the fires of their own forges."[3]

This early enthusiasm, however, did not persist. Soon the pronouncements of welcome to all and faith in Steelton's future progress[4] were challenged by doubts that harmony could continue. Especially in regard to the early black migrant, Steelton's old stock revealed increasing unwillingness to welcome minority groups. "The gang of imported Negroes doesn't seem to improve by living and associating with a civilized community," the *Item* complained. The paper admitted that some blacks were "respectable" but even they demanded protection from "this gang of ugly black heathens." As for the large number of black laborers, one critic lamented that, if the "colored men" recently employed by the steelworks were to be regarded as the "class and conduct" of the Negroes that inhabited the South, "we don't wonder much that the shotgun is used in ruling them."[5] The white press was most distressed by the "conduct and manners" of these blacks. Their dances, fighting, drinking, and "indecent language" were blatantly despised. Many blacks, moreover, too poor to build decent houses, constructed "shanties" along the Pennsylvania Canal near the steelworks and along Front Street. "If these persons are too poor to build respectable houses, let them select a place not quite so public as Front Street," a local editor demanded.[6]

The black migrants into Steelton, however, never became an

object of ridicule to the same degree as the white immigrants from southern Europe. Blacks were segregated in their own neighborhoods and forced to attend separate elementary schools, but Steelton's old stock directed most of its resentment and attention toward the "Huns"—the Croats, Serbs, Bulgarians, and Slovenes. American-born residents called them "Hunkies," a term which led to numerous street-corner brawls, but which the newcomers came to use among themselves.[7] Like the blacks, they were criticized for the poor social conditions in which they lived. Rumors held "Huns" responsible for the disappearance of stray dogs in town since they "frequently ate stray dogs for a feast."[8] One citizen complained to the *Reporter* that the tenement rows on the West Side stood in a low basin where all the waste water collected in ponds reeking with filth. "When the sun gets hotter," he wrote, "a poison will be emitted that will taint the atmosphere."[9] Besides complaints from irate citizens, countless stories filled the papers of immigrants involved with "trouble." Drinking was widespread among the immigrant population, and it was the center of much of the criticism leveled against the newcomers. Unscrupulous magistrates levied fines on foreigners whose only relief from the grind of the mill was "drinking on Sunday."[10] The U.S. Immigration Commission also did not form a very high opinion of the Slavs in 1910, regarding them as unacquainted with town life and imperfectly educated. It expressed fears that immigrants arriving in Steelton lacked "early training" and that the task of transforming them into "intelligent citizens" would be formidable.[11]

Residents formed a negative view of the newcomers, mostly single males, and their living quarters. At the lower or southern end, and on the West Side between the river and the canal, were rows of immigrant boardinghouses in an unsanitary environment. "The shanties are said to be occupied by a class of people who are a menace to the good and the welfare of the borough," Steelton's burgess claimed in 1900.[12] Another observer, who wrote to the *Reporter* asking that something be done about the living conditions of the "Hungarians," reported that "vermin and filth abound throughout the entire place. Disease is also lurking there. The buildings are dilapidated. . . . The scrubbing brush is also an unknown article and cleanser as soap is a perfect stranger. The stench arising when the thermometer reaches the 90's is almost unbearable to pedestrians."[13] The *Item* made similar statements as early as 1882. An editorial noted that authorities in Shenandoah, Pennsylvania, investigated the manner of living by the "Hungarians and the Polanders" and compelled them to live like human beings. "The Steelton authorities might," it said, "do likewise to improve the sanitary conditions of some neighborhoods."[14]

"Hungarian" wedding celebrations, involving prolonged drinking and merrymaking by these "so-called Americans," were also bitterly attacked. On several occasions city councilmen demanded greater police protection from the "disorderly conduct of the foreigners." In fact, in 1901, the town council empowered the burgess to swear in special officers to aid the constables on Saturdays and Sundays when the behavior of "Hungarians was dangerous and unsafe."[15] In 1908 after two men, Gittinger and Fisher, were accused of assaulting a young girl who claimed that they were Germans, the Trinity German Lutheran Church held an "indignation meeting" to publicize the fact that the accused men were "Hungarians."

Other incidents served to intensify the dislike of newcomers. In 1892 the town council received a letter from the secretary of the Pennsylvania Board of Health stating that the steamer *Switzerland* had arrived from a port which had an outbreak of cholera and that six of the passengers were destined for Steelton. When the news became public, the community was thrown into a near panic. Immigrants everywhere were suspect. The Steelton Sanitary Committee investigated immigrant neighborhoods with "reliable Hungarians and Polanders" to ascertain the names of recent arrivals. Rumors became rampant as citizens claimed that they had seen the infected "Huns" everywhere. The Sanitary Committee, after several surveys of boardinghouses, concluded that no new immigrants had arrived during the past few weeks and the six who were destined for Steelton had been hired by agents of "western firms" involved with labor trouble.[16]

Another complaint lodged against the immigrants was that they frequently intended to work in Steelton for only a few years and then return to Europe to live off their earnings. One editor claimed that it was a rarity for a "Hungarian" to become naturalized. Some immigrants secured "first papers" if they feared that they would not be able to return to Europe. The editor observed, however, that in the event of their return they gave their papers to a friend "and thereby beat the law."[17]

The most widespread criticism of the foreigner was that he drank too much. The average immigrant worked long hours in the most physically demanding occupations within the steel plant. He thus made his weekend (or Sunday) an occasion for celebration and enjoyment. "The Hungarians in Hun row were again in a turbulent state on Saturday night," a local editor frequently lamented. When members of a Serbian wedding party had been reveling for several days and rode through town on horses "in a most disgraceful and dangerous manner," a citizen complained that evidently the foreign element could do as it pleased.[18]

The outrage at immigrant drinking evoked a definite response on the part of the native white population. In the spring of 1882 Steelton saw the organization of the Sons of Temperance lodge. In the 1890s the Irish, not far removed from the immigrant experience themselves, formed the Total Abstinence Society. The Steelton Prohibition League was initiated in 1892, and the Women's Christian Temperance Union continually protested against immigrant use of alcohol.[19] The local YMCA took a survey in 1905 showing that more males in Steelton frequented bars in mid-week than religious services on Sundays.[20] When the Steelton town council considered a proposal for the erection of a brewery in 1905, George Sigler, pastor of the Main Street Church of God, wrote a revealing letter to the *Reporter*. Sigler noted that the Pennsylvania Railroad had ended the danger from flooding along the Susquehanna River, but "new sources of danger included foreigners who depreciate the value of property and of a brewery being located in Steelton. I shall not be surprised," he lamented, "if these two evils are allowed to exist that they will drive my church away from its present location."[21] In Sigler's mind, as in the minds of many of Steelton's residents, intemperance and immigrants were somehow agents rather than products of social change.

By a policy of restricting the consumption of alcohol, Burgess Jonah Diffenderfer won political acclaim in the community. In 1895, he began a crusade against "speak-easies." In his first raid, which received sensational coverage in the local press, Diffenderfer's forces entered the homes of Mike Viher, "Yohon" Prus, and Marko Viber of the "lower end." The news accounts reported in graphic detail what was found in the immigrant residences: "Twelve men were sitting around drinking beer and enjoying themselves. When the officers pounced in a general skirmish took place but all the doors and windows were guarded. A Hun attempted to interfere with the officers and was silenced. . . . Four quarter kegs of beer were confiscated."[22] The *Reporter* argued that many foreigners thought the American laws were only for the native born. The paper called upon all "good citizens" to assist in this endeavor.[23]

In 1905 Steelton officials sought to close down illegal beer traffic by passing a special ordinance. The law was aimed at Harrisburg brewery wagons that peddled beer among the Steelton immigrant population. Only beer that had been previously ordered and paid for could be delivered in Steelton according to town officials. This action was based on objections to drivers who simply sold kegs of beer from their wagons.[24]

Steelton's resentment manifested itself in other ways. In 1914 a No-License League was formed to protest the issuing of any more liquor licenses. A branch of the American Protective Association was started in 1896 to promote immigration restriction. An ordinance of the city council in the same year forbade sleeping by more than four persons in a room—a measure directly aimed at immigrant boardinghouses.[25]

In 1895 a Steelton Sunday Patriotic Association was formed by the local Protestant clergy in order to teach "Hungarians" how to observe "our Sabbath." The association considered it improper that at certain periods aliens would "have their jollification, which either extended into the Lord's day or began on that day."²⁶ This particular agitation became especially vocal after 1900 when waves of Serbs, Bulgarians, and Italians entered Steelton. In 1907, Thomas McEntee, an Irish burgess who was also a superintendent at the steelworks, issued orders to curb Sunday drinking and gambling among the foreign element. McEntee claimed that increased arrests would stop the problem entirely.²⁷

The frequent parades by immigrants on Sundays were another source of native discontent. In 1912 the town's white, Protestant, secret societies—such as the Junior Order of Mechanics, the Knights of Malta, and the Knights of Pythias—held joint meetings to protest the Sunday parades of the Bulgarians, Serbs, and Croatians. They complained that the parades upset people in church and led to "jollification" in the foreign quarter. Representatives of the secret societies presented a petition to the city council in August of that year asking for the suppression of these Sunday parades and the "desecration of the Sabbath day by the foreign element." The council acquiesced and passed an ordinance to outlaw Sunday parading—except for religious purposes.²⁸

In 1899 natives took action to provide for more law and order on their streets. A public meeting was held to devise means to enforce a better order on "our streets" and secure protection from the "lawless." The lawlessness was blamed on "colored youths" and "strangers" who never worked. The committee called upon the council to provide better police protection. "In the past the Pennsylvania Steel company exercised a great amount of discipline over its employees and enforced good order," the committee declared. The petitioners now felt, however, that the influx of hundreds of strangers were causing unprecedented problems.²⁹

The *Steelton Reporter* also praised a revenue measure, which the Pennsylvania legislature passed in 1897, to tax the incomes of alien workers. The paper noted that the measure was causing many foreigners to apply for steamship tickets back home.[30] In fact, it was Edward Beidleman, Dauphin County's representative in the Pennsylvania House, who introduced a measure in 1907 to prohibit unnaturalized foreigners from owning firearms. The *Reporter* lauded the bill and claimed that the citizens of Steelton were often in danger from the careless use of firearms by foreigners.[31]

Despite the hostility in Steelton, persistent attempts were made to ameliorate the condition of the immigrant. Originating largely from middle-class Protestants, attempts to aid the impoverished and inarticulate formed a pervasive theme in the industrial city. On the surface these efforts might appear somewhat contradictory since they came from the very classes that forced immigrants to stop parading on Sundays or made Negroes attend separate schools. But the same moralistic frame of mind forced the native classes to seek relief for the suffering and convert the "heathen" to American ways. The immigrant could be condemned and segregated but that was not enough to insure social stability. He also had to be instructed, made to understand "American ways," and, occasionally assisted.

With the increase of blacks and especially southern Europeans in Steelton after 1885, poverty became more of an issue. Failing to see the nature of the industrial transformation which was occurring, the local press displayed the characteristic nineteenth-century notion of attributing an individual's impoverishment to his own character deficiencies. "The poor are more extravagant than the rich," one local editor wrote, "and that is just what keeps them poor; for the sake of one feast they are willing to starve three days."[32] When the *Reporter* ran an extensive series on poverty in Steelton in 1889, its opening remarks attributed poverty to the lack of thrift. The basic assertion by its writers was that people were poor because they lived beyond their means, "spending more than they earned." The paper's editor, William H. Sieg, recalled an occasion when he saw a young steelworker at the opera house in Harrisburg sitting in the same row as one of the company's officials. "Can we justly endorse this act of extravagance," Sieg asked. In summary, he attributed poverty in Steelton to the poor "who failed to provide for a rainy day" as they should. He then asked why the poor did not improve their economic status. He claimed that they became "dazed by their condition." The poor felt that they had no chance of rising to a better social position: "Our poor people are not by their training prepared to rise. . . . They know of no way of living except up to the full amount of their income." Sieg then castigated the educational system because it failed to provide adequate instruction in household management for the workingmen. He argued that courses should be initiated locally to teach "domestic economy" as well as grammar.[33]

Sieg went on to compare the "American" and the "Hungarian." He claimed that they were alike only in their "animal phases." The "Hun" could sustain life on meat and vegetables alone, but the American also needed books, periodicals, and writing materials. A "Hun" was more likely to devote all his income to living expenses. "Lack of economy is the root of the whole matter," Sieg charged, "and it is useless to look for causes of hard times outside our homes."

These editorials provoked considerable dialogue. In letters to the editor, Steelton residents offered their own opinions on poverty. A "laborer" wrote that one should spend his money for the best pleasures he could get for "we do not know how long we have to live." Another worker admitted that he was making "big wages" but was "foolish" and spent everything. The *Patriot* was suspicious and declared that the entire series was intended to prepare the men for a wage cut. Sieg finally concluded with appeals to all of Steelton's workingmen to be contented. He told them to teach their children contentment by never complaining in their presence. "They should grow up believing that your condition in life is one in which it is possible to be happy and content," Sieg affirmed. As to wage problems, he asked the workingman not to find fault with wages but to study the economic conditions which determine wages.[34]

The chief cause, however, for low wages is the unkindness of workingmen to each other. Certain men will work for

less money than the people were paid who were doing it—
not only foreigners but full blooded Americans.

The greedy spirit must be weeded out root and branch.
And when workingmen love and respect each other, they
will be loved and respected by their employees and peace
and good will reign.[35]

While Sieg made an attempt to convince Steelton's lower
classes to be content with their station in life and instructed
them in the ways of avoiding poverty, economic and social conditions made it imperative that more than admonition and instruction be provided. In 1887 the first rudimentary attempts
at poor relief were made. Prior to that time the steel company
had cared for employees who were destitute. The *Reporter*
claimed that Pennsylvania Steel had lifted the burden of charity
considerably from the town and that tramps, who were not
included in the company's relief activities, would disappear if
they were arrested, leaving only a "few destitute" who could be
adequately cared for by local officials.[36] When several local residents, however, suggested that Steelton establish a charity fund
to help the "few destitute," the *Reporter* objected. If the town
dispensed aid, the journal argued, the number of applicants
would rapidly increase; public funds were often abused, "for
each mendicant imagines he has a right to all the help he thinks
he needs." The paper suggested instead that any needed charity be dispensed by the local churches but asked all citizens not
to foster pauperism through charity and "invite into our midst
the very class which is the curse of cities and towns all around
us." A meeting called in January 1888 to raise a charity fund
for the poor attracted only seven people.[37]

By 1893 the economic depression that was sweeping the nation also affected Steelton. Employment at the steel plant,
which had been over 4,200 in July 1893, fell to 1,093 by January 1894. Many immigrants, "Hungarians and Polanders," began leaving the borough for Europe. Several immigrant wom-
en earned money dispensing "medicine" to countrymen, while
jobless husbands remained with their families in barns which

served as homes in West Side alleys. Such impoverishment caused many Steelton citizens to reconsider their earlier stance against relief. In September 1893, at a joint meeting of representatives from the local chapter of the Grand Army of the Republic and the Lutheran church, a Benevolent Association was formed "to help the needy and protect the givers." Two men were appointed from each ward in the town to investigate all cases of reported destitution and to decide on their worthiness. Appeals were made for donations of food and clothing.[38]

The economic situation continued to worsen. In December, Samuel Felton announced that the steelworks would close the following month due to lack of business. When the plant reopened the following February, it was operated on a reduced work week. In an attempt to alleviate distress, the Steelton Store Company, owned by the steel firm, reduced prices on all items. Even the *Reporter,* which had been so adamant in its opposition to poor relief a few years earlier, pleaded during the winter of 1893–1894 for the more fortunate to aid the poor: "Don't ask the reasons, why, it [poverty] is one of the misfortunes of life. Just help if possible."[39]

As hundreds of idle men roamed the streets of Steelton, relief activities began to proliferate. In December 1893 several church groups banded together and fed 250 impoverished children a Christmas dinner. The wife of the steel company's superintendent headed a committee to raise relief funds, and the Benevolent Association increased its relief assistance to nearly 70 families a month. In fact, it was symptomatic that of 227 families aided by the association between September 1893 and January 1894, 144 lived in the fifth ward, the "lower end" where Slavic immigrants were heavily concentrated. Steelton even had a soup house which fed nearly 80 families per day.

By the end of 1894, employment at the steelworks was again approaching four thousand. Despite a minor recession in 1897, Steelton experienced relative prosperity during the next decade. The relief agencies which had sprouted up during the depression of the 1890s were closed. No permanent institution survived to aid the needy; yet the lessons of the past were not entirely forgotten. Steelton was more willing to help the poor during the panic of 1908. The industrial depression of that year had considerable effect upon Steelton and its ethnic communities. Whereas the net income of the Pennsylvania Steel Company exceded $5 million in 1907, it was less than $2 million the following year. In its annual report, the company's business outlook was not encouraging. Employment declined from seventy-eight hundred in 1907 to less than four thousand by November 1903.[40]

The United States Immigration Commission, which canvassed Steelton after the depression, found that the economic crisis had a serious impact on unskilled workers and particularly on recent immigrants like the Serbs and Bulgarians. Wage reductions were most severe in departments which employed mainly unskilled foreigners. All wages at the open hearth, for instance, were reduced 25 percent. Such a reduction combined with limited employment opportunities had disastrous effects on the well-being of immigrants. Native-born labor was hired for the openings that did exist. The yard-force superintendent, in fact, was instructed to favor Americans in hiring new men as long as opportunities were limited in 1908.[41]

As a result of limited employment opportunities and discrimination on the part of the company, hundreds of immigrants left Steelton for Europe and other American communities. Over twenty-four hundred aliens left Steelton between 1907 and 1908. More than one-half of them were Serbians and Bulgarians. Even the more "established" Croatians and Slovenes abandoned plans to build a new church in 1907. The aggregate membership of the immigrant fraternal societies, however, decreased by only three hundred. The worker affected most was the unskilled immigrant who had not yet acquired strong ethnic and economic ties.[42]

For a time, merchants helped the foreign population by extending credit to the boardinghouse keepers, but the volume of credit became so large that the policy was not continued. When further credit was refused, Serbs and Bulgarians, especially, were without any means of support and faced starvation. On the West Side, people subsisted on bread and water through the winter of 1907–1908. Immigrants and a few natives could be seen scouring the banks of the Susquehanna for driftwood which provided badly needed fuel.[43]

A relief committee was organized similar to the one that existed in the earlier depression. The committee began issuing tickets daily to over five hundred destitute workers. The tickets were used for rations of soup and bread which were distributed at two soup houses. Some 70 percent of the persons receiving the ration tickets were either Serbs or Bulgarians. The local press reported daily that lines of foreigners gathered to receive their allotments of food. The bread furnished by the relief committee was baked at the Bulgarian bakery with the help of immigrants who might otherwise have been jobless. The committee furnished the flour and the Bulgarian proprietor, Jordan Stancoff, baked and distributed the bread. On the West Side, the *Reporter* noted that "several hundred foreigners depended wholly on the soup house for subsistence." Stancoff and other immigrant businessmen eventually extended so much credit that they went bankrupt.[44]

The need to provide relief in Steelton was lessened by the exodus of immigrants. Indeed, the West Side soup house closed in April 1908, not because prosperity was restored but because so many impoverished Serbs and Bulgarians left the town to seek employment elsewhere or returned to Europe. In addition, the United States Immigration Service deported 190 aliens, most of them Bulgarians, on the ground that they had been solicited with the promise of work.[45]

Employment began to increase again by the autumn of 1908. The soup houses were gradually phased out, and the various relief activities were brought to a close. But this second depression had convinced much of official Steelton that poverty did not always stem from individual failings. Relief activities needed some continuity. As a local editor expressed it, "The best interests in the matter of relief and for the town would be served by establishing a permanent relief fund." In 1909 this suggestion was adopted by the Steelton

YMCA which organized a permanent Committee on Steelton Charities.[46]

In addition to conducting relief activities during periods of economic distress, Steelton's Protestant leaders subjected immigrants, more than blacks, to instruction in good citizenship. The superintendent of schools in 1902, at the peak of the Bulgarian, Serbian, and Italian influx, ordered all of Steelton's pupils to memorize certain patriotic songs such as the "Battle Hymn of the Republic" and "Columbia, the Gem of the Ocean." Several years later the superintendent issued instructions to teachers to emphasize patriotism and to teach all children the following pledge to the flag: "We pledge our heads, our hearts, our hands, to our country, one country, one language, one flag."[47]

The most active organization attempting to Americanize and proselytize among the local foreigners was the Steelton YMCA. It was established in February 1895, as an "arm of the church with sleeves rolled up, reaching and doing good where the church could not."[48] Its leadership was composed principally of leading Protestant ministers in the community, who began by providing a gymnasium and classes in English, arithmetic, and bookkeeping for all who were interested.[49] Before long, however, their efforts were directed almost entirely toward the Slavic immigrants. In 1903 the Dauphin County Bible Society, at the insistence of the YMCA, began distributing copies of the Bible written in Serbian, Croatian, Italian, and German. The Steelton Protestant Ministerial Association decided to form an educational branch of the YMCA in 1906. The local YMCA also looked into the living conditions of the "foreign element," and opened a special room for foreigners where periodicals in several languages were available and classes were held in Bulgarian and English. The ministers planned to concentrate their efforts among the Bulgarians and then gradually extend them to other nationalities. The Bulgarians were taught English and religion in a rented house on the West Side by an instructor familiar with their language, Bonis Najaroff of Philadelphia. One of his first presentations was an illustrated lecture "The

Life of Christ" in English and Bulgarian.[50] These ministerial efforts at no time included the Negro. In fact, soon after a foreign branch of the YMCA was established, blacks started a Colored Young Men's Christian Association which opened reading rooms of its own. This association was later accepted into the regular YMCA as a special branch.[51]

In 1909 the efforts of the YMCA were supplemented by the newly organized Municipal League of Steelton. The league included most of the town's elite such as Dr. William H. Siebert, L. E. McGinnes, superintendent of schools, Burgess T. T. McEntee, who was also a steel company official, and Dr. H. C. Myers. The avowed purpose of the league was to promote honest government, encourage and protect business and industrial interests, maintain parks and playgrounds, and make Steelton a more attractive place in which to live.[52]

Much of the impetus for the formation of the Municipal League came from investigations into the condition of immigrant boardinghouses in 1909. The city council surveyed the houses in foreign sections and found them extremely overcrowded and unsanitary. Tom Nelley, a councilman, was shocked that thirty or forty people would be crowded into four or five rooms. Another councilman suggested that a campaign of education in sanitary matters be commenced and that the board of health demonstrate to the "foreign element" the cost to their health and comfort in the way they were living. The council decided, after listening to reports on immigrant housing conditions, to issue literature in foreign languages which explained the dangers of unsanitary and crowded boardinghouses. Immigrants were warned that such conditions spread tuberculosis, fevers, and other contagious diseases. Landlords of tenement houses were gathered together by the board of health and reminded not only of the danger of tuberculosis but also of a state law which restricted the number of persons allowed to sleep in one room. Dr. William Siebert admitted, however, that it would be a hard matter to educate foreigners who had lived in "like circumstances in Europe."[53]

In the same year that the town council started to educate

immigrants on sanitation and the Municipal League was formed, Steelton also saw the formation of the Civic Club for the "betterment of social conditions." The Civic Club, a women's counterpart of the Municipal League, centered its activities on the West Side. It provided instruction for immigrant girls in gymnastics, sewing, and embroidery. Comparing the West Side or the "lower end" to the slums of London and New York, the Municipal League and the Civic Club started a "clean-up campaign." A five-dollar reward was offered for the most sanitary house among the foreign population. Another prize in the same amount was offered to the Negro residents. The *Reporter* praised these efforts of the Civic Club among the foreign women. It exclaimed that immigrants were ready and willing to learn the American way of living. "In another year," the paper predicted, "you will see them giving afternoon teas." The Civic Club also furthered the efforts of the board of health by obtaining translations of literature on sanitation in the Croatian, Italian, German, and Slovenian languages. A lecture on the prevention and cure of tuberculosis was held in Croatian Hall and drew over eight hundred Slavs. The talk was translated by two Slavs, Rev. Elias Gusic and Michael Horvath.[54]

By 1911, the YMCA was consolidating much of the reform activity into a Welfare Club where all foreigners could hear lectures, attend English classes, and receive proper instruction in health and sanitation. Steelton, indeed, had experienced a civic awakening. As L. E. McGinnes predicted, this movement would be recorded by all future historians of Steelton. McGinnes explained that the movement was intended to better the town and, in particular, to improve the conditions of the large foreign population.[55]

By World War I, Steelton had a Municipal League, and a permanent Charity Committee. The *Reporter,* which had blamed the poor for not exercising frugality in 1888, now expressed the hope that those who are blessed with "the full and plenty of this world's goods will lend a helping hand to the poor." The Methodist church even began to operate a "foreign school." Rev. J. D. Royer defended his school by claiming that a large number of foreigners could not become good citizens because they were unable to understand English properly. While their countrymen were gripped in a terrible war in Europe, Royer observed, foreigners in Steelton were "peacefully and fraternally studying to become good citizens under one flag."[56]

Despite the wide range of activities on the part of Steelton's native community, the welfare and educational reforms made few inroads into the immigrant communities and did little to remove the divisions that existed in residential patterns and social relationships. The Methodist school, for instance, attracted only twenty-two Italians, five "Hungarians," and ten Croatians. The YMCA never carried its work beyond eighty to one hundred Bulgarians. Indeed, Steelton's immigrant and black communities were largely preoccupied with their own particular problems before 1920. As the United States Immigration Commission, in explaining the failure of the YMCA to influence significantly the town's 4,000 aliens, observed: "The barrier of race and language has so far resulted in almost complete isolation of the foreign population. At the Y.M.C.A. it is stated that foreign men could not be induced to go to the association building; that they felt uncomfortable and awkward in the company of Americans, remembering no doubt, the open ridicule which 'Hunkies' often evoke from crowds of Americans youths standing on the streets."[57]

The native efforts at Americanization even extended into the realm of politics. As in most steel towns in America, Steelton's Slavic and Italian immigrants played a negligible role in local politics.[58] In some manner, however, nativists hoped to control and bring them into the mainstream of local party life. Local Republican leaders like Edgar Felton and Jacob Martin of the steel company took steps to gain immigrant loyalty, since the mass of newcomers constituted a potentially sizable voting block. Harrisburg lawyers, between 1912 and 1914, for instance, were frequently sent to meetings at Croatian Hall to explain the process of naturalization and voter registration. These meetings were ostensibly held under the auspicies of the

Croatian-Kreiner Political Club. One political organizer remembered, however, that after the people filled out their naturalization papers "we expected that they would become good Republican-Americans."[59]

Political loyalties among Steelton's immigrants were established by Tom Nelley, the political boss who welded the foreign population to the Republican machine. It was Nelley who arranged the "citizenship meetings" at Croatian Hall and, as the Immigration Commission noted, "cultivated and instructed" the immigrant worker with great care.[60] Although the *Reporter* proclaimed in 1900 that nothing was so repugnant to the American idea of government as the "boss," Tom Nelley experienced a meteoric rise to the top of Steelton's political structure.[61] A police sergeant in Harrisburg, he moved to Steelton around 1902 and was among a list of applicants for a hotel and liquor license in Steelton's first ward that year.[62] Several years later he purchased the Half-Way House tavern for a reported price of $37,500 and bought fourteen lots in Steelton's first ward.[63]

Nelley's move into the first ward at this time was politically significant. By 1902, the *Reporter,* which was adamantly Republican, constantly pointed out the potential of the naturalized immigrant vote and even urged the aliens to register as quickly as possible.[64] The first ward, moreover, was almost totally inhabited by Croats, Serbs, Slovenes, and a few Italians. Since there was only one liquor license allowed in each ward, the saloon, a gathering place for steelworkers, became a natural center of political life. Indeed, the granting of a saloon permit by Dauphin County judges was made with political considerations in mind. It was no accident that Nelley obtained the license in the first ward. M. Harvey Taylor, a power in Dauphin County politics, admitted that he "courted" Tom Nelley because the Republican Party was looking for leaders in Steelton.[65]

In 1906 Nelley was elected to the town council. Several years later he became head of the council's powerful police committee. Declaring that the power of his committee was final, he rejected any obligation to report to the rest of the city.[66] By

1917 Nelley was president of the council and responsible for bringing the bulk of Steelton's ethnics into the Republican fold.

Although Nelley was one of the few "Irishmen" in the first ward, he controlled the immigrant vote. His Half-Way House was strategically across the street from the steel plant. John Verbos, a Croatian and a Democrat, and a rival of Nelley in later years, admitted that the Croats thought the "sun rose and set over Nelley." Verbos recalled Nelley frequently attending the Croatian church on Sundays and "crackling a dollar bill" so all would know he had deposited it in the Sunday offering. Meter Dragovich remembered how Serbs were "kicked around" by local police and exploited by magistrates. Nelley promised to end such offenses if the Serbs would "follow him" to the naturalization office and take out citizenship papers.[67] Nelley was helpful in other ways. When an ordinance was proposed to raise water rents in 1910 to all nonusers of water meters, who tended to be immigrants, he successfully opposed the measure, since many in his ward "were unable to pay for the installation of a meter."[68] One Slovene stated that Nelley "would help you get a job when you couldn't speak English." One Croat woman insisted that Nelley was a friend of the Croatians and recalled several instances in which he purchased clothes so that their needy children could attend school and religious functions. He also secured jobs for Steelton's blacks and contributed to the AME Church. "He was about the kindest white person in Steelton to the colored people," one women affirmed.[69]

Nelley worked skillfully with spokesmen in each ethnic community who assisted him in maintaining the social status quo. Among Croatians, Nelley's organizers included Joseph Zerance and Joseph Sostar. Nick Klipa and Stan Dragovich became his assistants among the Serbs. The crucial point was that Nelley succeeded in keeping the bulk of Steelton's immigrant voters under his control and influence. In 1932, Franklin D. Roosevelt lost Steelton's first ward, which was nearly all Slavic, by nearly two to one.[70] By 1936, in spite of nationwide ethnic support for Roosevelt, Steelton's Republican registration still outnumbered the Democrats five to one.

A good example of an ethnic leader who was encouraged by Nelley but who supported the existing social order was Peter Blackwell, the dominant spokesman for blacks during the decade before World War I. Blackwell graduated from Harper's Ferry College and settled in Steelton around 1885. Within a year he had founded a night school for Negroes in the basement of the AME Church "in order to improve their education." During the late 1890s, Blackwell began publishing a Negro paper, the *Steelton Press.* Several years later he joined the executive committee of the National Colored Voters League. In 1903 Blackwell, along with Robert J. Nelson of Reading, was largely responsible for calling a national suffrage convention in Washington, D.C. One of the resolutions reached at the meeting was a demand that the Republican platform of 1904 contain a plank calling for the enforcement of the Fifteenth Amendment.[71]

By 1904, as Nelley was establishing himself on the Steelton council, Blackwell was seeking election as the first Negro councilman in Steelton, using the *Press* to push his campaign. Comparing his opponent to Ben Tillman of South Carolina, Blackwell declared that the "colored voters of Steelton were thoroughly aroused as to encroachment upon their rights by this class of men."[72] The Steelton *Reporter,* which frequently reflected the views of the steel company, even boosted Blackwell's candidacy: "There is no reason why any white or black Republican should vote against Blackwell. . . . This is a late day for the party to split upon the color line." The *Reporter's* kind view of Blackwell's candidacy is more understandable if one considers his remarks after he was elected. "Pennsylvania Steel holds a relative and corporate interest to the people of Steelton which demands that they should have a voice upon the floor of council at all times," the black councilman exclaimed. The company's spokesmen and Blackwell supported each other. The following year Pennsylvania Steel donated $500 to the AME Church to help it erect a new structure.[73] While blacks who lived in shanties were ignored, Pennsylvania Steel aided the "more stable" element.

Blackwell was elected as a Republican councilman by twenty-seven votes in a ward that had a majority of nearly 300 Republicans. The *Reporter* complained that at least 120 Republicans failed to support him because they refused to vote for a "colored man." Once on the council Blackwell immediately began to call for such measures as more police protection on Adams Street, where most blacks lived, and elimination of drinking and gambling halls. He insisted: "We want our young people to press onward and upward but the present incentives are the reverse."[74]

Blackwell further pursued his efforts to improve the situation of blacks through the Pennsylvania Afro-American League. Named the league's first president, he stated that the organization's objective was to further the interests of the Negro race along all lines tending to its elevation. "We feel that with proper and persistent effort the barriers of prejudice now existing in Pennsylvania will gradually be broken down and more opportunities will be open for us." By 1905, the league claimed a membership of over fifty-five thousand.[75] Black leaders such as William E. B. DuBois claimed the organization was essentially attempting to acquire political appointments for blacks. He suggested that the league was overlooking the crucial problems which affected Afro-Americans, and he denounced their "political morality" which merely sought favors for political support. DuBois called the league a small faction of "outs" who were striving to get "in."[76]

Despite such criticism, Blackwell's organization continued to seek political rewards for Pennsylvania's black voters. Robert Nelson of Reading, F. C. Battis of Harrisburg, N. H. Merriman of Pottstown, F. L. Jefferson, and Rev. W. R. Gullins of Steelton, all served with Blackwell as officials of the organization after 1904. They consistently backed Republican candidates. The *Steelton Press*, which became the league's official organ, not only carried lengthy endorsements of Republicans, but also called on Republican congressmen to oppose such activities as the disfranchisement and lynching of Negroes in the South.[77]

In 1903 the activities of the league illustrated clearly its attempt to secure political positions for blacks. Soon after Samuel Pennypacker took office as governor of Pennsylvania in January, F. L. Jefferson of Steelton, secretary of the Pennsylvania Afro-American League, and his fellow officials asked the new administration for the appointment of blacks to political offices. William Sample, of the league's executive committee, wrote: "In view of the large colored population of Pennsylvania with a voting strength of 51,668, nearly all of whom loyally support the Republican ticket, we go on record in expressing the belief that such loyalty is entitled to favorable consideration." Apparently the league was seeking to secure a position for one of its officials, Robert J. Nelson. During the election campaign Nelson had written a pamphlet, *Why the Colored Men Will Vote for Judge Pennypacker,* and distributed over thirty-five thousand copies of it. Blackwell continued to fight for the appointment of Nelson to some office, advising the governor that the time had come "when some substantial recognition should be accorded to the active colored men who help to make the Republican majority." Such an appointment, Blackwell felt, would gain Pennypacker widespread influence among Pennsylvania blacks. He would be the "Moses of the hour."[78]

The league was even able to enlist the support of Senator Boies Penrose. Penrose wrote to Pennypacker that the appointment of a Negro would disarm the criticism made of previous administrations that blacks were not sufficiently recognized.[79] After several months of waiting and pressuring, the league achieved its most significant, albeit modest, victory in 1903. Nelson was appointed to a clerical position in the Pennsylvania Bureau of Mines.

Blackwell continued to carry out his efforts in the *Press* to uplift Steelton's Negroes. He continually urged blacks to stand by the "party that broke the chains of slavery from your feet." Blackwell's editorials spoke out on a number of other issues. He frequently attacked lynchings in the South and called anyone who lynched a Negro a murderer. He urged blacks to take out insurance policies from Negro-owned concerns and to organize their own institutions. He supported the formation of a

Negro Savings Bank in Steelton, saying that "the time had come when the colored man must learn to foster his own institutions as much as possible. He must prepare the way for the rising generations of boys and girls."[80]

Blackwell even ranged into discussions on property ownership. He continually complimented Negroes who purchased property in the borough. If Negroes kept erecting homes, he claimed, it demonstrated that they were becoming aware of the need to become property owners. Blackwell felt that Negroes should earnestly save and acquire property.[81] Yet when a Harrisburg developer attempted to build new housing for Negroes in 1907, Blackwell protested. He expressed no objections to blacks buying property, "but we do object to them being herded together on one street and that street labeled at each end—nobody lives here but Black Folk."[82]

Blackwell offered Steelton's blacks a vaguely defined formula of success—purchase property, buy insurance, create all-black institutions such as banks—and attacked lynchings and disfranchisement in the South. But at no time did Steelton's black elite or Blackwell criticize either the social structure of Steelton which kept blacks on Adams Street or the pervasive power of the steel company. On the council, Blackwell supported Nelley, the local Republican party and the steel firm. Blackwell was a leading Republican in Steelton but was unable to enhance the social standing of Steelton's blacks.

The Pennsylvania Steel Company too attempted to regulate the behavior of the newcomer. The company realized that steelworkers often found at the local taverns a needed respite from the grueling work in the mills. Steel officials, however, felt that the temptation to drink was a threat to the prosperity of an industrial community. From the opening of its plant, Pennsylvania Steel limited alcohol consumption. If an individual was found indulging too frequently in intoxicants, he was put on a "black list" and discharged from his duties. The company officials warned men, "especially those who have families," to refrain from intoxication. "The company will employ only men of industry and sobriety," it announced.[83]

The steel company consistently opposed the granting of new liquor licenses in Steelton and desired all saloons and wholesale liquor places in the borough closed. In 1907, when Martin Kocevar, a Slovene, applied for a liquor license, however, Pennsylvania Steel attempted to solve the drinking problem once and for all with a unique plan. Kocevar had argued in court that the foreigners needed a place where they could spend a social evening and "be understood." J. V. W. Reynders, vice-president of the steel company, came to court and declared that he would like to see all drinking places in the town abolished. If the court were to grant an additional license, however, Reynders argued strongly that it should go to Kocevar, and the company would provide a place with music and sociability where "the big foreign element in Steelton could find decent recreation."[84] Reynders suggested that the company could in this way control the amount of drinking. No small saloons would exist; only "one big beer garden" in the foreign section with running water, trees, and shrubs. Reynders argued that "the foreigners are socially inclined and fond of music. We believe that if we provide a place where they can rest . . . and if we safeguard them properly the desired results will be obtained."[85]

Reynders was quickly challenged by lawyers of the local Anti-Saloon League. Rev. S. C. Nicholson, of the league, admitted that if Austrians could be segregated in the beer garden, little harm would be done. "People of other nationalities will go there, however," he said, "and the devilment will be done when they leave the place." Reynders defended the company's proposal. A conference was called of members of the different nationalities in Steelton, and Pennsylvania Steel pleaded its case. The company claimed that it now recognized the fact, after fighting liquor traffic for twenty years, that men had a natural desire for drink. What the company wanted to do was control the flow of liquor and "police the habit among foreigners" so that the drinking habits of its men would be tempered and made less dangerous to the community. "Our only reason for entering into this thing," Reynders said, "is to improve the condition of the foreigners."[86] The temperance forces in Steelton were too strong, however, and the company's proposal was rejected by the court. Despite the apparent intentions of the company, the *Reporter* felt that the Pennsylvania Steel Company had done a good job of regulating alcohol in Steelton and "there was no necessity for more liquor licenses."[87]

The company also attempted to control the foreign population by destroying the small, southern European businessmen in the borough. Immigrant workers and their families usually operated small neighborhood concerns, such as the "Slavish" Peoples Store, which were direct competitors of the steel company's store. These businesses were operated by men when they were not working in the mills, or by their wives. Immigrants not only preferred to deal with individuals of their own nationality but felt that the company store charged more to people "who bought on the book." In 1913 the steel firm prohibited company employees from engaging in outside business affairs. Within a few days many of the "cupboard business places" in the immigrant sectors were closed.[88]

At the same time the company promoted religious activity among the newcomers with financial contributions to the building and maintenance of various ethnic churches. This aid was regarded as a means of fostering a religious, and therefore stable, working class. The company contributed funds for the erection of the new Serbian church and even withheld church donations from employees' wages for all four Slavic churches. In 1905 the firm contributed $500 to the erection of the new AME Church. From time to time the mill also assisted in the purchase of church bells, as it did for the Slovenes, and other related items.[89]

The response of the upper class—the Anglo-Saxon ministers, editors, politicians, and business leaders, whose roots were firmly planted prior to 1890—to the inflow of southern Europeans and blacks was clear. Although some antagonism and denigration toward newcomers was expressed by company workers and average citizens, old-stock leaders attempted to define the terms by which southern Europeans and blacks would be allowed in the borough. Immigrant exclusion or complete cultural assimilation were little discussed. Newcomers were, after all, necessary for unskilled work and voting strength. Ethnic communites could remain as long as immigrants cleaned neighborhoods, ceased particular ethnic customs such as parading, limited their drinking, learned the lessons of Protestant Christianity, memorized patriotic songs, spoke English, voted Republican, and above all, were thrifty and content. If these exhortations had little effect on the immigrant communities, they nevertheless reflected the desire of the old stock to establish the ground rules by which newcomers could live in Steelton without sharing the power the old stock had acquired.

The strategy of old-stock leaders succeeded in maintaining their superior social position in the industrial borough. Southern Europeans, besieged by company regulations, Americanizers, proselytizers, nativists, and "prohibitionists," were denied any significant role in Steelton's affairs. The abandonment of their very language and culture was suggested as a prerequisite for even a modest amount of social acceptance. Consequently they had little choice except to turn inward and occupy themselves with their own problems.

6 The Newcomers Turn Inward

By attempting to retain their hegemony over the social order in Steelton, the old-stock leaders perpetuated its ethnic distinctions. These divisions not only insured the continued physical separation of the various ethnic communities, but also kept immigrants and blacks from playing any influential role in the borough's affairs. Confined in lower-level occupations in the steel plant, housed in separate row homes, unable to rise occupationally, subject to economic vicissitudes, and lacking positions of power in the steel town, the newcomers turned inward. Croats, Serbs, Slovenes, Bulgarians, and blacks displayed almost no regard for Anglo-Saxon concerns such as civic reform or local politics. Immigrants, especially, faced problems which concerned their own congregations, homelands, and ultimately their own identities. Unsure of their status in a new land and faced with rejection and criticism from the old stock, they debated issues that were peculiar to their own ethnic communities. And in the process, they acquired a new ethnic consciousness which surpassed anything they had known in Europe.[1]

All newcomers quickly began to establish a particular institutional framework which eased the transition to industrial society. Immigrant organizations proliferated and included societies that offered burial and unemployment benefits. Churches were also established, several years after the fraternal societies. Finally ethnic business establishments appeared. By 1910 Steelton had eighty-five immigrant business concerns alone, forty-five of which were operated by Jewish newcomers from Poland and Russia who were able to converse with Slavs. Of the eighty-five establishments, sixty were grocery stores and meat markets.[2]

During the 1890s an alliance of Croats and Slovenes slowly assumed institutional form. Feeling isolated and alone upon arrival in America, Croats and Slovenes found comfort in associating with one another. "Strangers amidst strangers," one Slovene recalled, "we lived in harmony with our Croatian brethren consoling one another."[3] In 1893, at the urging of a visiting Slovene priest from Joliet, Illinois, Croats and Slovenes organized a society which provided sick and death benefits. The Slovenian and Croatian Society of St. Nicholas elected Milo Mohorec as its president. Other leaders included Joseph Verbos, a Croat, and Marko Kofalt, a Slovene.[4] Five years later Croats and Slovenes organized a church of their own, St. Mary's Croatian-Slovenian Church.

By 1901 the nearly one thousand Serbs were also initiating their own institutions. Although several writers have concluded that most of the new immigrants were docile and dominated by their pastors, the impetus for organization came from the immigrants themselves. As churches grew out of fraternal lodges organized by Croatians and Slovenes, the Serbian Society of St. Nicholas was the forerunner of the development of the rest of the Serbian community. Even though Serbs were so poor they joined local fire companies in order to have a place to take a shower, they formed the St. Nicholas Lodge in 1901 to provide burial services for Serbian workmen.[5] The following year, through the efforts of such early leaders as Branko Pekich, a mass meeting of several hundred Serbs decided to organize a church. Funds for the purchase of a building were donated by the St. Nicholas Lodge.[6]

In 1903 St. Nicholas Serbian Orthodox Church became the fourth such parish in the United States. Its membership numbered nearly two thousand at the time of its dedication. Meter Dragovich remembered his father arriving late for the initial services because he had worked overtime at the mill. He kneeled outside in his work clothes, however, and cried in joy as Orthodox services were finally held in Steelton.[7] A Serbian school was founded in 1914; classes were conducted in Serbian, and English was taught one afternoon each week. The school was closed permanently in 1916 for, among other reasons, an insufficient student body.[8] Although the Italian, Croatian, and Slovene schools still exist, the Serbian school lasted only two years. Serbian traditions, however, persisted in Steelton to a greater extent than those of the Croatians and Slovenes. Countless ceremonies, conducted in conjunction with flag blessings, brought them together with Serbian visitors from nearby Lebanon. The Serbian Glee Club and a Serbian Athletic Sokol with several Serbian lodges provided additional social centers.[9] The celebrations such as the one which honored the late King Alexander of Serbia were especially colorful and popular. In 1908 the celebration honoring King Alexander lasted an entire week, culminating in a huge parade led by men who carried floral decorations inscribed with greetings in Serbian. Behind the floral decorations came men who bore portraits of the great heroes of Serbia. The main body of several hundred "foreigners" followed in the rear. The *Reporter* noted that the "mass of foreigners were so crowded on the pavement" that traffic of all kinds was held up.[10]

Perhaps the most important and popular event for the immigrants was the Orthodox Christmas. The Serbs, joined later by the Bulgarians, celebrated their Christmas on January seventh. All of Steelton would gaze on the hillside at the "lower end" of the town for it would be ablaze with the fires of pig roasts that marked the traditional Serbian celebration of Christmas. The labor departments at the mill always reported widespread absenteeism on such occasions. The festivities would last several days, with church services, pig roasts, dances, drinking, and games of strength. Straw for the Christ Child was placed under the tables in Serbian homes. The Serbs took these events so seriously that Meter Dragovich could remember as a boy seeing Serbs overturn the wagon of a huckster who was peddling potatoes on their Christmas day.[11]

Steelton's Italian and Jewish immigrants, although fewer in number, also began to create community institutions. Jews from Russia and Poland arrived mainly after 1900. In 1905 they banded together to build a small synagogue. Contemporary accounts noted that Steelton's Jews observed traditional religious services, especially the Jewish New Year. By 1909 Jews owned one-half of all immigrant business concerns in the town, had a Young Men's Hebrew Association, and had formed numerous fund-raising committees to solicit money for the relief of their coreligionists in Russia.[12] One account of the Hanukkah feast held in 1909 by the congregation of Pipereth Israel noted that traditional services were conducted with appropriate singing and chanting. The American flag was then waved by "enthusiastic children" as speakers compared George Washington to Judas Maccabaeus and American independence to the victory celebrated at Hanukkah. Once the "advanced disciples" were even dressed in red, white, and blue, with stars and stripes to represent Uncle Sam.[13]

By 1901 the Italian settlement had grown large enough to make preparations for a separate Catholic congregation. Until that time, Italians worshipped at St. James Church. In 1902 they began to hold their services separately in a rented hall with an Italian priest. They were finally able to erect a church in 1903 and a school in 1907, the congregation including many Italians from Harrisburg who did not have their own church.[14] By 1903 Italian community life was manifesting itself in other ways. The Italian Band, the Italian Citizens Society, and St. Michael's Fraternal Lodge were popular organizations. Every Saturday evening in 1903, Italians held a "festival and dance" in Croatian Hall where leaders asserted that "the best order will be preserved." And, in 1909, the first large-scale celebration of Columbus Day was held in Steelton with over two hundred Italians carrying the American and Italian flags through the streets.[15]

While creating an Italian community life, immigrants also took steps to ease their adjustment to a new land. At a meeting of the school board in 1904, sixty-three young Italians presented a petition asking school authorities to provide night classes for the instruction of foreigners. The young men who brought the petition forward were all unable to attend a regular school since they worked at the mill during the day. Interestingly enough, the school board rejected the request because many of the names on the petition had given the truant officers problems when they had earlier been enrolled as students. In 1911 Italian immigrants asked the state government to charter an Italian-American Citizen's Benefit Association "for the purpose of making American citizens of Italians, instilling patriotism and civic valor."[16]

Bulgarians, who were among the most impoverished of Steelton's immigrants, established organizations similar to those of other ethnic groups. The Holy Annunciation Macedonian-Bulgarian Orthodox Church was built in 1909, after Bulgarians from Steelton traveled throughout Ohio, Indiana, Michigan, and Canada to obtain contributions from fellow Bulgarian and "Macedonian benefactors." By 1910 the Bulgarian Synod sent the Reverend Theobald Theophilart to serve as pastor for the local congregation. After presenting his credentials to a committee at a poolroom on the West Side, he led a parade of nearly five hundred Bulgarians through the streets to dedicate their new church.[17]

The Bulgarians also had organized the Macedonian Band, the Christo Taleff Bulgarian Society, which provided sick and death benefits, and a Macedonian-Bulgarian Society of America, whose object was "to help in securing citizenship and developing closer ties between our people and Americans."[18] Among their religious customs two of the most important ones practiced in America were the celebrations in commemoration of Saints Cyril and Methodius, who brought Christianity to the Western Slavs in the ninth century, and the feast of the Epiphany, on January 19, which was an annual attraction for all of Steelton until World War II. Usually people waited along Franklin Street as the Bulgarians commemorated the baptism of Christ. After church services a gilded wooden cross was carried by the priest to the Susquehanna River and thrown into the icy waters. When the cross struck the water, young Bulgarian men dived for it. A pure white dove was then released, and the youth who secured the cross became the "hero of the day" at the festivities that followed. The event was annually headlined in the local press.[19]

Early institutional life among Bulgarians also included political organizations. The majority of Bulgarians were "unlettered peasants," but some were well-educated political opponents of the Turkish government who brought their political convictions to America. The first organization inaugurated by the Bulgarians, because of their close association with political events in Macedonia, was a revolutionary society which became affiliated with similar ones in other parts of the United States. The object of this organization was to publicize the atrocities committed by the Turkish administration in Macedonia, thus creating sympathy for the Macedonian cause. The executive committee of the organization, composed of twenty-five men, lived in its own boardinghouse in Steelton.[20]

As with southern Europeans, religious organizations played a leading role in the institutional life of the black community. The *Reporter* argued that the "colored churches" deserved credit for their moral endeavors. Sermons by Negro ministers frequently urged blacks to avoid "Sabbath breaking," drinking, gambling, and disorderly conduct. Blacks listened to sermons such as "The Future of the Negro in this Country" or "The Negro and the White Man of the South." The *Harrisburg Call* claimed that over seven hundred of Steelton's twelve hundred Afro-Americans were members of one of the three black congregations.[21] The African Methodist Episcopal Church, founded in 1871, was the first Negro congregation in Steelton. In 1884 the Mt. Zion Baptist Church was established and by 1895 blacks had organized the First Baptist Church.

The congregations, like their white immigrant counterparts, showed definite initiative on the part of laymen. They often formed their congregations before securing ministers, and, even after the arrival of a minister, laymen continued to exercise control. In July 1895, for instance, the deacons of the First Baptist Church concluded that the institution could not prosper as long as the pastor desired to run things "to suit himself." The deacons agreed to dispense with the services of the Reverend J. J. Jones. But Jones secured a temporary injunction from the Dauphin County Court to prohibit the deacons from interference with his preaching. When the deacons obtained a similar document to restrain the pastor, an impasse was reached and the church was closed. Jones finally was forced to leave after receiving three months' salary.[22]

Black institutional life, however, extended beyond the religious sphere. In 1888 Negroes formed the Home Club of Steelton to improve "home life" and advance the education of black children. A Negro Widows and Orphans Committee held frequent entertainments to raise funds for the needy. Other organizations included the Galilean Fisherman Lodge of Steelton and the Union Republic Club. The all-black Odd Fellows fraternal order, which paid sick and death expenses much like the white immigrant lodges, had less than one hundred members as late as 1910, indicating that it attracted only a small part of the black community. A Negro chapter of the American Legion, a separate Negro football team, and a black Young Men's Reform Association sought to end "rowdyism and drunkenness among their people."[23]

In all such activities Negroes acted separately from whites. While all Negroes were not fully integrated into it, a black community did indeed exist apart from the Irish, Croatian, German, and Italian communities in Steelton. The Negroes held separate Memorial Day parades, usually after the end of the "regular" one, conducted largely by Irish and German organizations; Slavic immigrant groups held no parade at all prior to 1910. The annual black Memorial Day parade was a source of friction among Negroes, and in 1894 feelings between Baptists and Methodists became so intense that two parades were held.[24]

Until after World War I, Negroes were required to attend an all-black school through the first eight grades. The *Reporter* observed: "In Steelton, the schools have been separated for several years and it has been found to work to the great interest and advantage of the colored children." The journal suggested that segregated schools and "colored teachers" ended all the bickering and dissension. "By all means," it said, "separate your schools." Negroes attended the Hygienic School Building, and

Charles F. Howard, a Negro, was principal. Commencement exercises for blacks who completed eight years of study were usually held in one of the black churches. Although the Afro-Americans could attend Steelton High School, many chose instead to seek employment. In the thirty years prior to 1910, less than forty Negroes had graduated from the high school.[25]

While blacks never seemed to protest the actual separation of educational facilities in the early years, they did make certain demands. In 1890 Negro citizens severely criticized a school board decision which leased an old hall to accommodate the "colored school." Blacks claimed that the hall was not the place for children to be educated and charged the school board with acting in a "prejudiced manner." They organized an American Protective Association, led by Joseph Hill and Peter Blackwell, which investigated the hall in question. The association found it unfit, and "demanded a proper school room for our children." The association also discovered that four classrooms were empty in the fifth ward and asked why blacks should be crowded into a room "unfit for school purposes." Blacks demanded either opening of rooms for Negroes in the present high school or the construction of new rooms. The black organization concluded by declaring that the school board was dependent upon the power of the local steel company to enforce its mandates, since the company discharged all men, black or white, who did not send their children to school.[26]

The issue was never fully resolved. The school board eventually found rooms for the blacks in the Hygienic School. But the *Reporter* declared that a debate should be held to examine whether the "colored in Steelton were receiving proper recognition" and whether Negroes failed to receive good positions "because they were not the same color as the managers of the steel company." The debate was never held. And in 1910, Steelton's blacks were aroused again when conditions at the Hygienic School became intolerable. They continued, however, to remain separated in the public schools.[27]

Although blacks could attend Steelton High School, they were barred from joining its very active alumni association. In

1902 Charles Howard, Franklin Jefferson, H. H. Summers, W. J. Bailor, and Vernon James started the Douglass Association. The organization, named for Frederick Douglass, was intended to be a black counterpart of the all-white Steelton High Alumni Association. Initially its stated objectives were "the promotion of education among our people, the encouragement of those who are seeking an education, and the mental and moral improvement of its members." The Douglass Association's annual banquet for its members became a social highlight of the black community. It persisted until after World War II.[28]

While blacks created a vital but segregated community, their attitude toward segregation in Steelton was muted by their lack of power. Although they demanded quality educational facilities for their children, they never openly protested elementary-school separation. Ironically, however, they protested quite loudly when the Pennsylvania legislature appropriated $20,000 for an Industrial School for Negroes in Philadelphia. Dr. Gullins, of the AME Church, spoke for a Steelton committee opposed to the project and claimed such an appropriaion constituted a "distinct drawing of the color line, which shall never be tolerated in Pennsylvania."[29] The appropriation was for the Berean Manual Training and Industrial School which was started in 1905 in the basement of the Berean Presbyterian Church in Philadelphia. Backed by William Wanamaker, Issac Clothier, and other members of Philadelphia's elite, the school hoped to train Negroes for industrial jobs.[30]

As with Slavs and Italians in Steelton, World War I tended to lessen the social divisions between Negroes and native white Americans for a time. While black soldiers were serving abroad, their pictures were carried in the local press along with those of white soldiers. One article carried the headline, "Our Negro Soldiers' Brilliant War Record." In the patriotic parades of 1918, Negroes, who had always marched separately, were permitted to march with the "regular" parade. And in 1919 both blacks and whites were urged to welcome Negro soldiers returning from France.[31]

Prior to community formation, newly arrived immigrants in

Steelton seldom manifested powerful strains of ethnic identity. The Croatians, for instance, were more conscious of their village ties and were deeply aware of distinctions among those arriving from Bjelovar, Voyvodina, and elsewhere. One immigrant child recalled that his parents, who had emigrated from Bjelovar, advised him not to marry a "Voyvodincia." Indeed, these two groups, who often argued over church affairs and such Old World customs as the proper ringing of the church bells, were reconciled only when the Slovenes established their own church in 1909.[32]

The early attachment to village loyalties was certainly not unique to Steelton. Immigrants, initially at least, defined themselves by the village of their birth, or by the provincial region that shared dialect and custom. Early immigrant organizations such as the Croatian fraternal lodges in Steelton were usually begun along local lines. At one time Steelton Croats had five different fraternal lodges which reflected generally the various European village origins of the immigrants.[33]

Not only did Croats retain their Old World loyalties, they displayed a growing reluctance to cooperate with Slovenes. Indeed, divisiveness crept into the Slovene-Croatian organizations in 1894 when Croatians began to feel that Slovenes were becoming dominant. Because of this discord, the St. Nicholas Society changed its name to the Slovene and Croatian Catholic Benefit Society of St. Nicholas. This move, however, was not enough to insure harmony after the Croatians decided to affiliate with the newly formed National Croatian Society in Pittsburgh. In 1895 the treasury of the St. Nicholas Society was divided among the membership. Although some distrusted an organization located "so far away as Pittsburgh," many Croatians joined to form the St. Lawrence Lodge in April of that year. The lodge was named after the patron saint of the people around Voyvodina in Croatia. At the same time the Slovenes organized the St. Aloysius Society.[34]

The St. Lawrence Lodge not only provided useful sick and death benefits of several hundred dollars, but also fulfilled a rising demand for social activities. Speakers were often brought from Croatia to lecture on events in the homeland. When an immigrant lost his job, lodge members held small parties to raise money so he could return to Europe or move elsewhere. Dances were usually held weekly. At funerals, lodge members always held formal marches. When Lawrence Rudman died in 1897, 150 members of the St. Lawrence Lodge marched with his body from Steelton to the cemetery in Harrisburg. At lodge meetings immigrants found a place to express themselves where they "felt safe from the American class of people."[35]

The first major organized activity of Croatians in Steelton was the blessing of a new Croatian flag by the St. Lawrence Lodge in June 1895. The affair was attended by Josip Ljubic, the Supreme President of the National Croatian Society, along with other Slavs from the community.[36] By 1902, with over one thousand Croatians in Steelton, the St. Lawrence Lodge had constructed a hall of its own and firmly established itself as a center for Croatian activity.[37] Whenever a Croat was killed at the steel mill, the lodge "took charge of the body." If Croatians were reported missing, lodge members searched the "hills in back of town" for their countrymen.[38] The celebration honoring St. Lawrence in August became a significant event among Steelton's Croatians.[39]

The flag-blessing ceremonies were among the most popular of the early social activities of the Croats. Early in the morning the members of the St. Lawrence Lodge organized and marched to St. James Church. After the church services, a procession moved down the town's main street with the American and Croatian flags at the head. A hired band furnished music, while three hundred members of the Croatian lodge marched in neat, dark blue uniforms. The parade then proceeded to Hess Island where a picnic was held. Croatians attended from as far away as Pittsburgh. The *Reporter,* after one such occasion, was quick to point out that the "best of order prevailed."[40]

As Croatian activities increased, they branched into various areas. In 1903 the St. Lawrence Lodge initiated a campaign to raise funds for the support of widows and children in Croatia whose husbands and fathers had been victims of recent troubles with Austria-Hungary. The *Reporter* carried an extensive interview with the Croatian pastor Rev. Francis Azbe concerning the drive. Azbe explained the alleged oppression of Croatians, citing cases of suppression of the press and exhorbitant taxes "which tends to keep the inhabitants in absolute poverty." Azbe continued: "We Croatians here are endeavoring to the best of our ability to relieve the sufferings of our fellow countrymen."[41]

By 1903 Croatians were making it known they desired to be considered respectable citizens. In August of that year, an immigrant named August Olshske was brutally assaulted. Harrisburg newspapers, in covering the incident, reported that the assault took place in the St. Lawrence Croatian Hall. This report was quickly challenged by Joseph Verbos, president of the Croatian Society, who argued that the assault did not occur at the hall, that the best of order was always maintained, and that beer and liquor were never sold there.[42]

In 1908 the Croatians began to prepare for the establishment of a local newspaper. Frank Horvath planned to become the publisher of *Hrvatski Dom,* which would be printed "in the interest of the Croatian workingman." But the project never materialized, apparently because agreements could not be worked out among the five local Croatian fraternal lodges that were supposed to support the publication. Croats did establish a "Hrvatska Citaonica" or Croatian library where immigrants could read books and newspapers in their own language.[43]

The St. Lawrence Lodge began a school to teach English to foreign residents in 1890. The school, headed by Michael Tenda, offered daily lessons in English for children too young to work. Weekend instruction was provided for those who worked in the mills. Croatian spokesmen hoped that the school would "give their children a better opportunity for advancement than they had."[44] By 1911, moreover, the Croatians had organized several Tamburitsa orchestras and a *sokol* or youth group which offered athletic activities to the young. In fact, the frequent gymnastic exhibitions were of special importance to the several Slavic groups in the town. They offered immigrant children an opportunity to participate in athletic competitions, since Slavs were not on the popular football and baseball clubs of Steelton in the early 1900s.[45]

On the eve of World War I, the Croatians were an active and thriving ethnic group. The spring of 1912 saw the "most pretentious procession of foreigners ever witnessed in the borough." A mammoth parade was sponsored by St. Marks National Croatian Society to honor the blessing of large silk American and Croatian flags which the lodge had just purchased. After the church blessing, over one thousand Croatians, Serbs, and Slovenes, some of whom came from Reading, Lebanon, Philadelphia, and South Bethlehem, marched in full regalia with red shirts, braided jackets, red caps, and black bands. Nearly all of the "foreign societies" in the town took part in the colorful parade. While many may have been studying and speaking English, ethnic self-consciousness among Steelton's immigrants was increasing.[46]

The religious needs of the early Croatian and Slovenian settlers were served by St. James Catholic Church. On certain feast days, such as the one honoring St. Lawrence, Croats would walk four miles or more into Harrisburg to attend St. Lawrence Catholic Church, since it reminded them of the old St. Lawrence Church in Voyvodina. At both St. James and St. Lawrence, however, most Croats admitted that they could not understand the priest, who spoke English.[47]

More than language differences caused the Croats and Slovenes to drift away from St. James Church. Steelton was in many respects, as Thomas Benkovic labeled it, "an Irish town." In the mill most of the supervisors and superintendents were Irish while the Slavs held the more menial occupations. This relationship was strained when Irish foreman extracted weekly "donations" for St. James from the Slavic paychecks. Such "donations," as one Croatian woman recalled, "made it hard on our people." St. James, moreover, operated a system of pew rentals which resulted in the more wealthy, such as the Doughertys and the McEntees, sitting in the front of the church. The Croats and the Slovenes inevitably sat toward the back or stood in the rear. Before long, Slavs took steps to create a Croatian-Slovenian Church of their own.[48] The separation of the Slavs from the Irish church reflected the deep ethnic divisions that were rising in the industrial city.

Since 1896 the Reverend Joseph D. Bozic had come occasionally from Allegheny City, near Pittsburgh, to conduct religious services in Croatian. On the occasion of his visits, the Slavs brought him from Harrisburg in a trolley decorated with American flags, accompanied by the Croatian band. Bozic accepted their invitation to settle in Steelton permanently in August 1898. By October, the first services were held at St. Mary's Croatian-Slovenian Church, an old Lutheran church purchased for $1,800. Bozic himself supplied nearly half the purchase price.[49] He had arrived in Pittsburgh in August 1894 and was the first Croatian priest among the "new immigrants." While serving the Croats of Allegheny City, Bozic published *Novi Svijet* (New World) and *Puco,* the first humorous Croatian paper in America. In Allegheny City, Bozic and the church committee disagreed over who actually would control the church. In Croatia the church was supported by the state. In America, however, Slavic immigrants felt that those who financially supported the church should control both it and the priest. This was quite possibly the reason that the Reverend Gorshe was transfered from St. Mary's in 1902. Nevertheless, Bozic, prompted by his troubles at Allegheny City, let the Slavs in Steelton know that he would not mind joining them permanently.[50]

The Croatian-Slovenian church alliance progressed smoothly for a while. The two groups were even able to organize the Croatian-Slovonic American Political Club. In 1903 they opened a school at St. Mary's with nearly one hundred fifty pupils. Both English and Croatian were taught. Emily Balch, an early observer of the Slav in America, felt that these schools only retarded the inevitable process of assimilation. Immigrants who built the school, however, had only one objective, as Thomas Benkovic expressed it, "to preserve the Croatian language."[51]

By 1908 ethnic tensions became so great between the Croatians and Slovenes that the unity of their congregation was threatened. The pastor of St. Mary's was now a Slovenian, the Reverend Francis Azbe. Since the Croats comprised nearly two-thirds of the congregation, they became increasingly disturbed by the fact that Azbe continually preached in Slovenian. A delegation of Croats went to Azbe and asked that the services be held more frequently in Croatian but Azbe was unable or refused to do so. One immigrant put it more forcefully, "We didn't want a Slovenian priest." Croatian delegates were sent to the bishop in Harrisburg and the Apostolic Delegate in Washington. The Croats asked for Azbe's removal.[52]

The Apostolic Delegate initially recommended that the Slovenes should receive a sum of money from the Croatians to form a new parish. The Croats rejected his suggestion. They also refused a request from Bishop Shanahan of Harrisburg to pay the Slovenians $7,000 to buy a lot and form a new parish and assume the debt of St. Mary's. When Shanahan issued a final decree, the Croatians acquiesced. In March 1909 they gave the Slovenes $6,500 from the church treasury, assumed the parish debt, and parted with the Slovenes. By May, the Slovenes had established St. Peter's Slovenian Church under Rev. Azbe. The Croats remained at St. Mary's, and the separation was complete.[53]

Like the Croatians and Slovenes, the Serbians suffered from internecine strife. Tensions in Serbian immigrant communities often centered on the rivalries between different fraternal lodges. The chief source of trouble, however, was the animosity between the Serbian laity and the pastors, who tended to be Russian. In 1913, for example, the Reverend Theofil Stefanovic, pastor of St. Nicholas, resigned and returned to Europe. Stefanovic indicated that he was disillusioned with the Serbian colony. He saw little harmony among the Serbs and claimed that contentions between the leaders and himself caused him to leave. The priest admitted that on his arrival in Steelton in 1907 he knew that the Serbian colony of Steelton was one of the "hardest to manage."[54] After Stefanovic left, Orthodox church officials in Philadelphia sent a new pastor. Upon his arrival, however, the Reverend M. D. Vukichevich was prohibited from entering St. Nicholas by the church committee. Although he brought suit against the committee, he was eventually forced to vacate the pulpit. Several months later a Reverend Jugovic from Pittsburgh read in a Serbian paper of the vacancy and volunteered to try to bring peace to the colony. Jugovic, however, soon became the third pastor within a year to leave Steelton over a rift with the church committee.[55]

There was more at stake in this controversy than the desire of the church committee to control the pastor and church affairs. Ethnic feelings again became crucial, as in the case of the Croatians and Slovenes. In this instance, the Orthodox church in America was controlled by Russian officials in this country. Serbians were convinced that the Russians were uninterested in Serbian parishes. "We do not want a Russian priest," one Serb recalled, "we wanted a Serbian priest."[56]

The Bulgarian community, like the other Slavic groups, could not escape the persistent factionalism which often grew out of ethnic and religious differences. From its inception the Macedonian-Bulgarian church was weakened by inner turmoil. Originally, in 1909, one section of the church wanted the congregation placed under the control of the Bulgarian Synod in Bulgaria. Another group, however, wanted greater lay control and a closer affiliation with the Serbian Orthodox Synod. In the initial dispute the faction favoring association with the Bulgarian Synod emerged triumphant. The controversy not only left a deep division within the Bulgarian community but also caused nearly a third of the immigrants to leave the Bulgarian church altogether or join the Serbian Orthodox parish.[57]

To a great extent European politics dominated the affairs of the Bulgarian community. In 1903 Bulgarians called a meeting of their countrymen and passed a resolution to condemn the czar of Russia for "intriguing" against the Macedonians in Europe. Ottoman oppression also was cited by the Bulgarians. An appeal to the president of the United States was included in the resolution, requesting him to cooperate with the powers of Europe and demand that Turkey cease oppression in Macedonia. It concluded: "We appeal to the American people to give the Macedonians their moral support and sympathy to a struggling and patriotic people who are fighting for the cause of freedom."[58]

The unrest among the southern Slavs prior to World War I was reflected by Steelton's immigrants, keenly aware of their own ethnicity. In addition to their obvious interest in the affairs of their homelands, the immigrants had many close relatives still living in southern Europe. In 1912 over seventy Bulgarians left for Macedonia in order to take up arms against the Turks. In the same year, Steelton Croats, who were growing increasingly hostile to Austro-Hungarian rule in Croatia, called a meeting of their fellow countrymen. The gathering condemned "the violence and tyranny that is ravaging Croatia." It called for a Pennsylvania federation of all Croats and Serbs to work for an independent Croatia. And they invited "all patriotic Croatians in America to organize a Croatian Political Association to collect funds for the former homeland "whenever the need arises."[59]

At the same time Slavs went out of their way to affirm their loyalty to America. In 1913 the *Harrisburg Patriot* reported that there would be "little stirring" to mark the celebration of Independence Day. "But the foreigners will have a big day," the paper noted; several Slavic groups had planned large parades. The Serbs were also holding a series of athletic events with visiting Serbs from Philadelphia, South Bethlehem, and Lebanon.[60]

The outbreak of the Second Balkan War in 1913 further aroused Steelton's immigrant population. The Bulgarian church conducted prayers for victory in behalf of the Serbian and Bulgarian armies at Adrianople. Some former residents of Steelton, who had been forced to return to serve in the armies of their homeland, were reported killed in action. The Serbian *sokol* gave gymnastic exhibitions in Harrisburg to raise funds for the Red Cross in Serbia.[61]

As war rapidly approached in July 1914, tempers flared among Croats, still loyal to the Austro-Hungarian government in Vienna, and Serbs. The assassination of the Austrian Archduke by a Serb created "bitter feeling" between them.[62] The situation was inflamed when Ivan Kresic, the editor of *Novi Hrvat,* a Croatian paper in New York, wrote an editorial bitterly attacking the Croatian pastor in Steelton, Anton Zuvic. Kresic, who had been invited by the local Croatian *sokol* to help celebrate the Fourth of July in Steelton, wrote, "When I came there I found our Croatian and Serbian sokols divided into two bitter factions. . . . This was caused by the Rev. Anton Zuvic . . . who is planting hatred among these people." The pastor, according to Kresic, used the pulpits to preach against the Serbians "with whom he has nothing to do."[63] This editorial immediately stirred the ire of the Croatian population. Croatian leaders, like Spiridion Furich, an immigrant banker, claimed Zuvic was working hard "for the advancement of our people," and he described Kresic as "undesirable." In fact, the tensions between the two groups resulted in the Croatian *sokol* abandoning its plans to hold a street parade along with the Serbians. One Croat was even stabbed in a brawl between Croats and Serbs.[64] Finally, on July 19, members of the Crotian and Serbian *sokols* met in the Croatian Hall to mediate their differences. After impassioned pleas by Steve Memonic and Mile Bogdonovic, it was decided to lay aside all past differences and work together, "for the mutual benefit of all." Once the war actually erupted, animosity between the two was superseded by a growing resentment against Austria-Hungary and a consuming interest in the events of the war itself.

As hostilities developed in Europe, orders were received in Steelton from the Austro-Hungarian consul at Philadelphia to the effect that all subjects of his government should be ready at a moment's notice to "take up arms against Serbia." The Austrian consul came to Steelton several days after war was declared in Europe and told a meeting of Steelton's Slovenes, Croats, and Serbs that a general amnesty had been given to anyone who had left his homeland to avoid military service. He called on the Slavs to return and fight. Probably about eight hundred men were eligible for induction into the Austro-Hungarian armed forces. The *Harrisburg Telegraph* estimated that there were some thirty thousand eligible in eastern Pennsylvania.[65] The number of Slavs who actually returned to serve in the Austrian army was negligible. In the first week of August about fifty Steelton "reservists" received notices to report for duty with the Austrian forces. Steelton steamship agents reported in the same week, however, that no Serb or Croat had left for Europe. On the contrary, most Serbs and a growing number of Croatians and Slovenes not only had no intention of going to war but also were growing more sympathetic with the Serbian cause.[66]

On August 3 a mass meeting of Slavs was called to formulate plans to aid Serbia. A committee was appointed to collect funds for the Serbian Red Cross. The committee consisted of representatives for the Serbs (Voja Yovanovic), Croats (Steve Srbic), and Slovenes (Stephen Koncar). Following the delivery of patriotic speeches by the Reverend George Popovic of St. Nicholas Serbian Church, twenty-five young men volunteered for military service with the Serbian forces. Many of the volunteers soon left their jobs at the Pennsylvania Steel Company and headed for Europe. The *Telegraph* expressed amazement that, although many of the foreigners were of Austrian birth, "their sympathies to a man seem to be with Serbia."[67]

Activity through the early months of the war continued at fever pitch. Countless events and meetings were held to raise money for Serbian relief in Europe. The *Telegraph* had special stations set up in town where bulletins of the war were sent and translated. The news was then carried throughout Steelton's immigrant neighborhoods. News of relatives, former Steelton residents, in addition to the progress of the war, was anxiously awaited. Kazmir Pozega, a Croat spokesman and one of the translators for the *Telegraph,* told an interviewer: "What the United States fought for in 1776, Serbia is fighting for today. I do not believe it is just for an emperor to . . . crush a little country that is beginning to cherish dreams of political freedom. That is why I am for Serbia." Apparently most of Steelton's Slavs were supporting Serbia by the end of August 1914. Indeed, Meter Dragovich recalled a Serbian flag flying over one of the departments at the mill for the duration of the war.[68]

The war affected Steelton's immigrant population in other ways as well. The Bulgarians, for instance, were unable to secure a priest from Bulgaria and did without one for awhile. Business was slack in 1914 at the steel mill, as many foreign orders had been curtailed, and men were working fewer hours. The steel officials, however, were hopeful that the future would be bright since "war munitions business was immensely profitable."[69] Anton Zuvic now began to preach to his Croatian congregation the importance of owning one's home and becoming an American citizen. He felt that the war in Europe had decimated Croatia to such an extent that it would be useless to attempt to return.[70] When war demands again increased production at the mill, moreover, work became plentiful, and many were further convinced that it would be better to stay in America. As Meter Dragovich expressed it, "I didn't want to go to Yugoslavia."[71]

Local officials grew increasingly concerned about the heightened activity among the foreign population. Steelton's burgess, "an Englishman by birth," issued an order to prohibit sympathizers with any of the belligerent European nations from holding street parades or war demonstrations of any kind. He further advised Slavs to remain quiet and refrain from discussing the war situation with "any adherents of the opposing forces." The town officials attended a fund-raising meeting at the Croatian Hall which was packed "to almost suffocation." After receiving enthusiastic shouts of "Zivio! Zivio!" the burgess spoke. "Steelton is a cosmopolitan town, containing many subjects of every one of the nations now at war. We are all members of one family and we should sympathize with our brothers of all nations. . . . You are here in a neutral country. You can have no part in the struggle. Don't let your enthusiasm get away with you. Street demonstrations of any warlike nature are forbidden. . . . Now you are all poor men; we don't want to fine you for you can use the money in other ways."[72]

Once America entered the conflict, the company too became

concerned about immigrant loyalty. Bethlehem Steel, which had purchased the Steelton works in 1916, took a survey in 1918 during a Liberty Loan campaign and revealed that nearly one-fifth of its thirty thousand employees were "foreigners." The study also noted that about four out of every ten of these foreigners wanted to return to their homeland after the war.[73] The Bethlehem Company began to conduct a series of "get-together" meetings at its Steelton works. In an attempt to whip up patriotism and loyalty among the nearly ten thousand workers, the firm brought in military men who had seen active service at the front. A British army officer told some six thousand workers on the day shift that their cooperation was needed "to make the world safe for democracy." He described the steelworker as a soldier in the thick of the fight and gave a brief account of the life of "American boys" in the trenches. Then he urged his listeners to support their relatives and friends in Europe with a "100% output." Following this particular address, the Steelton Band played, and patriotic songs were sung. Bethlehem felt such meetings not only fostered loyalty but also stirred up enthusiasm for the plan of its president, Charles Schwab, to build "a bridge of ships" for the war effort.[74]

Patriotic activity was also rampant in the community. An "alien squad" composed of ten American soldiers of different nationalities appeared at Steelton High School to raise funds for the fourth Liberty Loan drive in 1918. The Italian Citizens Society of Steelton and Harrisburg passed a resolution to "stand by the government and President Wilson during the present crisis." In fact, the Sons of Italy held several parades, with children in military dress, to show their "American spirit." The Steelton Knights of Columbus formed a committee of forty to conduct a Liberty Loan drive. Of the forty, all were either Irish or German. No one elected to take German language study at Steelton High School in 1918 and 1919. Jews initiated their own war fund drive. The Bulgarians raised $2,000 during the third Liberty Loan campaign.[75]

Like other ethnic groups, the Croatians often seemed as anxious to prove their unquestioned loyalty as government and industry were to instill it. The Croatian *sokol* held several dances to raise funds for the Red Cross. The Croatian lodges took an active part in the Liberty Loan drives. The Croats and Serbs, moreover, found time to participate in demonstrations in Washington calling for freedom of the "Southern Slavs" from Austria. Yet when a group of Serbs wanted to parade with a banner that read, "The Kingdom of Serbs, Croats, and Slovenes," the Croats and Slovenes refused to participate. They were eager to show their appreciation in every possible way for the fact that America was their liberator, said Michael Horvath, a Croatian printer. "They will never follow a banner of a Kingdom."[76] Kasmir Posega, an interpreter by occupation, advised on the Fourth of July, 1918, that all foreigners "gradually become Americanized." Posega used the example of the Fothergill School in Steelton, saying that there one could find children of different nationalities, creeds, and religions. He exclaimed, however, "They were only American."[77]

The Croatian press was especially sensitive to the accusations and implications that immigrants were not completely loyal. One of the strongest statements affirming Slavic loyalty appeared in *Zajedničar* in 1918. The Croatian organ claimed in an editorial on "dangerous foreigners" that Slavs had never been properly understood by the Americans. The paper failed to see how foreigners constituted a risk for America or her industries. It cited the absence of Slavic leadership or participation in recent labor disturbances as evidence of immigrant loyalty. Then the journal confronted the charge that immigrants did not know the English language. "What of it? Their children do. They would know English too if they were given an opportunity. You would have to show us the man who has worked ten and twelve hours everyday in any one of our steel mills, mines, or freight yards, and is brick enough to go to school." After expressing the immigrants' bitterness toward corporations for not being interested in the education of their foreign workmen, the editorial concluded that certainly the Slavs loved the land of their birth, but their patriotism in America, "with the exception of a few sporadic cases, is beyond reproach."[78]

In January 1918 the Croatians of Steelton, in what represented an extreme effort by newcomers to demonstrate that they belonged in a foreign land, organized the George Washington Lodge. The lodge's objectives and its name displayed graphically the manner by which immigrants were attempting to define their identity. While the lodge was named after an American president and was intended to show Croatian loyalty to the United States, it simultaneously promoted the separation of Croatia from Austria-Hungary. The point is revealed clearly in a letter sent by Joseph Verbos and Lawrence Rudman on behalf of the lodge to Woodrow Wilson: "The Croatians of Steelton . . . applaud most heartily the declaration of war upon the treacherous Austro-Hungarian government and beg to assure you that in offering our services we are actuated by sentiments of loyal patriotism and a desire of aiding the United States in this struggle for democracy and freedom of small nations, which we hope will mean freedom for the Croatians."[79]

Most of the immigrants who formed the George Washington Lodge feared being labeled as unpatriotic because of the small socialist group that existed among Steelton's Croats in 1918. Traces of socialist thought appeared in the Croatian *sokol,* and Croats were well aware of those who held socialist beliefs, especially when they abstained from regular church attendance. Of those individuals identified as sympathetic to socialism, few were laborers. Indeed, the socialist sympathizers Kasmir Posega and Michael Horvath were two of the most articulate and educated persons in the Croatian community. Posega was a frequent spokesman for the Croatians in their relations with the local press. Horvath, who at one time planned a Croatian paper for Steelton, became an editor for one in Pittsburgh.[80]

The flurry of patriotic statements on the part of Slavs seemed to signal a departure from the theme of a growing ethnic consciousness. The positions of Posega and Horvath, who simultaneously defended fellow Slavs as good Americans and held socialist beliefs, were apparently contradictory. It was certain that newcomers were being pulled from opposite directions. The larger community was suspicious of foreigners and demanded a display of patriotism. Slavs, however, had deep personal views on European politics and developments and, as Posega and Horvath illustrated, on domestic politics as well, which often conflicted with one-hundred-percent Americanism. Croat spokesmen, for instance, were forced continually to reassure the old stock that their loyalty was beyond reproach. But such assurances had strategic value for newcomers. They allowed Slavs to pursue ethnic interests, such as Croatian independence, while allaying the suspicions of the old stock.

The loyalty crusade hit a peak in the summer of 1918 during the Independence Day parade at Harrisburg. The parade that day was the first recorded instance when Negroes, Italians, Slavs, and native white Americans marched together. Blacks and Slavs had each marched separately on Independence Day and never with the native population. The practice of integrating parades was not continued after the war. But in 1918 the *Telegraph* observed that Americans were now compelled to forget the "hyphenated names" after seeing the "patriotic spirit with which they marched." The paper remarked that the Steelton Bulgarian-Balkan Band and the First Cornet Negro Band received much applause. Governor Sproul of Pennsylvania added: "When we entered the war . . . we looked upon this great body of foreign-born people as a menace. . . . We have found in the hearts of the foreign-born an unexpected depth of patriotism. They could be a great asset in the future of our state if properly led."[81]

During World War I Slavs were forced to mediate between Old World interests and one-hundred-percent Americanism. Just as internal turmoil in Steelton's immigrant churches had heightened ethnic awareness, the war years again raised the issue of ethnic identity. This internal conflict not only solidified individual ethnic communities but also caused immigrants to discard the localism of their European upbringing. European ties and perspectives were weakened, but their relations with Steelton's old stock remained distant once the war was ended. Unable or unwilling to return to the homeland and consigned to lower-class status, the only alternative was to preserve the ethnic communities which had been molded in America.

Blacks also continued to live their lives apart from the various white communities. The war years had temporarily narrowed the gulf between immigrants, who were urged to demonstrate their loyalty, blacks, whose soldiers were celebrated, and the old stock. Peace abroad, however, did not signal the dawn of social harmony at home. Once the war ended, Steelton's people wasted little time in retreating to their separate communities.

7 Continuity and Change

Although immigrants had acquired a foothold in Steelton, they were not able to ease their way into the mainstream of life between 1920 and 1940. Immigrant children matured but occupied lower-level jobs and compensated for their inferior status as their fathers had done: by supporting the ethnic community institutions and selecting marriage partners within their own group. Anglo-Saxon leaders kept their higher social status intact and dominated skilled trades and local political and civic affairs. The company continued to influence local affairs and keep labor quiescent.

While Slavic and Italian newcomers and their progeny now comprised nearly one-half the white population of the town, they were not integrated into the community. Of 1,759 foreign-born adult males in 1920, 1,100 still had not secured their first citizenship papers. Only 3 percent of the town's residents were the children of "mixed" immigrant and native-born parents in 1920 and only 4 percent in 1930. Immigrants had an English illiteracy rate which was over twenty-seven times greater than the rate for native whites. The children of newcomers were also underrepresented in Steelton's schools.[1] Whether immigrants and their children could improve their social standing and integrate themselves more fully into Steelton life remained for the future to tell.

Immigrant customs were prevalent in Steelton well after 1920. The Orthodox Christmas celebration was still the major annual cultural event for the Serbs and Bulgarians. Throughout the 1930s fires from Serbian pig roasts, which culminated the Christmas ceremonies, still lit up the winter sky each January.[2] During the two decades after 1920 the Bulgarians continued to commemorate the Epiphany each winter.[3] The social activities of immigrants and their children continued to revolve around the ethnic congregations. One of the largest Croatian celebrations in the entire decade of the 1920s was the commemoration of the twenty-fifth anniversary of St. Mary's Church. Hundreds of Croats who had formerly resided in Steelton returned for the ceremony. Residents of other Croatian colonies in steel towns such as Lackawanna, New York, and South Bethlehem, Pennsylvania, sent delegations to the anniversary as they had done for two decades.[4]

Anniversary celebrations strengthened ethnic awareness as newcomers began to perceive a history of their own. Early pioneers and settlers were celebrated for the hardships they endured and the institutions they forged. One Slovene remarked in 1939 that the youth were unable to visualize "how unpleasant was the life of our pioneers."[5] Bulgarians praised their early settlers: "They met with accidents and illness. Having no one to take care of them, the Macedonians were claimed by death. They were called 'backward foreigners' for lack of formal American schooling. . . . Friends were few. The 'strange people' failed to extend sympathy or a helping hand. Humiliation and aggression seized them. . . . As a result they decided to organize and pool their talents, labors, spirit and enthusiasm. Their combined efforts produced a House of prayer, a Macedonian-Bulgarian Orthodox Church."[6] Such celebrations usually ended with expressions of gratitude for the sacrifices of the pioneers who created a settlement in Steelton and exhortations to maintain the ethnic ways. "Because of the hardships," a Serbian-American wrote, "we are now able to fully enjoy the fruits of the labor of these pioneers. . . . May you keep the faith," he added, "as your fathers kept it before you."[7]

Many new ethnic organizations were formed by the second generation after 1920. Both the Slovenian club, which was instituted in the late 1920s, and the Steelton Italian club held weekly dances. The Croatian Boys' Club was organized after 1930 and sponsored dances during the depression years. The largest gatherings of the Slovenia Ladies Union occurred in 1934. The Croatian-American Civic and Educational Club was initiated the year before, along with the Hrvatimati Hrvaticama theatrical group. Throughout the 1930s the Serbs still celebrated the creation of Yugoslavia as a nation and invited officials to speak at Serbian Hall annually. Serbian basketball teams came regularly from Cleveland and Pittsburgh to play against the Steelton Serbian teams. Even the traditional roast lamb was still served at the South Slav wedding feasts.[8]

Several Croatians who grew up in the 1930s recalled the friction that persisted between themselves and native-born residents. Croatian children were admonished not to visit Pine Street where most of the company officials and town professionals lived. In retaliation for persistently being called "hunkies," Croatian children decided among themselves to sit alone at high-school football games and label any Anglo-Saxon a "cake eater" because Croats considered cake a luxury.[9] Typically, the children of newcomers did not even enter Steelton High School. The Croatian school, which contained elementary grades only, had over five hundred students by 1927 and was forced to build a larger structure. Few Slavs remained in school past the eighth grade before the late 1930s. In 1920 the Steelton public schools graduated 131 eighth-grade students. Only three Croats and Slovenes were on the graduation list and no Serbs or Bulgarians whatsoever. Only one Steelton Slav had completed the public high school by 1920; no facilities existed for parochial education at the secondary level. By 1924 only three Slavs could be found among the 67 high-school graduates, and two were girls. Two years later, two Croatian boys and an Italian represented the newcomers on the graduation list. In 1927 six Slavs were found among 80 graduates, although a Serb was yet to earn a local high-school diploma. The first Croat to finish college was Lawrence Gustian in 1927, nearly a half century after the arrival of Croats in Steelton.[10]

Education was invariably terminated in favor of work. Children were expected to assist with family maintenance and usually turned their earnings over to their mothers. One Slovenian child cried when she was forced to leave school following the sixth grade, but her father argued that a girl didn't need an education to put diapers on babies. She began working in a neighboring boardinghouse for one dollar a week washing clothes and peeling potatoes for sixteen boarders. Catherine Lescanec left school at age fifteen and studied sewing and dressmaking from a "German lady" in Steelton. Boys often worked in the cigar factory or as "water boys" in the mill. One Slovene who sent his son to college in 1918 was mocked by the "foreign people" who thought that the boy should be sent to work in the mill.[11]

Internal disputes continued to plague the ethnic communities. In the 1920s the Macedonian Political Organization (MPO) revived. It was concerned ultimately with sending men and money to Europe to create an autonomous Macedonia, activities which disturbed Bulgarians who did not believe their church should serve as a center for European-oriented political activity. The MPO was tolerated, however, until 1934 when the pastor, the Reverend David Nakoff, decided to dissociate his church from the Bulgarian Synod. This move splintered the church into three factions: the Nakoff group, the synod faction which supported the original church charter, and the MPO. The synod group, now backed by the MPO, warned Nakoff that if he did not follow the original charter which affiliated the congregation with the Bulgarian Synod, he would be considered a trespasser on the church grounds and subject to ejection. The Bulgarian Orthodox Mission for the United States and Canada started court proceedings to oust Nakoff, while Alexander Kormushoff, president of the congregation, called a meeting and declared that only the congregation had the right to hire or dismiss pastors, and the one in Steelton, which was "one-hundred percent naturalized," totally supported Nakoff.[12]

Proclamations did little to restore unity to the congregation. The synod adherents, known also by the names of their leaders, the Minoff brothers, brought a lawsuit against Nakoff in 1937 in Dauphin County Court. One of the Nakoff followers contended, "We didn't want to have anything to do with that government in Bulgaria because we believe the American Church belonged to the people." The court, nevertheless, upheld the original charter and the Minoff faction prevailed.[13] Its decision forced the Nakoff followers to leave the Holy Annunciation Church and form a separate congregation in Steelton. However, when Nakoff died during World War II, his supporters lost the leadership that had held them together, and they were readmitted into the Holy Annunciation Church.[14]

The importance of ethnic activities to immigrants and their children was demonstrated most graphically in the selection of marriage partners (see table 16). Very few of the sons of Croatian, Serbian, or Bulgarian immigrants married into the native American community. Between 1920 and 1939, 88 percent of the Croatian and Slovene sons married within their own ethnic group. Of the 12 percent who married non-Croatians or non-Slovenes, approximately one-half married second-generation Italians. Serbians and Bulgarians also married along ethnic lines. In the two decades after 1920 only one out of every ten sons of Serbian immigrants selected a non-Serbian mate. In the same time period, every Bulgarian son married a partner of similar parentage.

Likewise, Steelton's American-born Irish, English, and German sons almost always married within the native-born, old-stock community. Ninety-one percent of all native-born whites married native-born individuals. Of the 9 percent of the native-born, old-stock population who married immigrant children after 1920, all selected partners of either Scotch, Irish, or German descent. In no case did a native-born, old-stock male select a mate of Slavic descent.

TABLE 16: *Marriages of Steelton Males, 1920–1939*

Nationality of Father	Number	% Marrying Within Group
Native born	500	91
Croatian-Slovene	188	88
Serbian	102	90
Bulgarian	·32	100

Source: Dauphin County Marriage License Dockets.

The children of new immigrant groups were also experiencing less intergenerational occupational mobility than the progeny of English, Irish, German, and native whites had several years before (see table 17). About one-half of the sons of unskilled, native-born white workers rose to positions higher than those attained by their fathers between 1888 and 1905. The children of English, Irish, and German immigrants showed an even greater tendency to surpass their fathers. In surveys of the sons of unskilled workers who appeared in the 1880 federal census, an average of 47 percent of the sons of native white laborers attained higher skill classifications than their fathers. Among the sons of Irish, English, and German immigrants, however, an average of 59 percent of the male children rose above their fathers. Nearly one-half of both native-born whites and old-immigrant sons who advanced moved into skilled and nonmanual jobs. While the children of native whites in some measure rose above their fathers before 1905, the sons of unskilled blacks were rarely able to do so. The ratio by which they surpassed their fathers was less than one in five or about 18 percent.

Since blacks and the English, German, and Irish immigrants were almost all in the unskilled categories in 1880, the determination of intergenerational mobility for other categories was not possible. Among native white groups, however, sufficient data was available to investigate intergenerational mobility at all levels (see table 18). In all occupational classes of native whites of native parentage, nearly 20 percent failed to attain a level that was at least equal to that of their fathers. Some 30 percent of the sons advanced to positions beyond those attained by their fathers. The most common experience, however, was that a native white son achieved about the same occupational status as his father.

While nearly six out of every ten male children of English, Irish, and German immigrants surpassed their fathers, the sons of Slavic and Italian newcomers did not do nearly as well. The ratio at which they overtook their parents was much closer to that of the blacks (see table 19). Slavic children surpasssed their

TABLE 17: *Intergenerational Mobility of Sons of Unskilled Workers, 1888–1905*

Ethnic Classification of Father	1888 Group				1896 Group				1905 Group			
	No.	% Moving Up	% Moving Down	% No Change	No.	% Moving Up	% Moving Down	% No Change	No.	% Moving Up	% Moving Down	% No Change
Native white	41	45	2	53	53	47	3	50	47	50	2	48
Black	9	0	0	100	18	22	0	78	19	31	1	68
English, German Irish	15	46	0	54	29	55	0	45	23	76	0	24

Source: Individuals were identified from the "Tenth Census, 1880."
Note: Read "45 percent of native-white sons held a higher occupational classification in 1888 than their fathers did in 1880."

TABLE 18: *Intergenerational Mobility of Sons of Native Whites, All Skill Categories, 1888–1905*

Position Attained	1888 (N=67)	1896 (N=101)	1905 (N=89)
Above father	28%	31%	33%
Below father	22	22	17
Same as father	50	47	50

Source: Native whites listed in the "Tenth Census, 1880."

fathers after 1920 in only one out of four instances. This ratio was considerably less than the 59 percent achieved by sons of the old immigrants and certainly less than the 31 percent revealed by native whites between 1888 and 1905.

The second-generation Slavs and Italians were no more successful in escaping unskilled and semiskilled status than their parents' generation had been. Twenty-nine percent of the first-generation Italians and Slavs who had resided in Steelton since 1905 climbed out of low manual jobs between 1915 and 1925. In an additional group residing in Steelton in 1915, 22 percent moved upward in the same decade. But the second-generation workers escaped from low manual callings at a rate of 22 percent between 1920 and 1945, a lower rate than that of their fathers (see Appendix 1, table H). Moreover, whereas roughly three-fourths of all first-generation Slavs and Italians continued in the same occupation between 1905 and 1925,[15] immigrant sons showed a total continuity rate of 60 percent. Continuity rates were lower in unskilled occupations because more opportunities existed for modest advances. Upward mo-

TABLE 19: *Intergenerational Mobility of Sons of Slavs and Italians, 1920–1939*

Position Attained	Slavs (N=282)	Italians (N=58)
Above father	24%	38%
Below father	14	10
Same as father	62	52

Source: Children were identified in Dauphin County Marriage License Dockets and the "Twelfth Census, 1900," then traced in *Boyd's Directory of Harrisburg and Steelton.*

bility, however, usually stopped at the semiskilled level which had a continuity rate of 70 percent among the sons of new immigrants.[16]

Since kinship and ethnic ties were used to secure jobs, many second-generation Slavs and Italians occupied positions in the same category as their fathers. Joseph Kovach, a milkman, was the son of a cigarmaker; Joseph Milletics was a tinner in the mill just like his father. Joseph Santana was a fruit merchant like his father before him. Anton Tezak, whose father was a tinner, became a melter. Joseph Bruno and his father were both helpers in the open hearth. Mark Slabonik became a steam fitter while his father had been a laborer, and Anthony Sinkovita became a butcher after his father had worked in the local cigar factory. Some rose above their immigrant fathers in the steel town but they were in a minority. The promise of American life held no guarantees.

While Slavic and Italian children did not match the mobility of the sons of the old immigrants, their rates were not incommensurate with those of the blacks after 1920. Sons of both blacks and Slavs surpassed their fathers at about the same rate, one out of four.[17] Italians fared slightly better. There were only 58 Italians, however, considerably fewer that the 282 Slavs and 216 blacks investigated. Nevertheless, the figures do suggest that the extent to which sons could surpass their fathers between 1920 and 1939 was substantially smaller for children from black and newer immigrant homes than it had been for children from the ethnic groups which formed the basis of Steelton's pre-1920 power and elite structure.

In a comparison of blacks and immigrants after 1920, however, the stronger position which Afro-Americans held earlier over Slavs and Italians was now completely reversed. Whereas blacks had a lower proportion of their workers listed as unskilled in 1905 and 1915 than did southern Europeans, only 33 percent of all Slavs and Italians were unskilled between 1920 and 1939 as compared with 67 percent of the Negroes (see Appendix 1, table D). While a greater percentage of blacks than of immigrants were semiskilled prior to 1920, 47 percent of the Slavs and Italians were now semiskilled as compared to 27 percent of the blacks. In skilled trades neither blacks nor newcomers made significant inroads. The relative preponderance of immigrants over blacks in nonmanual fields continued at about the same rate.

The improvement of the Slav and Italian in relation to the Negro was modest in many respects. While the percentage of immigrants in unskilled jobs declined from 78 in 1915 to only 33 in the 1920–1939 group, eight out of every ten immigrants were still in a blue-collar job after 1920, exactly as they had been in 1905 and 1915. Immigrants shifted from unskilled to semiskilled positions. Thomas Benkovic, a Croatian, for example, moved from the brutal heat of shoveling in the open hearth to a position as a crane operator in a career that spanned over fifty years.[18] Immigrants enjoyed upward mobility but on a limited and modest basis.

Blacks were surpassed by Slavs and Italians after 1920 and remained at about the same occupational level as before (see tables 20, 21). The ratio of Negroes in unskilled positions remained fairly constant throughout the period. The results were similar for the semiskilled categories. In fact, both southern Europeans and Negroes remained primarily in unskilled and semiskilled jobs throughout the first four decades of this century. As the semiskilled segment of the work force expanded, these positions were assumed at a more rapid rate by new immigrants and their sons than by Negroes. Neither blacks nor immigrants ever escaped blue-collar work in any large numbers. More than eight out of every ten immigrants worked in blue-collar positions throughout their lifetimes. For blacks, over nine out of every ten entered low-level jobs.

Geographical mobility also served to distinguish blacks from southern European immigrants. Between 1920 and 1939, of 332 Slavic immigrant sons applying for marriage licenses in Steelton, 87 percent were born in the town, but of 373 black applicants during the 1920s and 1930s, only 11 percent were born locally. The blacks who married in Steelton between 1920 and 1939 were not the children of residents who had lived in

TABLE 20: *Occupational Distribution of Blacks, 1905–1939*

	1905	1915	1920–1939
Unskilled	60%	70%	67%
Semiskilled	33	26	27
Skilled	0	0	0
Nonmanual	3	1	6

Sources: Table 12; Appendix 1, table B.

the community during the first two decades of the century, while immigrant children were largely the sons of those who persisted in Steelton (see Appendix 1, table D). Immigrant children, the second generation, were reluctant to marry outside their ethnic group or to move far from their homes and weaken kinship ties. Seventy-seven first- and second-generation Slavs were interviewed in Steelton about their careers and those of friends and relatives who moved away. This technique revealed information not only on the persisters but on the movers as well. Of 150 second-generation Slavs born in Steelton before 1930, 77 percent still lived in the Steelton-Harrisburg area in 1974. Even more striking, 56 percent were still in Steelton and the adjacent working-class settlement of Bressler. Among the 23 percent who had left the immediate Steelton area, only five had left Pennsylvania.

Most children in the steel town attained occupations roughly comparable to their fathers. About 65 percent of all sons occupied the same status as their fathers after 1920. Thus, even if upward intergenerational occupational mobility was attained by a quarter of the black and Slavic children, immigrants, blacks, and their children were still lodged in unskilled and semiskilled categories. Those groups that held a dominant position before 1920 continued to do so afterward.

TABLE 21: *Percentage of Immigrants and Blacks in Unskilled and Semiskilled Jobs, 1905–1939*

	1905	1915	1920–1939	Average
Slavs, Italians	83	88	80	84
Blacks	93	96	94	94

In political affairs as well as economic ones, immigrant Slavs and their children were unable to make significant inroads before 1940. Throughout the 1920s Slavs were not found among the ten members of the town council, the police force, or in other public office. Steelton politics remained under the influence of Thomas Nelley and Bethlehem Steel. In fact, the town burgess in the early 1930s was John C. Craig, superintendent of the rolling mills. Frank A. Robbins, the superintendent of the entire plant, was on the city council and also the head of the school board. Robbins even asked his superintendent in the frog and switch department to run for the school board when a vacancy occurred in 1929, thus increasing the company's representation.[19]

In 1924 a group of young Croatians challenged Steelton's power structure. Michael Horvath, a printer, and John Verbos, who was a laborer in the open hearth, agreed to join in an effort to "break the stranglehold which the politicians were beginning to exercise on a great majority of our people." Verbos and Horvath, both Democrats, argued that insignificant favors, "the usual tools of the politician," were being used to forestall any attempts by Slavs to make their own selection. Claiming that such political practices could not be endured by the American-born Croatian youth, they decided to oppose the Nelley political machine despite the fact that it was one of the most powerful in the state. While Verbos, running as a Democrat, lost in the local council race to Nelley in 1924, he and Horvath felt that they had begun to break the ties of "our people" to the old practices of the "politicians."[20]

No Slavs appeared in responsible political positions until after 1930—over forty years after the arrival of the first Slavic immigrants. In 1932 Joseph Zerance, a Croatian mill worker, appeared on the borough council. Soon after Steven Suknaic was elected to the council, Frank Simonic became a constable, and in 1939 a Croatian, Joseph Sostar, became chief of police. When John Verbos was nominated for the position of local postmaster by President Roosevelt in 1934, *Zajedničar* proclaimed: "This appointment should serve to raise our people in

Steelton to a new and higher level. If they will continue to stick together, there is little doubt that the pride they share now is only a stepping stone to something bigger and better."[21]

In 1933 several Slavs again challenged the Nelley machine. Lewis Balkovic unsuccessfully ran against a Nelley candidate for justice of the peace. Dr. Frank Cunjack actually ran against Nelley for the council seat from the heavily Slavic first ward. Cunjack and John Verbos held several rallies that year at Croatian Hall and claimed the Republicans and Nelley were not using enough available funds for local welfare. Verbos frequently criticized the way Nelley "ran" Steelton and claimed the Democrats would fight harder for "labor's view." Nelley countered with rallies of his own. At one meeting Meter Dragovich, president of the St. Nicholas Serbian Church, presided and called for Nelley's reelection. Nelley was always certain that the Croatian orchestra played when meetings were held at Croatian Hall.[22]

Nelley's political machine was strong enough to beat back this challenge to its power. Less than one-half of the immigrant generation was naturalized, a fact which facilitated Nelley's control among the few who did vote. Even though the challenge came from the members of the ethnic groups who provided him with much of his support, Nelley had long ago established his base by performing numerous favors. Prominent Croatians like Michael Horvath claimed that the machine would cause a man to lose his job if he did not follow its instructions. Indeed, Nelley retaliated against the challenge to his power in 1933 by directing an obedient town council to fire three policemen whose relatives worked against him in the campaign. He also demanded that Frank Cunjack be removed as physician for the county poor board.[23] Steelton's power structure remained intact.

Residential segregation patterns which existed before 1920 continued afterward as well. Cottage Hill remained an enclave of company-built superintendents' homes where Slavs, Italians, and blacks could not hope to settle. The leading officials of the local plant continued to reside on Pine Street, while the

West Side and the "lower end" remained working-class neighborhoods.[24]

In 1930, when Steelton celebrated the fiftieth anniversary of its incorporation as a borough, the immigrants were conspicuously absent from the celebration. The borough council appointed a planning committee including representatives from the town council, the Kiwanis Club, the American Legion, and the Civic Club, which continued its Americanization work well into the 1930s. A complete list of the fifty citizens appointed to the committee included two blacks, Charles F. Howard and Peter Blackwell, and one Croatian, Joseph Zerance. No Serbs, Slovenes, or Bulgarians were on the list despite the fact that in 1930 approximately one-half of Steelton's population was either of first- or second-generation immigrant stock. At the celebration itself the honored guests were all former officials of the local steel company: Quincy Bent, J. V. W. Reynders, and Edgar Felton.[25]

While Steelton's long established elite generally excluded immigrants from participation in civic affairs, the company maintained a firm hand on the organizing activities of its workers. Since the strike of 1919, Steelton was relatively free of any overt form of labor protest. The major instrument in keeping unionism out of the town was the company's own employee representation plan.[26] In 1918 the National War Labor Board had ordered the Bethlehem Steel Company to provide opportunities for its employees to bargain collectively. Bethlehem, following the board's directives, prepared a plan of employee representation. The plan, which went into effect in October 1918, provided ways and means for workers to discuss with management problems that affected their working conditions: employees organized into twenty-two divisions, elected representatives to serve on various committees dealing with specific problems and grievances. The plan was soon endorsed by Bethlehem's president, Eugene Grace, in a letter to employees: "It is with keen satisfaction that the Management offers to you a voice in the shaping of policies affecting your conditions of employment combined with a means of dealing with the Management in the equitable solutions of matters arising for adjustment. . . . The Plan of Employee Representation in industry is essentially the same as the theory of popular government."[27] For the next twenty years the plan was strongly supported by Bethlehem officials. In a pamphlet printed in 1920, *Hints to Foreman in Meeting the New Employee,* the company stressed that the employee should be impressed with the fact that the plan represented the employer's desire to retain a close personal relationship with workers and that it was not just for handling grievances but for bringing the management and employees closer together.[28]

The plan, of course, was the company's surrogate for independent unionism. In frequent communications to the men, Grace stressed that no outside agency could take the place of the employee representation plan without destroying the all-essential direct contact and relationship so necessary to insure employees the best possible working and living conditions. In 1937, when pressure began to mount from the Steel Workers Organizing Committee of the Congress of Industrial Organizations, Bethlehem increased its publicity campaign at its plants in Steelton and elsewhere on behalf of the plan. The company insisted in numerous posters that the CIO organizers were claiming that union membership would be necessary to hold a job. Steel officials maintained, however, that the right to hold or reject membership in any organization was an individual right guaranteed by the United States Constitution and recognized in the company's representation plan.[29] When CIO strikes erupted at Bethlehem and Johnstown, Steelton remained calm. Hundreds of Mexican steelworkers and farmers from rural Pennsylvania were brought to Steelton by the company. These newcomers, who were hardly aware of union activity elsewhere, combined with a substantial number of layoffs to blunt any strike efforts locally. Steelton also lacked union organizers. Several steelworkers who wanted to sign up were confused about how to do so.[30] Steelton still had no outside union.

In the ranks of labor some division existed between skilled employees, usually native born, old stock, and unskilled workers who tended to be Slavic or black. Walter Lang, who was the superintendent of the frog and switch department, recalled that the unskilled "grinders" who were mostly foreigners were very much in favor of the CIO. They consequently incurred the wrath of the more skilled workers who were less than enthusiastic about the outside union.[31]

In 1939 the National Labor Relations Board declared that Bethlehem's promotion of a company union was an unfair practice because it prohibited employees from exercising the freedom to choose their own labor organization. Bethlehem was ordered to terminate such a practice at all of its facilities and desist in interfering with their employees' right of self-organization and collective bargaining.[32] For the first time since 1866, Steelton workers could unionize without interference from management.

If the antiunionism of the company, limited occupational mobility, and the old-stock dominance conspired to maintain immigrants and blacks in inferior social positions, the depression of the 1930s certainly defeated much hope for improved conditions in the steel town. Hard times were not unusual for Steelton's newcomers and their progeny. Hundreds had left the borough in the winter of 1893–94. Thousands, especially Bulgarians and Serbs, had returned to Europe in 1907 or moved to other cities in search of jobs. But in 1933 few immigrant children were ready to leave for Europe, and job opportunities appeared no better elsewhere.

In 1931 nearly five thousand men were employed at the steelworks, about the same number as in 1928. Employment dropped drastically, however, between 1931 and 1935. Only about twenty-seven hundred men had jobs, only half as many as in 1928. The company even made a 15 percent reduction in its pension payments.[33] Despite rumors of a large order for steel rails by the Pennsylvania Railroad, which were continually circulated in the press, Steelton was unable to escape hard times during the mid-1930s. By 1938, about five thousand were again employed, but thousands were on relief. In April 1933, over seven thousand families were seeking relief in Dauphin

County. By far the largest group of unemployed were general laborers, of whom the bulk (3,586) were employed at the Steelton plant.[34] Such figures set local relief agencies into action once again. In 1933, Frank A. Robbins, president of the Steelton Welfare Association and superintendent of the steel mill, raised over $9,000 in a campaign for funds. The Bethlehem Steel Company also began to distribute aid from a modest relief fund of its own. Even the local American Legion had a welfare committee to serve its own members.[35]

The nature of the Steelton Welfare Association's efforts indicated by whom the depression was felt most. The association, for instance, established milk clinics for "white and colored persons." Milk was distributed at the Croatian school on Tuesdays, the Italian school on Wednesdays, the Slovene school on Thursdays, and to the "colored children" on Fridays.[36] After 1932 local relief organizations in Pennsylvania were assisted by federal funds. The most active federal project in Steelton was sponsored by the Civil Works Administration (CWA) but never employed more than one hundred men. It put men to work constructing sewers, repairing local boardwalks, building new stands at the local football fields, and painting local schools. The pay for these men usually averaged about twelve dollars a week.[37]

The wives of many first- and second-generation Croatians, Slovenes, and Serbs found employment. Outside the General Cigar Factory in Steelton, which continued to operate, lines of women formed daily, waiting to be called for work. Steelton women working at dress factories in Harrisburg recalled waiting in line to get a piece to sew and women on piece work fighting over a garment. Many families planted large gardens, which they were forced to guard at night with weapons. Soup lines also provided needed food and shoes periodically. Many families' savings were exhausted.[38]

Heavy Croatian unemployment drained the reserves of the Croatian Fraternal Union, so many men were signing up instead for sick benefits. Local lodges could not always meet their assessments regularly because their members were unable to pay monthly dues. By March 1933, nearly one-half the entire membership of the Croatian Fraternal Union was unemployed and nearly all members were drawing on the reserve accumulation of their insurance policies. Steelton's St. Lawrence Lodge could not even sponsor its Croatian basketball team which had played Croatian teams throughout the East.[39]

Economic circumstances did not allow newcomers or their children to make significant occupational advances. Among those who managed to hold a job, work was usually on a reduced basis. Often men who represented the company union were the last to be laid off from work and the first to return. Immigrant children suffered in particular since they were just beginning their careers and lacked training and experience to obtain positions elsewhere.[40]

Immigrants and their children, moreover, maintained their own ethnic organizations and institutions. By choosing marriage partners from within the group, and settling within the same community, the children insured the continuance of the ethnic community. Indeed, the very existence of strong ethnic communities by the late 1930s revealed an inability and an unwillingness on the part of immigrant children, partly because of limited upward mobility and old-stock dominance, to leave the ethnic enclaves their fathers had established. In many instances they created new ethnic organizations and celebrated their parents as pioneers. Their integrative development being arrested, the insulated world of the ethnic group afforded the same retreat for the second generation as it had for the first. Ethnicity was the answer of immigrants and their children to exclusion and working-class status.

At the end of the 1930s the division which had characterized social relationships in Steelton was still discernable. Newcomers and their children confined their social activity to ethnic communities. The Irish-German-English melange provided civic and political leaders and dominated the social and economic life of the town. The burgess and tax collector were still Irish, and company officials still headed the school board.[41] A pattern which was noticeable at the turn of the century remained distinguishable: ethnic consciousness was more acute among the working class than among Steelton's native, English, Irish, and German middle and upper classes. As Warren Eyster observed in his novel of Steelton: "Nothing had been solved, nothing was being solved. Only human spirit and human dignity, caught in little corners of little hearts, promised a future, after the last banners had fallen in the dust. And perhaps it was even less than this which mankind had to look forward to, not a future only a continued existence."[42]

While the profile of Steelton society seemed static, however, the seeds of social change were taking root almost imperceptibly for the post-1940 period. The central event in precipitating this change in the town's social relationships and eventually in its social structure was the establishment of the local CIO. Meeting secretly in private homes or fire houses, walking past company guards who "took names," workers from various departments of the plant signed a charter of the Steel Workers Organizing Committee, Local 1688, in late 1939. Two years later the company recognized the local as the collective bargaining agent for its members. For the first time the southern Europeans, with assistance from the blacks, created a unified organization which challenged the power of the steel company and the dominance of the old-stock political machine of Tom Nelley. Once such a challenge was effected, newcomers would gradually enter other areas of Steelton life previously denied them.

The leadership of the charter group indicated both the degree of ethnic cooperation in the new organization and the newer attitude of the second-generation southern European who saw his future in Steelton. The most prominent local supporters were Paul Dragas, a Croat who worked in the frog and switch department; Oscar Daniels, a black; Joe Basdar, a Serb; Buck Magnelli, an Italian; and John Madden, an Irishman. Somewhat later the group included Joe DiSanto, an Italian; Dave Moore and George Pinkney, both black; Steve Klipa, a Serb; and Louis Cerjanic, a Croat.[43] The ethnic mix of the group was unique in Steelton's labor history. Prior to 1939 ethnic and racial differences had deeply divided the town's working class. Blacks were left out of workers' organizations in 1891 and Slavs were neglected in 1919. Even various departments in the mill reflected ethnic divisions. In 1939, however, Steelton's newcomers and blacks exhibited an emerging, working-class consciousness which overlooked traditional ethnic barriers. Due to limited occupational mobility, Slavs and blacks had remained in tightly knit ethnic communities which prevented them from seeing goals they may have shared with others. But the shared experience of the depression tended to move steelworkers to common action. Men who were unemployed for over two years lost all seniority and now sought job security. Speaking as workers rather than as ethnics, several Serbs declared that a union was needed to improve job security. One Italian supported the CIO to prevent a return to "those goddam depression days"; another blamed the depression on the local steel company and suggested that the union would be necessary in order to "straighten things out."[44]

Dragas was a particularly good example of the ethnic who was acquiring stronger working-class perceptions. Active in local Croatian societies and a frequent reporter on local Croat activities to *Hrvatski List,* a Croatian paper in New York City, Dragas also espoused strong feelings about the value of hard work. In 1936, in a strong, somewhat anticlerical letter to the paper, Dragas expressed his displeasure over the indebtedness of St. Mary's Croatian Church, which he attributed partially to the "capricious nature" of the local pastor, Irenaeus Petricak. Revealing his working-class predilections, Dragas suggested that the cleric accept "honest work" (*postenoga rada*) at the Bethlehem Steel Plant and experience "sweat and perspiration" as a means of acquiring an appreciation for hard-earned money.[45]

Steelworkers of diverse ethnic and racial backgrounds called for a united action by their respective groups. Dave Moore, a black who worked on the plant's narrow-gauge railroad, recalled how both Paul Dragas and Oscar Daniels came to his home to elicit union support. They told Moore of "old times" when men failed to receive bonuses that the company had promised during World War I, and of the lack of compensation for unemployment. Dragas and Daniels argued that the union would allow both the Croats and blacks to obtain better jobs. The trend toward working-class cooperation was highlighted by George Medrick, the chief CIO organizer in Steelton between 1939 and 1942. Medrick continually called for increased "integration" of the mill's departments, a stance which won him substantial Slavic and Negro support.[46]

With the establishment of the CIO, alterations began in Steelton's social order. Although change came slowly, it did come. Steelworkers won wage advances in 1942 and carried out the first successful strike in Steelton in 1946. The first southern European to sit on the school board, an Italian, was elected in 1947. Although no Slav had ever served on the school board prior to 1960, a few began to appear on the board and town council thereafter. The hold of the Irish-Americans on the offices of burgess and tax collector was broken after 1957. Croatians finally became foremen in the open hearth in 1960 when Nick Cackovic, John Backeric, and Steve Vergot were promoted. The first black helpers in Steelton appeared in the same year, while the initial black craneman came in 1963.[47] The CIO also helped erode another foundation of Steelton's old-stock control by launching widespread voter registration drives to enlist steelworkers and their families into the Democratic party. Such activity permanently weakened the traditional Republican support of the Nelley machine. Steelton's immigrant wards began to vote consistently for Democratic candidates.[48]

The Anglo-Saxon domination of Steelton was at an end. Irish, German, and English residents had minimized their ethnic differences and were secure in their higher-class status. They displayed almost no overt manifestations of ethnic culture or identity. But they had exploited the ethnicity of the working class. Anglo-Saxons attempted to regulate immigrant culture in Steelton but not destroy it. Tom Nelley had cleverly cultivated ethnic alignments rather than attacked them. The company also assisted by maintaining an ethnic pattern in its mills. When a more unified working class weakened its position of privilege, the old stock simply began to abandon the borough. As southern Europeans and blacks entered local political offices, company officials and professionals such as doctors and lawyers left the town for more desirable suburbs near Harrisburg. The exodus of the old stock was apparent from population figures. While the community's population remained stable at thirteen thousand from 1920 to 1940, it fell rapidly after 1950. By 1970 Steelton had less than nine thousand individuals, no leading company officials, and only one doctor.[49]

The flight of the old stock is also revealed in persistence rates after 1930 (see table 22). Long the most stable element of Steelton's generally transient population, the old stock began leaving the borough steadily during the 1930s and 1940s. The Slavs, on the other hand, were increasingly making Steelton their home. Between 1930 and 1950, 66 percent of a sample of old-stock residents living in Steelton in 1930 moved away, while the same percentage of Slavs remained in the borough throughout the two decades.

TABLE 22: *Persistence Rates, 1930–1950*

	Number in 1930	% Remaining in 1940	% Remaining in 1950
Slavic	320	78	66
Old stock	300	60	34

Sources: Polk's Harrisburg and Steelton City Directory, 1930, 1940, 1950.

The community left behind by the old stock displayed little to justify the optimistic assertions of 1880 when Steelton's progress appeared inevitable. A planning study conducted by the borough council in 1958 concluded that the community contained an undesirable mixture of residential and commercial properties and explained that housing was generally unsound, streets were narrow and congested, recreation areas were scarce, and usable vacant land was at a premium.[50] The community had twice the statewide rate of deteriorating housing in

1960 and ten times the Pennsylvania average for dilapidated homes. Its medium family income, as in the steel towns of McKeesport, McKees Rocks, and Monessen, was about four hundred dollars below the Pennsylvania average.[51] Individuals between fifteen and twenty-five, moreover, were rapidly leaving the town, an indication that the third generation of newcomers were joining the exodus of the old stock.[52]

The children of Steelton's newcomers now dominated the town. The community was almost entirely working class and, consequently, much of the residential separation characteristic of the past was gone. Blacks, Italians, and Slavs could be found everywhere. Seven of the ten town council members were Slavic, Italian, or black, and no company officials or old stock served on it or the school board any longer. With its older homes and smoky mills, the town became the resting place for southern Europeans and an increasing number of blacks who were unable or unwilling to leave. Steelton now belonged to the newcomers. No one else wanted it.

8 Conclusion

The evolution of social relationships in Steelton reflected broad changes in American society after 1870. Rapidly modernizing under the weight of industrialization and urbanization, the American social order was assuming recognizable forms. Considerations of status and class became paramount to skilled workers, businessmen, and other professionals who stood to lose most by a radical alteration in the social structure. As Herbert Gutman has found for Patterson, New Jersey, industrial towns were not controlled by industrialists alone. Similarly, a melange of groups in Steelton subjugated religious and ethnic differences to a comprehensive program of status preservation. This was especially true of skilled workers who were becoming less in demand than the semiskilled sector of the work force. Thus Steelton's old stock worked feverishly at shaping rather than resisting the course of social change by controlling the institutions that regulated labor, civic, political, moral, and educational activities before 1940.[1]

Impoverished newcomers from southern Europe and American blacks, unable to participate in the exercise of community power, established alternative mechanisms for dealing with the pressures of transiency, economic fluctuation, and inferior status. The outstanding example of this adaptive behavior was a growing reliance on the ethnic group rather than on kin alone. This process began in the migration experience itself and was reinforced by exclusion from community power and lack of occupational mobility in Steelton. Ironically, while ethnicity was somewhat of a divisive force before 1930, it was actually laying the basis for the type of cooperation that would be necessary for the eventual triumph of the CIO. The reliance on the ethnic community taught newcomers the value of confronting social problems and economic difficulties with large, formalized institutions and organizations rather than with isolated kin groups. The lessons of institutionalization and formalized cooperation to gain socioeconomic goals were actually being learned in the ethnic communities which appeared so isolated to American observers. The experience of the Great Depression reinforced this growing awareness for the need for sophisticated institutions. Hard times underscored the inadequacies of ethnic institutions in dealing with economic problems, for instance, and accelerated the drift toward formal organizations.[2]

The reaction of the old stock and the newcomers to industrialization was somewhat similar. All migrants to the industrial town came either as individuals or in small family units. Whether they sought to return to Europe or prosper in Steelton, migrants moved within these smaller frameworks. But after settlement in the mill town, security was sought within the context of larger ethnic and class aggregations. Both the old stock and the newcomers began to create a formalized, institutional framework for achieving their respective and somewhat similar goals of status preservation and security. Class and ethnicity were not ends in themselves but instruments which assisted various groups in their attempts to preserve a sense of order in a rapidly changing and increasingly unpredictable industrial environment. The fundamental fact about social relationships in Steelton, shown by the growth of poor relief, ethnic organizations, and ultimately the labor union, was that they were increasingly formalized and institutionalized.

On a larger level the Steelton community evolved into a system not of competing individuals but of competing organizations. Prior to 1900, the paternalistic company and the business elite shared power. With the growth of a distinct laboring class in the two decades before World War II, a period of structural stagnation was reached. The formal reins of power were held exclusively by the early settlers and their children, yet a vast portion of the town was composed of separate ethnic and racial communities having little institutional or social contact with the old stock. After 1930, with the rise of the second generation and the prolonged depression, this community order was upset. The larger Steelton community began gradually to fall to the newcomers.[3]

Some recent historians have attempted to reinterpret the impact of industrialization upon social behavior. Certainly the rapid assimilation of skilled Irish steelworkers, the formalization of social relationships, and the increase in residential segregation indicate the transformative nature of the process.[4] But the new interpretation denies that industrialization was primarily a destructive, uprooting force, and stresses instead cultural continuity from preindustrial to industrial society. Newcomers are viewed as positive—not disillusioned—agents who actually influence the system that modernizes them. The religious and familial traditions of southern and eastern Europeans, for instance, survived the move to an urban, industrial setting.[5]

But Steelton's immigrants and migrants were neither tradition-bound peasants nor disillusioned settlers. The error many students of industrialization and modernization have made is to equate disintegration and change. Transition from preindustrial to industrial society involved a process of accommodation rather than of uprooting. After several decades in the industrial environment, the displaced peasants of southern Europe were neither wandering adrift, embracing traditional American middle-class values, nor living European life-styles. They were creating a new milieu which was a blend of their cultural heritage and emerging working-class status. At the confluence of ethnicity and class, this new milieu included a way of life which allowed them to adjust to the routine of the work week, the uncertainties of the economy, the paternalism of the higher classes, and the confinement of their socioeconomic status. The components were clearly evident. The traditional church and kinship ties remained strong. But new elements were added: residential cohesion, declining European regionalism, fraternal insurance, exaggerated displays of patriotism, declining transiency rates, heavy drinking, countless parades and celebrations, general disinterest in the civic, political, and educational affairs of the larger community. Ethnic consciousness itself was actually heightened, embellished, and tenaciously sustained.[6] Perhaps the relationship between community and industrialization in Steelton best illustrates the multifarious impact of industrialization. An axiom of the social sciences has held that community disintegration inevitably accompanied urban, industrial growth.[7] Michael Frisch, in a study of Springfield, Massachusetts, argued that the concept of community became more abstract and less personal with urban and industrial growth.[8] In Steelton, and similar areas such as South Chicago, industrialization actually accentuated the desire of the working class to form deep communal ties.[9] Ethnic communities were nurtured in working-class neighborhoods as a means of adjustment and were even encouraged by industrial managers. The Steelton community became more segmented by 1910 than it had been in 1870. But communal ties were not destroyed by modern change, they were redefined. The larger community became an exclusive concern of those who prospered in it. Resourceful immigrant workers, denied equal participation, prosperity, and opportunity, discovered a basis for their own particular communities in the web of ethnic, kinship, and religious ties they brought with them.

This framework of social relationships did not dissolve rapidly. Old-stock leaders were not about to relinquish their social dominance. Immigrants and their progeny had little upward mobility and, as an analysis of their marriage and residential patterns suggested, were unwilling to weaken their own ethnic ties. An important difference occurred, however, in the experience of the second generation. While their parents were highly transient and either returned to Europe or moved elsewhere when work was scarce, the immigrant children planned to stay in Steelton.[10] Indeed, since the immigrant had already weakened parental ties by his move to America, he may have been more willing to move in search of work than his American-born children. Ironically, the high transiency rate of the early immigrants may have permitted the continued supremacy of ethnic over class considerations. When economic troubles occurred, it was easier to move to another ethnic settlement in another coal or mill town than to fight for social or political change. But the second-generation Slavs were more likely to settle in Steelton than the old stock or blacks whose predecessors had been dislodged by the huge immigrant waves, and they were less spatially mobile than their parents. Having little desire to abandon the Steelton area and seeing that opportunities were limited elsewhere, this generation was particularly distressed during the Great Depression. Ethnic fraternal associations and institutions proved inadequate to meet "hard times." For the first time, socioeconomic considerations such as job security became more important than traditional ethnic parochialism. Thus John Verbos challenged the Nelley political machine and Paul Dragas joined Italian and black leaders in organizing the local CIO. Working-class matters, always below the surface, rose to a primary position. In another twenty years, the newcomers' children would inherit Steelton.

The evolution of social relationships in Steelton not only illustrates the complexity of the effects of industrialization upon community but casts doubt upon a long-accepted interpretation of ethnic groups in modern America. Impressions of ethnic settlement in industrial America have frequently included reference to the "replacement theory."[11] In short, a succession of ethnic groups was assumed. The newest group held the lowest socioeconomic position because of its recent arrival from preindustrial areas. A group would climb upward over several generations and be replaced at the bottom of the "social heap" by more recent arrivals. This view assumed that social mobility was an inevitable by-product of industrial society and that it operated independently of the surrounding culture. Ethnicity and race were implicitly discounted as variables in mobility, and rigidity in the industrial social structure was minimized.

The Steelton experience revealed, however, that the formula did not work for blacks and Slavs and that a community's particular social structure influenced the pattern of social mobility. As Stephan Thernstrom found in Boston, blacks in Steelton were driven down and out rather than upward by later immigrants.[12] The pattern for Slavs further revealed that the identification of replacement with social mobility was overly simplistic. Slavs encountered only limited mobility. They gained influence in community affairs, not because they rose to share power with the old stock, but because Steelton became almost completely working class and was no longer important to the Anglo-Saxons. Newcomers did not advance because the system did not encourage mobility, although the early Irish and Germans who arrived with skills and intentions of staying achieved some success. Generally it was only through intervention in the system that workers secured or retained some degree of community power. Prosperity continued to be elusive. But the creation of formal organizations enabled newcomers to maintain some security in spite of the workings of the American industrial system.

The embracement of Steelton by the children of newcomers and its abandonment by the old stock were symptomatic of a larger pattern of suburbanization. While suburban growth was facilitated by improved means of transportation, it was also motivated by a desire of the more affluent middle classes, largely old stock, to escape the working-class mill towns and urban neighborhoods which were simultaneously less desirable environments and more difficult to "control." Left behind were "white ethnics," clinging to communal ties which had been nurtured over several generations, and an increasing number of blacks. It is little wonder that modern America has witnessed the spectacle of working-class ethnics and blacks struggling over the issues of urban housing, inadequate tax bases, and busing. Abandoned by the affluent old stock, these two groups were left alone in the urban arena to face its awesome problems. The legacy of enforced isolation which characterized their historical experiences, however, left them unprepared to deal not only with these problems but with each other.

APPENDICES

NOTES

BIBLIOGRAPHICAL ESSAY

INDEX

Appendix 1
The Steelton Work Force

TABLE A: *Average Yearly Earnings in Steelton by Nativity, 1910*

	Number	Average Yearly Earnings
Native-born white, native father	46	$402
Native-born white, foreign father		
English	21	556
German	34	426
Irish	38	504
Foreign-born		
Bulgarian	46	179
Croatian	123	256
German	104	324
Irish	20	457
Serbian	112	175
Slovenian	48	381

Source: U.S. Immigration Commission, *Reports of the United States Immigration Commission: Immigrants in Industries, Part 2: Iron and Steel,* 2 vols., S. Doc. 633, 61st Cong., 2nd sess., serial 5669 (1911), I, 631.

TABLE B: *Ethnic Composition of the Steelton Plant, 1910*

	Number Surveyed	Blast Furnace	Bridge & Construction	Foundry	Frog & Switch	Labor	Merchant Mill	Machine Shop	Open Hearth	Rail Mill	Slab Mill
American	2,084	16	415	114	484	9	194	156	48	146	38
Bulgarian	61	3	—	—	—	15	2	—	17	4	7
Croatian	774	85	77	32	21	15	136	4	257	37	27
English	71	—	6	1	25	—	4	11	2	6	—
German	456	15	44	23	60	10	87	49	18	40	3
Irish	123	5	6	5	14	1	2	18	26	7	8
Italian	100	—	13	2	46	1	2	3	14	2	—
Magyar	284	13	109	—	2	55	43	—	3	10	2
Negro	198	15	14	2	4	3	31	2	27	20	20
Serbian	319	7	4	100	9	7	81	—	7	60	25

Source: Reports of the Immigration Commission: Iron and Steel, I, 651.
Note: Figures are given only for the principal departments in the plant.

TABLE C: *Persistence Rates for Steelton, 1880–1925*

	Unskilled	Semi-skilled	Skilled	Nonmanual	Total
1880 group	(N=398)	(N=93)	(N=68)	(N=47)	(N=606)
1888	44%	60%	50%	80%	50%
1896	75	75	85	80	77
1905	70	76	86	72	73
1905 group	(N=1219)	(N=1051)	(N=387)	(N=681)	(N=3338)
1915	41%	38%	27%	37%	39%
1925	50	54	60	53	50
1915 group	(N=1421)	(N=1196)	(N=330)	(N=639)	(N=3586)
1925	35%	33%	42%	36%	35%

Sources: For the 1880 group, "Tenth Census, 1880"; *Boyd's Directory for Harrisburg and Steelton,* 1888, 1896, 1905. For the 1905 and 1915 groups, Boyd's directories, 1905, 1915, 1925.

Note: Read "44 percent of 398 unskilled workers living in Steelton in 1880 continued to reside in the town in 1888; of those men persisting to 1888, 75 percent continued to persist until 1896."

TABLE D: *Occupational Distribution of Steelton's Work Force, 1920–1939*

	Native-born White (N=514)	Foreign-born Slavic, Italian (N=293)	Native-born of Native Parents Black (N=372)	Native-born of Native Parents Slavic, Italian (N=397)	German, English, Irish (N=78)	Avg. % (N=1,655)
Unskilled	12%	33%	67.0%	16%	20%	30%
Semiskilled	52	47	27.0	60	45	46
Skilled	11	9	00.5	4	15	6
Low non-manual	20	8	04.0	13	12	12
High non-manual	7	3	02.0	7	8	6

Source: Dauphin County Marriage License Dockets, 1920–1939 (Microfilm, Pennsylvania Historical and Museum Commission, Harrisburg). These records, after 1920, gave the age, place of birth, and occupation of the applicant as well as the place of birth and occupation of his father. The 1,655 men represent all male applicants from Steelton from 1920 to 1939.

Note: Due to rounding, totals in columns 1 and 3 exceed 100%.

TABLE E: *Occupational Mobility of Native-born Whites, Immigrants, and Blacks in Steelton, 1880–1905*

1880 Census Group	No.	1880–1888				1888–1896				1896–1905			
		No.	Moving Up	Moving Down	No Change	No.	Moving Up	Moving Down	No Change	No.	Moving Up	Moving Down	No Change
Unskilled	398	175	34%	—	66%	131	8%	6%	86%	92	3%	7%	90%
Semiskilled	93	54	11	15%	74	41	17	7	76	21	20	3	77
Skilled	68	34	0	21	79	29	7	10	83	25	0	0	100
Nonmanual	47	37	0	11	89	29	0	10	90	21	0	0	100
Total	606	300	—	—	—	230	—	—	—	169	—	—	—
Avg. %	—	—	22	6	72	—	9	6	85	—	5	4	91

Sources: The 1880 group includes all adult male workers in Steelton in the "Tenth Census, 1880." These individuals were divided into skill categories and traced in *Boyd's Directory of Harrisburg and Steelton,* 1888, 1896, 1905.

Note: Upward mobility for unskilled workers means, for instance, movement to a semiskilled job such as a crane operator; downward mobility means a skilled machinist dropping to a semiskilled rank of bricklayer. The distinction between low and high nonmanual was not made because such a definition would obscure the mobility from unskilled to semiskilled and from semiskilled to skilled manual ranks that was so frequent among those in Steelton who moved upward at all. For the classification system used in this study, see chapter 4, n. 28.

TABLE F: *Occupational Mobility of Native-born Whites, Immigrants, and Blacks in Steelton, 1905–1925*

| | 1905 | | 1915 | | | | 1925 | | | |
	No.	No.	Moving Up	Moving Down	No Change	No.	Moving Up	Moving Down	No Change
Unskilled	1,219	496	9%	—	91%	250	12%	—	88%
Semiskilled	1,051	390	7	5%	88	214	9	5%	86
Skilled	387	106	—	15	85	64	—	15	85
Nonmanual	681	254	—	9	91	136	—	1	99
Total	3,338	1,302	—	—	—	664	—	—	—
Avg. %	—	—	6	3	91	—	6	2	92

Note: For an explanation of the methods used to identify native whites, immigrants, and blacks and to trace their careers, see chapter 4, and tables 9, 10, and 12.

TABLE G: *Occupational Mobility of Native-born Whites, Immigrants, and Blacks in Steelton, 1915–1925*

| | 1915 | | 1925 | | |
	No.	No.	Moving Up	Moving Down	No Change
Unskilled	1,421	510	21%	—	79%
Semiskilled	1,196	397	8	5%	87
Skilled	333	141	—	15	85
Nonmanual	639	231	—	6	94
Total	3,586	1,288	—	—	—
Avg. %	—	—	10	4	86

Note: For an explanation of the methods used to identify native whites, immigrants, and blacks and to trace their careers, see chapter 4, and tables 9, 10, and 12.

TABLE H: *Mobility and Continuity Among Second-Generation Slavs and Italians, 1920–1945*

	Sons Born 1900–15 (N=180)
Mobility	
Sons of lower-class	
families moving up	22%
Sons of middle-class	
families moving down	43
Continuity rate by occupation of father	
Unskilled	35
Semiskilled	70
Skilled	43
Low nonmanual	80
High nonmanual	80
Avg. %	60

Sources: Second-generation Slavs and Italians were identified in the Dauphin County Marriage License Dockets. Of 340 Immigrant sons identified, 180 were found in subsequent years in *Boyd's Directory of Harrisburg and Steelton.*

Note: The lower-class category included all sons of unskilled and semiskilled fathers; the three remaining ranks were regarded as middle class. John Josef Barton, *Peasants and Strangers: Italians, Rumanians, and Slovaks in an American City, 1890–1950* (Cambridge, Mass.: Harvard University Press, 1975), and Stephan Thernstrom, "Immigrants and WASPS: Ethnic Differences in Occupational Mobility in Boston, 1890–1940," in *Nineteenth Century Cities,* ed. Stephan Thernstrom and Richard Sennett (New Haven: Yale University Press, 1969), p. 140, measured occupational mobility as movement between manual and nonmanual occupations. Thernstrom calls this measure a "crude one." However, such a methodology would be misleading in Steelton. The mobility experienced by Steelton's workers was much more modest and within manual or nonmanual ranks. Most of Steelton's upwardly mobile laborers moved to semiskilled or skilled positions. For a further discussion of classification schemes, see Clyde Griffen, "Occupational Mobility in Nineteenth-Century America: Problems and Possibilities," *Journal of Social History* 5 (1972), 310–30.

Appendix 2
Social Mobility in Steelton
and Other Cities

The historical study of social mobility in American cities is a very recent development. The extent to which upward mobility was achieved by the "new immigration" has, until now, scarcely been measured at all. The following tables make some attempt to compare the results of the Steelton study with studies done in other urban areas.

The limited amount of upward mobility experienced by immigrants and other workers in Steelton was not particularly exceptional, as table I indicates. Fifteen percent of the native-born manual workers in Boston were propelled into white-collar jobs during the 1880s. This was three times the rate experienced by native-born workers in Steelton in the same decade.

Among immigrant workers, the ratios for Steelton, Boston, and Cleveland were quite similar. In the 1880s, 7 percent of Boston's foreign-born workmen moved from manual to white-collar callings. In Cleveland, between 1910 and 1920, some 9 percent of the Slavs and Italians moved upward. About 5 percent of Steelton's Italians and Slavs climbed into nonmanual positions in the decade after 1905 and 5 percent in the ten-year period after 1915.

The sons of immigrant workers tended to surpass their fathers' status at a slightly lower rate in the small mill town, as table J suggests, than they did in the large industrial city. Among second-generation Slavs and Italians born in Cleveland between 1901 and 1910, one-fourth climbed above the occupational status of their fathers. Among those born between 1911 and 1920, 30 percent moved upward. In Steelton, however, among second-generation Slavs and Italians born between 1900 and 1915, only 22 percent surpassed their fathers.

Finally, table K reveals clearly not only the extent to which workers tended to remain in the same occupational strata throughout their lifetimes, but also the extent to which blacks were excluded from skilled positions. In Poughkeepsie, 92 percent of the blacks in low manual jobs remained in them throughout their careers. Of blacks who remained in Steelton, 86 percent stayed in the same occupational strata during the 1880s. Among the Irish immigrants in Poughkeepsie, 82 percent of the low manual workers remained in the same callings throughout their careers. Among Irish and English workers in Steelton, 70 percent continued in low manual jobs. In Steelton and Poughkeepsie blacks were seldom able to enter high manual or skilled trades.

TABLE 1: *Occupational Mobility and Continuity in Boston, Cleveland, and Steelton*

	Native Born			Foreign Born		
	Boston 1880–90 (N=210)	Steelton 1880–88 (N=206)	Boston 1880–90 (N=211)	Cleveland 1910–20 (N=300)	Steelton 1905–15 (N=127)	Steelton 1915–25 (N=261)
Interclass mobility						
Manual workers moving up	15%	5%	7%	9%	5%	5%
White-collar workers moving down	8	6	12	22	3	10
Continuity by rank						
Unskilled	57	54	77	70	94	74
Semiskilled	68	76	68	72	76	88
Skilled	81	76	91	73	100	100
Low nonmanual	72	80	75	55	81	77
High nonmanual	89	93	90	79	96	90
Avg. %	75	70	81	70	90	79

Sources: For the Cleveland figures, Barton, *Peasants and Strangers*, p. 112. For the Boston figures, Thernstrom, "Immigrants and WASPs," p. 138.
Note: The foreign born in Cleveland were Slovaks, Rumanians, and Italians. In Steelton they were Croatians, Serbs, Bulgarians, Slovenians, and Italians.

TABLE J: *Mobility and Continuity Among Second-Generation Slavs and Italians in Cleveland and Steelton, 1920–1950*

	Cleveland		Steelton
	Born 1901–10 (N=81)	Born 1911–20 (N=92)	Born 1900–15 (N=180)
Workers of lower-class origin moving up	25%	30%	22%
Workers of middle-class origin moving down	70	50	43
Continuity rate by rank of father's last job			
Unskilled	26	21	35
Semiskilled	0	20	70
Skilled	40	33	43
Low nonmanual	17	10	80
High nonmanual	0	75	80
Avg. %	26	25	60

Source: For Cleveland, Barton, *Peasants and Strangers,* p. 107.

Note: See note to table H for class categories. Barton used a manual category instead of "lower class," including skilled as well as unskilled and semiskilled workers. For him, mobility constituted a move between manual and nonmanual ranks. If this criterion were used in Steelton, only 7 percent of workers of manual origins would move up, and 7 percent of those of nonmanual origins would move down. When upward mobility rates include movement from un- skilled and semiskilled ranks to skilled and nonmanual, the results more nearly approximate the patterns of a large urban area which offered a great diversity of positions. Only 5 percent of Steelton's work force was low nonmanual (e.g., clerks) in 1880. On the other hand, 11 percent of the workers in Boston in 1880 were low nonmanual, and 8 percent in Poughkeepsie. See Clyde Griffen, "Making it in America: Social Mobility in Mid-Nineteenth Century Poughkeep- sie," *New York History* 51 (1970), 484.

TABLE K: *Mobility of Low Manual Workers, Poughkeepsie and Steelton*

	Steelton 1880–88		Poughkeepsie 1850–80	
	Blacks (N=38)	Irish-English (N=44)	Blacks (N=64)	Irish (N=208)
Remain low manual	86%	70%	92%	82%
Climb to high manual	3	23	2	10
Climb to nonmanual	8	7	6	8

Source: For Poughkeepsie, Griffen, "Making it in America," p. 494.

Notes

INTRODUCTION

1. Dean R. Esslinger, *Immigrants and the City: Ethnicity and Mobility in a Nineteenth-Century Midwestern Community* (Port Washington, N.Y.: Kennikat, 1975); Stephan Thernstrom, *Poverty and Progress: Social Mobility in a Nineteenth-Century City* (Cambridge, Mass.: Harvard University Press, 1964); Josef John Barton, *Peasants and Strangers: Italians, Rumanians, and Slovaks in an American City, 1890–1950* (Cambridge, Mass.: Harvard University Press, 1975); Thomas Kessner, *The Golden Door: Italian and Jewish Immigrant Mobility in New York City, 1880–1915* (New York: Oxford University Press, 1977); Humbert S. Nelli, *Italians in Chicago, 1880–1930: A Study in Ethnic Mobility* (New York: Oxford University Press, 1970).

2. See David Brody, *Steelworkers in America* (Cambridge, Mass.: Harvard University Press, 1960); Herbert Gutman, "The Worker's Search for Power: Labor in the Gilded Age," in *The Gilded Age*, ed. H. Wayne Morgan (Syracuse, N.Y.: Syracuse University Press, 1963), pp. 38–68. Studies of smaller industrial towns have included Donald B. Cole, *Immigrant City: Lawrence, Massachusetts, 1845–1921* (Chapel Hill; University of North Carolina Press, 1963); Stanley Buder, *Pullman, an Experiment in Industrial Order and Community Planning, 1880–1930* (New York: Oxford University Press, 1967); Thernstrom, *Poverty and Progress.*

3. Samuel P. Hays, "Social Structure is the New Urban History," manuscript in the author's possession; Sam Bass Warner, "If All the World Were Philadelphia: A Scaffolding of Urban History, 1774–1930," *American Historical Review* 74 (1968), 26.

4. See Barton, *Peasants and Strangers.* Stephan Thernstrom, "Immigrants and WASPS: Ethnic Differences in Occupational Mobility in Boston, 1890–1940," in *Nineteenth Century Cities*, ed. Stephan Thernstrom and Richard Sennett (New Haven: Yale University Press, 1969), pp. 125–64, has no precise information on the identity of Boston's immigrants after 1890 except that they were foreign born. See also Samuel P. Hays, "Historical Method and Technique," *Journal of Interdisciplinary History* 4 (1974), 475–82.

5. See Niles Carpenter, *Nationality, Color, and Economic Opportunity in the City of Buffalo* (Buffalo, 1927), pp. 190–91; Paul Worthman, "Working-Class Mobility

in Birmingham, Alabama, 1880–1914," in *Anonymous Americans,* ed. Tamara K. Hareven (Englewood Cliffs, N.J.: Prentice-Hall, 1971), p. 192.

6. Richard N. Juliani, "The Social Organization of Immigration: The Italians in Philadelphia" (Ph.D. diss., University of Pennsylvania, 1971), pp. 228–29; Victor Greene, "For God and Country: The Origins of Slavic Catholic Self-Consciousness," *Church History* 35 (1966), 446; Timothy L. Smith, "Religious Denominations as Ethnic Communities: A Regional Case Study," ibid., 226; Nelli, *The Italians in Chicago,* pp. 156–70; Caroline F. Ware, ed., *The Cultural Approach to History* (Port Washington, N.Y.: Kennikat, 1940), pp. 63–82.

7. *Social Mobility in Industrial Society* (Berkeley and Los Angeles: University of California Press, 1959), p. 105. Certain sociologists have suggested that blocked mobility can "reinforce" the norms of ethnic communities. For instance, the ties of Irish Catholics to the Democratic party were a direct result of their concentration in ghettos where machine politics flourished. See Robert Dahl, *Who Governs* (New Haven: Yale University Press 1961) and Nathan Glazer and Daniel Moynihan, *Beyond the Melting Pot* (Cambridge, Mass.: M.I.T. Press, 1963). This is not to say, however, that once upward mobility occurred, ethnicity rapidly diminished. David Knoke found that upwardly mobile white Protestants continued to vote Republican, while upwardly mobile Catholics still voted Democratic. He concluded that ethnic communities "socialize" their members into a political tradition which persists when the ethnics achieve higher occupations. See "Community and Consistency: The Ethnic Factor in Status Inconsistency," *Social Forces* 51 (1972), 23–33.

8. Victor Greene, *The Slavic Community on Strike* (Notre Dame, Ind., 1968); Victor Greene, *For God and Country: The Rise of Polish and Lithuanian Ethnic Consciousness in America, 1860–1910* (Madison, Wis.: State Historical Society of Wisconsin, 1975); Barton, *Peasants and Strangers;* Edward R. Kantowicz, *Polish-American Politics in Chicago, 1888–1940* (Chicago: University of Chicago Press, 1975). No student of Slavic Americans should overlook the brilliant discussion of ethnic accommodation in South Chicago in William Kornblum, *Blue Collar Community* (Chicago: University of Chicago Press, 1974).

9. Walter Warzeski, *Byzantine Rusins in Carpatho Ruthenia and America* (Pittsburgh: Byzantine Seminary Press, 1972); Greene, *The Slavic Community on Strike.*

CHAPTER 1: EARLY STEELTON

1. Studies of smaller industrial cities include Donald B. Cole, *Immigrant City: Lawrence, Massachusetts, 1845–1921* (Chapel Hill: University of North Carolina Press, 1963); Stanley Buder, *Pullman, An Experiment in Industrial Order and Community Planning, 1880–1930* (New York: Oxford University Press, 1967). Stephan Thernstrom, *Poverty and Progress: Social Mobility in a Nineteenth-Century City* (Cambridge, Mass.: Harvard University Press, 1964), was concerned primarily with social mobility in Newburyport, Massachusetts. See also Michael

Weber, *Patterns of Progress: Social Mobility in a Pennsylvania Oil Town, 1897–1910* (University Park, Pa.: Penn State University Press, 1976); Gordon Kirk, "The Promise of American Life: Social Mobility in a Nineteenth-Century Immigrant Community, Holland, Michigan, 1847–1894," (Ph.D., diss., Michigan State University, 1970); Margaret Byington, *Homestead: The Households of a Mill Town* (New York: Russell Sage Foundation, 1910); and Horace B. Davis, *Labor and Steel* (New York: International Publishers, 1933), pp. 31–72.

2. *Steelton Plant* (n.p.: Bethlehem Steel Co., 1953); Peter Temin, *Iron and Steel in Nineteenth-Century America* (Cambridge, Mass.: Harvard University Press, 1964), p. 170; A. Howry Espenshade, *Pennsylvania Place Names* (State College, Pa.: Pennsylvania State College, 1925), pp. 203–04. See also Pennsylvania Steel Company, *Descriptive Catalogue, 1883* (n.p., n.d.) in the Pennsylvania Steel Company Collection, Eleutherian Mills Historical Library, Greenville, Del.

3. Felton, as president of the Philadelphia, Wilmington, and Baltimore Railroad in 1861, was credited with enabling Abraham Lincoln to pass unrecognized through Baltimore on his way to his inauguration. The episode is documented in the Samuel M. Felton Papers, Historical Society of Pennsylvania, Philadelphia. See also "A History of the Steelton Plant, Bethlehem Steel Corporation, Steelton, Pennsylvania," unpublished manuscript at the Steelton Municipal Building and also in the author's possession; Burton J. Hendrick, *The Life of Andrew Carnegie*, 2 vols. (Garden City, N.Y.: Doubleday, Doran, 1932), I, 200; S. K. Stevens, *Pennsylvania, Titan of Industry*, 3 vols. (New York: Lewis, 1948), II, 104–05; *Harrisburg Telegraph*, 19 Sept. 1891, pp. 9–12. *The Steelton Reporter*, 26 Jan. 1889, provides further biographical data on Felton.

4. *Souvenir Booklet, Hygienic Hose Company* (Steelton, 1910), pp. 1–8, 20 (this book was kindly loaned by Mr. Harold Kearns); U.S. Immigration Commission, *Reports of the United States Immigration Commission: Immigrants in Industries, Part 2: Iron and Steel*, 2 vols., S. Doc. 633, 61st Cong., 2nd sess., serial 5669 (1911), I, 581 (herafter cited as *Reports of the Immigration Commission, Iron and Steel*); W. H. Kent, "History of the 100 Years of the Harrisburg and Dauphin County Y.M.C.A.," *Dauphin County Historical Review* 4 (1955), 4–16; William H. Egle, *History of the Counties of Dauphin and Lebanon* (Philadelphia, 1883), pp. 400–04; Frederic A. Godcharles, *Chronicles of Central Pennsylvania*, 4 vols. (New York: Lewis, 1944), III, 137.

5. "A History of the Steelton Plant"; James M. Swank, "The Iron and Steel Industries of Pennsylvania," in Commonwealth of Pennsylvania, *Annual Report of the Secretary of Internal Affairs, Part III: Industrial Statistics*, 1881–82 (Harrisburg, 1883), p. 36; Stewart H. Holbrook, *Iron Brew: A Century of American Ore and Steel* (New York: Macmillan, 1939), pp. 324–25.

6. *Souvenir Booklet, Hygienic Hose Company.*

7. *Reports of the Immigration Commission, Iron and Steel*, I, 591; interview with Margaret Dailey, 27 Aug. 1971 (see the Bibliographical Essay for description and location of all oral interviews cited in the text); *Souvenir Booklet, Hygienic Hose Company*, p. 26.

8. This portrait of Steelton was pieced together from the tenth census, 1880. (For complete citations of census manuscripts and published volumes, see the Bibliographical Essay.)

9. *Eleventh Census, 1890*, p. 533. The proportion of southern Europeans is an estimate arrived at by the author after studying names listed in *Boyd's Directory of Harrisburg and Steelton*, 1890 (Harrisburg, 1891).

10. *Eleventh Census, 1890*, p. 533.

11. Ibid. For a more complete description of the occupational stratification of Steelton see chapter 4.

12. *St. John the Evangelist Church, Dedication Booklet* (Steelton, 13 Aug. 1953). *Reporter*, 12 Jan. 1889, p. 4; ibid., 5 July 1901, p. 4; ibid., 22 Aug. 1902, p. 4.

13. *Golden Jubilee of St. James Church* (Steelton, 1929), pp. 5–6; *Souvenir Booklet of St. James Church* (Steelton, 1900), p. 3; *Reporter*, 6 Sept. 1890, p. 4; *Item*, 29 Sept. 1882, p. 5.

14. Quincy Bent, "Looking Backward," May 1949, a booklet in Charles Schwab Memorial Library, Bethlehem Steel Company, Bethlehem. Bent also recalled rivalries between the Irish and German shifts at the mill. *Reporter*, 20 Aug. 1892, p. 4.

15. *Reporter*, 1 Oct. 1892, p. 4; ibid., 23 July 1893, p. 4; ibid., 20 Nov. 1897, p. 1; ibid., 24 Feb. 1899; ibid., 22 Sept. 1922, p. 1; *Souvenir Booklet of St. James Church*, p. 3. *Reports of the Immigration Commission, Iron and Steel*, I, 730, stated that in 1910 the German and "British Races" were no longer thought of as foreigners in Steelton.

16. *Reports of the Immigration Commission, Iron and Steel*, I, 582; *Boyd's Directory of Harrisburg and Steelton*, 1887, 1888, 1889.

17. The biographical details in this and the following five paragraphs, unless otherwise noted, are from W. H. Egle *et al.*, *Commemorative Biographical Encyclopedia of Dauphin County Containing Sketches of Prominent and Representative Citizens and Many of the Early Scotch-Irish Settlers* (Chambersburg, Pa., 1896), pp. 1, 230, 967–77, 984–85, 991–95, 1030.

18. See *Reporter*, 6 June 1885, p. 4.

19. 16 Sept. 1881, p. 1.

20. *Reporter*, 18 Nov. 1893, p. 4.

21. 15 Jan. 1887, p. 4. See also *Reporter*, 29 May 1886, p. 4; David Brody, *Steelworkers in America* (Cambridge, Mass.: Harvard University Press, 1960), pp. 118–19.

22. *Reporter*, 18 July 1885, p. 4.

23. 25 July 1885, p. 4.

24. 7 Nov. 1885, p. 4.

25. 20 Jan. 1894, p. 5.

26. *Reporter*, 1 Nov. 1890, p. 4; ibid., 17 Jan. 1891, p. 4; ibid., 28 March. 1891, p. 4; ibid., 24 Jan. 1891, p. 4.

27. *Item*, 3 June 1881, p. 4; ibid., 7 Oct. 1881, p. 5; Brody, *Steelworkers in America*, p. 116. Steel company officials continued to serve on the school board

through 1920. Quincy Bent, in 1918, was simultaneously president of the school board and general manager of the plant. Luther Bent headed the group which formed the Steelton National Bank in 1886. See *Reporter*, 13 Nov. 1886, p. 4.

28. 7 Oct. 1881, p. 5.
29. *Reporter*, 17 July 1886, p. 1.
30. *Reporter*, 30 May 1885, p. 4.
31. *Reporter*, 11 July 1885, p. 4; ibid., 19 July 1884, p. 4.
32. *Reporter*, 11 July 1885, p. 4; ibid., 13 June 1885, p. 4.
33. *Harrisburg Daily Patriot*, 17 Sept. 1885, p. 1.
34. *Reporter*, 12 Sept. 1885, p. 4; ibid., 19 Sept. 1885, p. 4.
35. Warren Eyster, *No Country for Old Men* (New York: Random House, 1955), p. 412. Eyster was a native of Steelton.
36. A list of all borough officers and school board members can be found in the annual editions of *Boyd's Directory of Harrisburg and Steelton*, 1880–90.
37. *Reports of the Immigration Commission, Iron and Steel*, I, 589.
38. Ibid., p. 707. See also Commonwealth of Pennsylvania, *Annual Report of the Secretary of Internal Affairs, 1907, Part III: Industrial Statistics* (Harrisburg, 1908), XXXV, 73.
39. *Reports of the Immigration Commission, Iron and Steel*, I, 707.
40. The thirteenth census gave the country of origin of Steelton's foreign-born population in 1910: the immigrants included 2,265 from Austria (mostly southern Slavs); 552, Hungary; 374, Turkey; 317, Italy; 174, Russia; 102, Ireland; and 28, Wales. *Thirteenth Census, 1910*, p. 679. The report in the 1920 census was more accurate because officials were more aware of the precise points of origin of immigrants. It listed Steelton's foreign born as including 1,294 from Yugoslavia; 421, Hungary; 368, Italy; 161, Greece (probably Bulgarians); 134, Russia (mostly Jews); and 100, Germany. *Fourteenth Census, 1920*, pp. 872, 883–86.
41. 14 Mar. 1896, p. 4. See also *Fiftieth Anniversary of West Side School* (Steelton, 1940).
42. *Reporter*, 1 Oct. 1898, p. 4.
43. *Reporter*, 29 May 1903, p. 4; ibid., 29 Dec. 1905, p. 1.
44. For a slightly different pattern see Howard Chudacoff, "A New Look at Ethnic Neighborhoods: Residential Dispersion and the Concept of Visibility in a Medium-Sized City," *Journal of American History* 60 (1973), 76–93.
45. *Item*, 10 Mar. 1882, p. 20.
46. Commonwealth of Pennsylvania, *Annual Report of the Secretary of Internal Affairs, 1886, Part III: Industrial Statistics* (Harrisburg, 1887), p. 25.
47. *Reporter*, 9 Jan. 1886, p. 4. See also ibid., 11 May 1889, p. 4.
48. *Reporter*, 7 Mar. 1902, pp. 1–4.
49. Commonwealth of Pennsylvania, *Annual Report 1886, Part III*, pp. 25–26.
50. *Reporter*, 22 Aug. 1886, p. 4; ibid., 10 Sept. 1887, p. 4; interviews with Rev. Jerome Kucan, 30 June 1971, and Steve Suknaic, 6 Oct. 1971. See also chapter 2.

51. *Reports of the Immigration Commission, Iron and Steel,* I, 569–660.

52. The *Library Journal* 80 (1955), 1140, described Eyster's work as one which dealt with the rise of the American laboring class, the demise of the craftsmen, and the social effects of industrialization in a small town.

CHAPTER 2: STRATEGIES

1. *Reports of the Immigration Commission, Iron and Steel,* I, 582; U.S. Congress, Senate, *Report on Conditions of Employment in the Iron and Steel Industry in the United States,* 4 vols., S. Doc. 110, 62nd Cong., 1st sess., serial 6098 (1913), II, 11–64.

2. George J. Prpic, *The Croatian Immigrants in America* (New York: Philosophical Library, 1971), p. 18; Gerald G. Govorchin, *Americans from Yugoslavia* (Gainesville, Fla.: Florida State University Press, 1961), p. 10. Yugoslavia is a multinational state consisting of the republics of Slovenia, Croatia, Serbia, Macedonia, Montenegro, and Bosnia-Herzegovina. In addition it contains the autonomous regions of Voyvodina, where most of Steelton's Serbs and Croats came from, and Kosmet.

3. Prpic, *Croatian Immigrants,* pp. 91–93; interview with Steve Suknaic, 6 Oct. 1971; Emily G. Balch, *Our Slavic Fellow Citizens* (New York: Charities Publication Committee, 1910), pp. 402 ff.; Govorchin, *Americans from Yugoslavia,* p. 14; Joseph Roucek, "The Yugoslav Immigrants in America," *American Journal of Sociology* 40 (1935), pp. 602–04; U.S. Immigration Commission, *Abstracts of Reports of the Immigration Commission,* 2 vols. (Washington, 1911), I, 226. An interesting account of Croatian immigration can be found in Louis Adamic, *From Many Lands* (New York: Harper, 1949), pp. 55–67. See also Stjepan Gazi, *Croatian Immigration to Allegheny County, 1882–1914* (Pittsburgh: Croatian Fraternal Union, 1956), pp. 2–4; and *Zaciatky Ceskej Slovenskej Emigracie Do U.S.A.* (Bratislava, 1971).

4. *750 Years of the Serbian Church, 1219–1969* (Cleveland, 1969), p. 127; Chedomir Pavich, "Serbs and Serbian Organizations," *American Srobran,* 19 June 1918, p. 1.

5. *Reporter,* 24 Apr. 1897, p. 1; ibid., 5 May 1899, p. 1; ibid., 24 Aug. 1906, p. 1.

6. *Fiftieth Anniversary, Holy Annunciation Macedonian-Bulgarian Church* (Steelton, 1959), pp. 1–8; David Nakoff, *A History of the Macedonian-Bulgarian Church of Steelton Pennsylvania,* (Steelton, 1939), pp. 2–3.

7. *Reporter,* 4 May 1890, p. 4; *Reports of the Immigration Commission, Iron and Steel,* I, 602; *Reporter,* 4 May 1889, p. 4.

8. *Press,* 29 Aug. 1903, p. 1; *Telegraph,* 7 Apr. 1917, p. 11; ibid., 12 July 1918, p. 12; ibid., 9 May 1918, p. 4; *Reports of the Immigration Commission, Iron and Steel,* I, 602; *Reporter,* 4 May 1889, p. 4; ibid., 7 July 1894, p. 4; ibid., 21 July 1894, p. 4.

9. 5 July 1912, p. 4. See also "Immigrant Labor" in Commonwealth of

Pennsylvania, *Annual Report of the Secretary of Internal Affairs, 1883, Part III: Industrial Statistics* (Harrisburg, 1884), XII, 63–67. Labor shortages became so acute during World War I that the Steelton plant used female manual laborers. See also Pennsylvania Department of Welfare, *Negro Survey of Pennsylvania* (Harrisburg, 1927), p. 35.

10. Interview with Walter B. Lang, 7 Sept. 1973 (Lang was a department superintendent); David Brody, *Labor in Crisis: The Steel Strike of 1919* (Philadelphia: Lippincott, 1965)), p. 15; Allan Nevins, *Abram S. Hewitt* (New York: Harper, 1935), p. 422. Nevins wrote that Andrew Carnegie, David Morell of the Cambria plant in Johnstown, Joseph Warton of the Bethlehem Company, and Felton paid their workingmen no more than unprofitable industries and thus were making enormous fortunes. See also Burton J. Hendrick, *The Life of Andrew Carnegie*, 2 vols. (Garden City, N.Y.: Doubleday, Doran, 1932), I, 213.

11. *Patriot*, 15 Mar. 1902, p. 1.

12. *Reports of the Immigration Commission, Iron and Steel*, I, 602.

13. *Reporter*, 19 Feb. 1898, p. 1; ibid., 26 Feb. 1898, p. 1.

14. Interview with Thomas Benkovic, 11 July 1971.

15. "Twelfth Census, 1900."

16. *Reports of the Immigration Commission, Iron and Steel*, I, 603.

17. Ibid.

18. Ibid., 603–04.

19. Ibid., 892; interviews with John Badovinac, president of the Croatian Fraternal Union of America, 4 Jan. 1972; and Rev. Jerome Kucan, 30 June 1971. Many of the South Italians came from Cataleone Posentina in Calabria. See *Reports of the Immigration Commission, Iron and Steel*, I, 593.

20. *Reporter*, 18 May 1886, p. 1; ibid., 18 May 1889, p. 4; ibid., 8 Nov. 1907, p. 1; ibid., 1 May 1889, p. 4; *Reports of the Immigration Commission, Iron and Steel*, I, 591.

21. Passenger Lists of Vessels Arriving at Philadelphia, 1883–1945, Microfilm Series T-840, vol. 128, reel 79, Federal Archives and Records Center, Philadelphia.

22. *Zacetek Sloveneske Naselbine v Steeltonu, Pennsylvania* (Steelton, 1939), p. 1; *Pozdrav in Castitke, 1909–1945* (Steelton: St. Peter's Church, 1945), p. 18; interviews with Anna Lopert, 17 Aug. 1971; and with Martin Tezak, John Tezak, and Mary Krasovic, 25 Mar. 1976.

23. Vera St. Erlich, *Family in Transition: A Study of 300 Yugoslav Villages* (Princeton, N.J.: Princeton University Press, 1966), p. 32.

24. Interviews with Louis and Catherine Lescanec, 17 June 1976.

25. Josip Lakatos, *Narodna Statistika* (Zagreb: Tiskom Hrvatskog Stamparskog Zavada, 1914), pp. 62–64; Johan Chelmar, "The Austrian Emigration, 1900–1914," *Perspectives in American History* 7 (1973), 291–92, 341.

26. Frances Kraljic, "Croatian Migration To and From the United States Between 1900 and 1914" (Ph.D. diss., New York University, 1975), pp. 1–7. Branko M. Colakovic, *Yugoslav Migrations to America* (San Francisco: R and E

Associates, 1973), p. 58, found 70 percent of a sample of seventy-seven Yugoslavs immigrating before 1910 intending to return.

27. The information on incoming Croats was pieced together from the Passenger Lists of Vessels Arriving at Philadelphia.

28. Interviews with Charles Bojanic, 13 Aug. 1971; Thomas Benkovic, 11 July 1971; and Meter Dragovich, 27 Oct. 1971. Ema Umek, "Prispevki K Zgodovini I Zseljevanja Iz Kranjske v Ameriko v Le̒tih, 1910–1913" [Contributions to the History of Emigration from Carniola to America, 1910–1913], *Slovenski Izseljenske Koledar* 14 (1967), 199–207.

29. *Spomen Knijizica Četrdeset Godišnjice, 1898–1938, Hrvatske Rimokatolicke Župe Uznesenja Bl. Dj. Marije* (Steelton, 1938), pp. 1–4. This account of Steelton's Croatians was written by early Croatian settlers still living in 1938. I am indebted to Harold Kearns and Rev. Jerome Kucan for assistance in locating and translating this document. See also interview with Thomas Benkovic, 11 July 1971.

30. Michael Anderson, *Family Structure in Nineteenth-Century Lancashire* (London: Cambridge University Press, 1971), p. 154.

31. Josef John Barton, *Peasants and Strangers: Italians, Rumanians, and Slovaks in an American City, 1890–1950* (Cambridge, Mass.: Harvard University Press, pp. 55–56.

32. The twelfth census, 1900, revealed that the average age of 108 Slavic immigrants was thirty-four and that they had been here an average of 1.2 years. Thus the mean age at the time of arrival was 32.6. Fifty-eight percent of this group was married and the men had been married an average of nine years.

CHAPTER 3: STEELWORKERS

1. *Reporter*, 12 May 1888, p. 4; ibid., 20 Apr. 1895, p. 4; ibid., 14 Apr. 1899, p. 4; ibid., 13 May 1905, p. 1; *Annual Report of the Pennsylvania Steel Company, 1902–13* (Bethlehem Steel Company Library, Bethlehem).

2. *Reports of the Immigration Commission, Iron and Steel,* I, 606; *Harrisburg Patriot,* 26 Sept. 1913, p. 1; Arundel Cotter, *The Story of Bethlehem Steel* (New York: Moody, 1916), pp. 46–47.

3. Interview with Joseph DiSanto, 19 Apr. 1974; Minutes of United Steelworkers of America, Local 1688, Harrisburg. Mr. DiSanto kindly allowed me to see the historical records he has kept pertaining to the Steelton plant.

4. *Reports of the Immigration Commission, Iron and Steel,* I, 650–52. The ethnic character of various departments was revealed repeatedly in interviews with Joseph DiSanto, 19 Apr. 1974; Dave Moore, 25 Mar. 1974; Meter Dragovich, 24 Mar. 1974; and John Verbos, 24 Mar. 1974.

5. *Pennsylvania Labor News,* Local 1688 Edition, 15 Apr. 1960, p. 1; interviews with Joseph DiSanto, 19 Apr. 1974; and Dave Moore, 25 Mar. 1974.

6. See John A. Fitch, *The Steel Workers* (New York: Charities Publication

Committee, 1910), pp. 29–30, for a description of the steelworker's working conditions. See also *Zajedničar*, 29 Aug. 1934, p. 7; Harrisburg Board of Trade, *Industry and Commercial Resources of the City of Harrisburg* (Harrisburg, 1889), p. 26.

7. *Reports of the Immigration Commission, Iron and Steel*, I, 650–51.

8. Ibid., 633.

9. Ibid., 654.

10. Ibid., 611.

11. See Appendix 1, table A.

12. *Report on Conditions of Employment in the Iron and Steel Industry*, IV, 161–64; *Reporter*, 9 May 1902, p. 4; ibid., 30 Mar. 1906, p. 1; *Reports of the Immigration Commission, Iron and Steel*, I, 643–44.

13. *Reports of the Immigration Commission, Iron and Steel*, I, 656, 583.

14. Copy in Samuel W. Pennypacker Papers, R. G. 171, Box 55, Pennsylvania Historical and Museum Commission, Harrisburg (hereafter cited as Pennypacker Papers). See also *Reporter*, 20 Oct. 1905, p. 1.

15. Brody, *Steelworkers in America*, pp. 119–20; *Harrisburg Patriot*, 11 Sept. 1913, p. 5; *Reports of the Immigration Commission, Iron and Steel*, I, 596–61.

16. *Reporter*, 17 July 1886, p. 1.

17. 9 June 1882, p. 2.

18. *Reporter*, 14 Feb. 1891, p. 4; ibid., 9 May 1891, p. 4; ibid., 11 July 1891, p. 4. See Brody, *Steelworkers in America*, pp. 51, 80, 96, on the movement of the Amalgamated eastward into Lebanon and Norristown after 1890.

19. 18 July 1891, p. 4; *Iron Age* 48 (23 July 1891), 143.

20. *Reporter*, 18 July 1891, p. 4; *Iron Moulders Monthly Journal*, 10 July 1891, p. 1.

21. *Telegraph*, 22 July 1891, p. 1; ibid., 23 July 1891, p. 1; ibid., 28 July 1891, p. 1; *Reporter*, 18 July 1891, p. 4; 25 July 1891, p. 4; 1 Aug. 1891, p. 4; *Reports of the Immigration Commission, Iron and Steel*, I, 645; *Iron Moulders Monthly Journal*, 10 Aug. 1891, p. 19.

22. *Reporter*, 18 July 1891, p. 4; *Telegraph*, 30 July 1891, p. 1; *Iron Age* 48 (6 Aug. 1891), 217.

23. *Iron Age* 48 (30 July 1891), 190.

24. *Telegraph*, 30 July 1891, p. 1; ibid., 1 Aug. 1891, p. 1; ibid., 10 Aug. 1891, p. 1.

25. *Reporter*, 16 Jan. 1892, p. 4; ibid., 13 Oct. 1888, p. 1; ibid., 18 Dec. 1886, p. 4; ibid., 1 Aug. 1891, p. 4.

26. *Telegraph*, 23 July 1891, p. 1. For additional criticism of the Amalgamated treatment of Negroes see Richard P. Wright, *The Negro in Pennsylvania* (New York: Arno Press, 1969), p. 98.

27. *Reporter*, 1 Aug. 1891, p. 4; ibid., 8 Aug. 1891, p. 4; ibid., 14 Feb. 1891, p. 4. Brody, in *Steelworkers in America*, pp. 112–13, found similar sympathy for the company's view in other steel towns. Herbert Gutman, "The Worker's Search for Power: Labor in the Gilded Age," in *The Gilded Age*, ed. H. Wayne Morgan

(Syracuse, N.Y.: Syracuse University Press, 1963), pp. 36–68, has argued that small communities tended to support strike movements because of preindustrial traits holding the workingman in high regard. Steelton was created as an industrial town and had no real preindustrial past, although many of its workers were from rural backgrounds.

28. *Reports of the Immigration Commission, Iron and Steel,* I, 645.

29. *Reporter,* 7 July 1894, p. 4; *Telegraph,* 9 July 1894, pp. 1, 5.

30. *Reporter,* 1 July 1904, p. 4; *Patriot,* 30 June 1904, p. 3.

31. *Patriot,* 7 Mar. 1906, p. 1; *Reporter,* 9 Mar. 1906, p. 4; *Lebanon Daily News,* 7 Mar. 1906, p. 1; ibid., 8 Mar. 1906, p. 1.

32. 8 Mar. 1906, p. 1; 9 Mar. 1906, p. 1.

33. *Patriot,* 18 July 1912, p. 7; ibid., 19 July 1912, p. 2; ibid., 23 July 1912, p. 7; *Telegraph,* 13 July 1912, p. 1. For similar occurrences see *Patriot,* 7 July 1914, p. 10.

34. *Telegraph,* 15 Aug. 1918, pp. 1, 6; ibid., 20 Aug. 1918, p. 1; ibid., 22 Aug. 1918, p. 4; ibid., 29 Aug. 1918, p. 4.

35. Brody, *Labor in Crisis,* p. 54.

36. *Telegraph,* 28 Aug. 1918, p. 4.

37. Grace is quoted in Brody, *Labor in Crisis,* p. 76. Considerable literature exists on the steel strike of 1919. See U.S. Congress, Senate, Committee on Education and Labor, hearings, *Investigation of the Strike in Steel Industries,* 66th Cong., 1st sess. (1919), pp. 480–83. William Z. Foster, *The Great Steel Strike and Its Lessons* (New York: International Publishers, 1920), and Marshall Olds, *An Analysis of the Interchurch World Movement Report on the Steel Strike* (New York: G. P. Putnam, 1923), p. 226, attributed the strike to Slavs. While the Senate report was disturbed by the "radicalism" of the strikers, the Interchurch World Movement was more sympathetic to the union's demands for collective bargaining.

38. *Telegraph,* 12 Mar. 1919., p. 15; ibid., 19 Mar. 1919, p. 17; ibid., 22 Mar. 1919, pp. 1, 8.

39. *Telegraph,* 5 Apr. 1919, pp. 3, 6; ibid., 26 Apr. 1919, p. 7.

40. *Telegraph,* 21 May 1919, p. 8; ibid., 22 Mar. 1919, p. 8; ibid., July 23 1919, p. 1.

41. *Telegraph,* 19 Sept. 1919, p. 7; ibid., 22 Sept. 1919, pp. 1, 15; ibid., 23 Sept. 1919, p. 1; ibid., 27 Sept. 1919, p. 1.

42. *Telegraph,* 29 Sept. 1919, pp. 19, 29.

43. *Telegraph,* 30 Sept. 1919, p. 1. The policy committee consisted of L. G. Barlets, J. M. Brown, C. Kauffman, Frank Kennedy, James Snavely, Frank Tourison, and Percy Zinn.

44. *Telegraph,* 1 Oct. 1919, pp. 1, 13; ibid., 2 Oct. 1919, p. 1.

45. *Telegraph,* 3 Oct. 1919, p. 10; Brody, *Labor in Crisis,* pp. 132, 181, 196; interviews with Thomas Benkovic, 11 July 1971; and John Verbos, 12 July 1971.

46. *Radnik,* 17 Oct. 1925, p. 1. Few Croatian papers commented editorially on the 1919 strike. This should not be surprising since most of the immigrant

press was controlled by fraternal organizations which were middle class in their orientation and seldom assumed a strong position on labor matters. A good example of their noncommital reporting on the strike is an editorial in *Narodni List,* 24 Sept. 1919, p. 2. A Slovak paper, *Narodne Noviny,* refused to take a stand on the strike itself. It strongly protested, however, in a series of editorials, that the "steel interests" were attempting to blame the strike on the foreign-born workers. *Narodne Noviny* claimed that it was a "cheap trick" on the part of steel interests to stir up the race question. While the paper thought the strike was an "ill chosen weapon," it claimed that Slavic immigrants were "tired of being the goat of both capital and labor alike." The journal continued that the strike was not the work of foreigners or foreign agitators: "There is not one foreigner as an officer in the union [AFL]." It charged the "steel interests" with attempting to identify Americanization with industrial submissiveness. See *Narodne Noviny,* 2 Oct. 1919, p. 4; ibid., 19 Oct. 1919, p. 4; ibid., 16 Oct. 1919, p. 4.

47. Interviews with Lewis Zuvic, 25 Aug. 1972; Gustav Belsak, 25 Aug. 1972; and Anonymous, 14 May 1976. A number of other immigrants, who requested anonymity on this point, confided to the author that they were "suspicious" of certain union organizers in Steelton in 1919. Brody, *Steelworkers in America,* pp. 260–61, argues that unskilled immigrants played a vital role in the 1919 strike and were active strikers. This appears to be true in certain areas such as Pittsburgh. In Homestead the local paper claimed that 95 percent of the strikers were "foreign-born, unskilled men." See *Homestead Daily Messenger,* 23 Sept. 1919, p. 1; and the Interchurch World Movement, *Public Opinion and the Steel Strike* (New York: Harcourt, Brace, 1921). In Bethlehem, Pennsylvania, however, the situation was similar to that in Steelton, and immigrants were kept on the periphery of the strike. See Thomas Vadaz, "The History of an Industrial Community: Bethlehem, Pennsylvania, 1741–1920" (Ph.D. diss., College of William and Mary, 1975). One possible explanation for the difference was that Pittsburgh had more labor organizers from western Pennsylvania coal areas who had worked with Slavs for years. Eastern areas like Bethlehem and Steelton lacked such influence. See interview with John Czelen, 26 Feb. 1973.

CHAPTER 4: COMMUNITY AND MOBILITY

1. Thernstrom, *Poverty and Progress,* p. 58. The belief that American immigrants experienced steady occupational advancement has been affirmed in numerous works. See W. Lloyd Warner and Leo Srole, *The Social Systems of American Ethnic Groups* (New Haven: Yale University Press, 1945), p. 63. Warner and Srole wrote that the occupational history of ethnic groups in Yankee City paralleled their residential history. Workers of the newly arrived groups started at the very bottom of the occupational hierarchy and, after several generations, climbed up to jobs with higher pay and increased prestige. Each new ethnic group tended to repeat the occupational history of the preceding one. By 1933, most had attained positions in the industrial life of the community which approximated that of the

native group. Timothy L. Smith, in citing reasons for religious voluntarism among American immigrants, attributed it partly to the "extensive second stage mobility of immigrants during the years after they had settled in the United States." See "Lay Initiative in the Religious Life of American Immigrants, 1880–1950," in *Anonymous Americans,* ed. Tamara K. Hareven (Englewood Cliffs, N.J.: Prentice Hall, 1971), p. 242. Brody, *Steelworkers in America,* p. 107, concluded: "The crucial fact was that in the steel mills the immigrants did rise." Brody atrributed "stability" in the unskilled ranks partially to upward mobility. Upward mobility is also stressed by Thomas Kessner, *The Golden Door: Italian and Jewish Immigrant Mobility in New York City, 1880–1915* (New York: Oxford University Press, 1977); Humbert S. Nelli, *Italians in Chicago, 1880–1930: A Study in Ethnic Mobility* (New York: Oxford University Press, 1970); and Cecyle Neidle, *The New Americans* (New York: Twayne, 1967), p. 43.

2. 18 Dec. 1886., p. 1.

3. 12 May 1888, p. 4.

4. *Reporter,* 10 June 1893, p. 4; ibid., 2 June 1894, p. 4; ibid., 6 June 1891, p. 4.

5. Interviews with Lewis Zuvic, 25 Aug. 1972; Thomas Benkovic, 11 July 1971; Meter Dragovich, 29 Aug. 1971; Hope Kormuschoff, 19 Sept. 1971; Charles Bojanic, 13 Aug. 1971; and Steve Suknaic, 6 Oct. 1971.

6. Ivan Mulacek, "Nase Iseljavanje v Stevlikah," *Cas* 7 (Ljubljana, Slovenia, 1913), 26–29.

7. 16 Sept. 1922, p. 1. The literature on social mobility and even expectations on the part of the "new immigrant" is still slim. See Barton, *Peasants and Strangers;* John Bodnar, "Immigration and Modernization: The Case of the Slavic Peasant in Industrial America," *Journal of Social History* 10 (1976), 44–71; John Bodnar, "Materialism and Morality: Slavic American Immigrants and Education," *Journal of Ethnic Studies* 3 (1976), 1–20; Kessner, *The Golden Door.* Brody, *Steelworkers in America,* p. 107, claims that immigrants did rise but offers no substantive or quantitative evidence. See also Joseph S. Roucek and Francis J. Brown, "The Problem of Negro and European Immigrant Minorities: Some Comparisons and Contrasts." *Journal of Negro Education* 3 (1939), 299–312. Roucek and Brown claim that although "some sons of the 'old World' have become successful, we know very little about the millions of forgotten small men whose high hopes have been buried." One Slavic immigrant priest suggested that Slavs lived "underneath America" and experienced no upward movement at all. See Balch, *Our Slavic Fellow Citizens,* p. 419.

8. 24 Dec. 1921, p. 1.

9. Thernstrom, *Poverty and Progress,* pp. 84–85; *Reporter,* 1 Apr. 1910, p. 1; ibid., 25 July 1902, p. 4.

10. U.S. Immigration Commission, *Reports of the Immigration Commission, Immigrants in Industries,* S. Doc. 633, 61st Cong., 2nd sess. (1911), XVIII, 331–42.

11. *Reporter,* 28 Mar. 1891, p. 1; *Telegraph,* 4 Aug. 1891, p. 1; *Reporter,* 24 Oct. 1902, p. 1.

12. *Reporter,* 6 Jan. 1911, p. 1. Immigrant papers carried numerous inducements by western mining companies to attract immigrants. See *Narodni List,* 2 July 1898, p. 3.

13. *Consecration and Sixtieth Anniversary, Holy Annunciation Macedonian-Bulgarian Orthodox Church* (Steelton, 1970), pp. 1–2; *Radnik,* 17 Oct. 1925, p. 1.

14. *History of St. Peter's* (Steelton, 1959), pp. 1–3.

15. *Reporter,* 26 Oct. 1911, p. 4.

16. John Verbos, "The St. Lawrence Story," *Zajedničar,* 15 Apr. 1970, p. 4. The economic effect of the depression could be gauged partially by the fact that in 1907 Steelton's immigrants sent nearly $700,000 to families in Europe. In 1908, they were able to send only $200,000. See *Reports of the Immigration Commission, Iron and Steel,* I, 589, 594.

17. *Reports of the Immigration Commission, Iron and Steel,* I, 594–95.

18. *Reporter,* 23 Dec. 1910, p. 4; ibid., 30 Dec. 1910, p. 1; ibid., 23 Sept. 1910, p. 4; ibid., 13 Jan. 1911, p. 4.

19. *Patriot,* 9 July 1913, p. 12; *Reporter,* 9 July 1909, p. 4; ibid., 24 Nov. 1911, p. 4.

20. *Patriot,* 8 Nov. 1913, p. 16.

21. See Peter R. Knights, "Population Turnover, Persistence, and Residential Mobility in Boston, 1830–1860," in *Nineteenth Century Cities,* ed. Stephan Thernstrom and Richard Sennett (New Haven: Yale University Press, 1969), p. 256.

22. These results were computed on the basis of data used in preparing table 5.

23. See table 5. For reasons that cannot be explained, the 1905 group of unskilled workers showed a higher persistence pattern in the ensuing decade than skilled or nonmanual workers. One possible explanation might be the gradual replacement of skilled workers by technology at this time.

24. For the manner in which blacks were identified see the note to table 12.

25. See table 14 for data on immigrant and black occupational mobility.

26. See Thernstrom, *Poverty and Progress,* pp. 84–90. A similar conclusion was reached for Newburyport, Massachusetts.

27. *Diamond Jubilee of St. Mary's Croatian Church* (Steelton, 1958), p. 4.

28. The classification of workers into skilled, semiskilled, and unskilled was devised from published wage figures provided in the *Reports of the Immigration Commission, Iron and Steel,* I, 612–25. The wages are hourly rates.

Skilled	
Machinist	39 ¢
Carpenter	32
Patternmaker	31
Heater	29
Semiskilled	
Moulder	26
Melter	25

Electrician	24
Blacksmith	22
Crane Operator	20
Foreman (labor)	17½
Blower	17
Engineer	16
Keeper	16
Charger	16
Unskilled	
Ladleman	13½
Helper	13
Fireman	13
Laborer	11

For a more extensive discussion of categorizing the work force, see Clyde Griffen, "Occupational Mobility in Nineteenth-Century America: Problems and Possibilities," *Journal of Social History* 5 (1972), 310–30.

29. "Tenth Census, 1880."

30. The most complete listing of "new immigrants" in Steelton is to be found in the "Twelfth Census, 1900," and in the "Alien Lists" of the Annual Enumeration of All Persons, Places and Things for Steelton in 1903 and 1905 located at the Dauphin County Court House, Harrisburg. These lists were special surveys of the immigrant population by assessors so that aliens could be taxed. The alien lists were more comprehensive in enumerating immigrants than the federal census partially because the peak years of Italian and Slavic immigration were after 1900. Thus, it was more reasonable to compile an aggregate sample of new immigrants from several sources between 1900 and 1905 and use 1905 as a starting date for tracing. If only individuals from 1900 census had been used, the sample would have been considerably smaller.

After the immigrants were identified, they were traced in *Boyd's Directory of Harrisburg and Steelton* for 1905, 1915, and 1925. The total of 403 Slavs and Italians appearing in 1905 in the city directory, moreover, represented only about 25 percent of the more than 1,800 Slavs and Italians appearing in the 1900 census and alien lists. Unfortunately the alien lists did not indicate an immigrant's occupation. Clearly city directories tended to be less accurate in the coverage of unskilled and semiskilled workers. Thus, the overall limited occupational gains of the immigrants and blacks in this study were in all probability even more modest than indicated here. See also Peter R. Knights, "A Method for Estimating Census Under-Enumeration," *Historical Methods Newsletter* 3 (December 1969), 5–8, and Charles M. Dollar and Richard Jensen, *Historian's Guide to Statistics* (New York: Holt, Rinehart, and Winston, 1971), p. 12.

31. See table 11.

32. Before the onset of heavy Slavic and Italian immigration in 1900, the

geographic mobility rates of blacks had been decreasing. After 1900 they began to increase. See the discussion of geographic mobility below.

33. For other comparisons of the black and immigrant experiences see John J. Appel, "American Negro and Immigrant Experience: Similarities and Differences," *American Quarterly* 18 (1966), 95–103; and Roucek and Brown, "The Problem of the Negro and European Immigrant Minorities." Competition between Irish, Negro, and Jewish workers is treated in chapter 1 of Carolyn Golab, "Polish Communities of Philadelphia, 1870–1920: Immigrant Distribution and Adaptation in Urban America" (Ph.D. diss., University of Pennsylvania, 1971). See also Stephan Thernstrom, *The Other Bostonians: Poverty and Progress in the American Metropolis, 1880–1970* (Cambridge, Mass.: Harvard University Press, 1973).

34. See chapter 7 for a further discussion of the impact of immigration upon the black worker.

35. See table 5. Obviously a trace of individuals can only relate the experiences of steelworkers who remained in the town. Evidence on the achievements of outward migrants from Steelton is difficult to obtain. The study has suggested that workers who were geographically mobile tended to experience less upward mobility than those remaining in a community. See also Gordon W. Kirk and Carolyn Tyirin Kirk, "Migration, Mobility, and the Transformation of the Occupational Structure in an Immigrant Community: Holland, Michigan, 1850–1880," *Journal of Social History* 7 (1974), 157.

36. Emmet Larkin has suggested that the Irish immigrants of the later years of the nineteenth century were a "vast improvement" over the Irish newcomers of the generation before. They were less impoverished and better educated. See "The Devotional Revolution in Ireland, 1850–1875," *American Historical Review* 77 (1972), 625–52.

37. The data on the percent of the total work force achieving upward mobility between 1880 and 1925 were drawn from Appendix 1, tables E, F, and G. Nine percent of entire work force experienced some form of advancement between 1888 and 1896; 5 percent between 1896 and 1905; and 6 percent between 1896 and 1915; and 6 percent between 1915 and 1925.

38. Katherine Stone, "The Origin of Job Structures in the Steel Industry," *Radical America* 7 (Nov.–Dec., 1973), pp. 30–34; *Report on Conditions of Employment in the Iron and Steel Industry,* III, 81.

39. Charles Reitell, *Machinery and Its Benefits to Labor in the Crude Iron and Steel Industries* (Menasha, Wisconsin: Banta, 1917), pp. 16, 32.

40. Paul Worthman's study of working-class mobility in Birmingham, Alabama, shows also that in the early twentieth century the large influx of white migrants, some of them Russians, "Hungarians," and Italians, brought into Birmingham mills from the North, helped erode black domination of some trades. See "Working-Class Mobility in Birmingham, Alabama, 1880–1914," in *Anonymous Americans,* ed. Tamara K. Hareven (Englewood Cliffs, N.J.: Prentice-Hall, 1971), p. 185. Worthman also states that unfortunately he could not

systematically examine immigrant patterns of mobility since no information was available about the place of birth of workers in 1890 and 1899. Thernstrom similarly found Irish immigrants surpassing blacks in Boston in the late nineteenth century. See *The Other Bostonians*, pp. 186–87.

41. See John A. Fitch, *The Steel Workers* (New York: Charities Publication Committee, 1910), pp. 29–30.

42. Reitell, *Machinery and Its Benefits*, p. 10; interviews with Martin Tezak, John Tezak, and Mary Krasovic, 25 Mar. 1976; and Jerome Kucan, 30 June 1971.

CHAPTER 5: MAINTAINING THE SOCIAL ORDER

1. *Item*, 9 Jan. 1880, p. 5.

2. *Item*, 30 June 1882, p. 5.

3. *Item*, 9 Jan. 1880, p. 5; ibid., 20 May 1881, p. 5; ibid., 27 May 1881, p. 5; *Reporter*, 22 Dec. 1894, p. 4.

4. *Item*, 17 June 1881, p. 4; ibid., 27 May 1881, p. 6; ibid., 16 Sept. 1881, p. 5.

5. *Item*, 6 Jan. 1882, p. 5; ibid., 2 Sept. 1881, p. 5.

6. *Item*, 20 May 1881, p. 5; ibid., 3 June 1881, p. 2; ibid., 9 Sept. 1881, p. 5; ibid., 7 July 1882, p. 5.

7. Interview with John Verbos, 12 July 1971. During the 1890s the Pennsylvania legislature passed a series of nativistic measures including one in 1895 which permitted only the employment of American citizens in the erection or improvement of public buildings or public works. One legislative committee investigating conditions in the anthracite region even concluded that prosperity would be impossible unless immigration was restricted. See Commonwealth of Pennsylvania, *Legislative Record* (Harrisburg, 1895), III, 1380–81; "Report of the Committee to Investigate Conditions Among Employees of the Anthracite Coal Regions," *Legislative Record* (Harrisburg, 1897), III, 2667–69.

8. *Reporter*, 15 May 1886, p. 4. See also R. G. Kirk, "Hrvatski Harlequin," *Saturday Evening Post*, 6 Aug. 1927, pp. 12–13, 85.

9. *Reporter*, 9 June 1905, p. 1.

10. *Reporter*, 27 Jan. 1905, p. 1. Four immigrants in 1905 were charged with murder for shooting two men who claimed the foreigners were not "Americans."

11. *Reports of the Immigration Commission, Iron and Steel*, I, 723.

12. *Reporter*, 7 Dec. 1900, p. 4; ibid., 20 July 1900, p. 4; George L. Laverty, *History of Medicine in Dauphin County, Pennsylvania* (Harrisburg, 1967), p. 63.

13. 17 Aug. 1900, p. 4.

14. 14 Aug. 1882, p. 5.

15. *Reporter*, 11 Sept. 1897, p. 1; ibid., 13 Sept. 1901, p. 4; ibid., 10 Jan. 1908 p. 44; ibid., 17 Sept. 1909, p. 1.

16. *Reporter*, 10 Sept. 1892, p. 4.

17. *Reporter*, 19 Aug. 1893, p. 4; ibid., 20 Oct. 1894, p. 4; ibid., 7 Dec. 1900, p. 4.

18. *Reporter*, 13 Sept. 1890, p. 4; ibid., 27 June 1891, p. 4; ibid., 31 Jan. 1891, p. 4; ibid., 9 Sept. 1893, p. 1; ibid., 25 Aug. 1894, p. 1; ibid., 10 July 1903, p. 1; ibid., 6 Sept. 1912, p. 1.

19. *Item*, 19 May 1882, p. 5; *Reporter*, 5 Nov. 1892, p. 4; ibid., 13 June 1893, p. 4.

20. *Reporter*, 27 Jan. 1905, p. 4.

21. *Reporter*, 28 Apr. 1905, p. 4.

22. *Reporter*, 18 May 1895, p. 4; ibid., 15 June 1895, p. 1.

23. *Reporter*, 15 June 1895, p. 4; ibid., 22 June 1895, p. 4.

24. *Reporter*, 5 May 1905, p. 4.

25. *Harrisburg Patriot*, 1 Apr. 1914, p. 9; *Reporter*, 25 Jan. 1896, p. 4; ibid., 9 May 1896, p. 4; ibid., 4 July 1902, p. 1.

26. *Reporter*, 18 Apr. 1896, p. 4; ibid., 26 Oct. 1895, p. 4.

27. *Reporter*, 23 Apr. 1907, p. 4.

28. *Reporter*, 14 June 1912, p. 4; ibid., 9 Aug. 1912, p. 1; ibid., 18 Oct. 1912, p. 1.

29. *Reporter*, 29 Sept. 1891; ibid., 27 Oct. 1899, p. 1.

30. *Reporter*, 26 June 1897, p. 1; Commonwealth of Pennsylvania, *Legislative Record* (Harrisburg, 1898), I, 2168. The measure passed the Pennsylvania House by a vote of 142 to 2. It was later declared unconstitutional by a federal judge in Pittsburgh. *Reporter*, 28 Aug. 1897, p. 4.

31. *Reporter*, 14 Dec. 1906, p. 4; ibid., 25 Jan. 1907, p. 4. For other expressions of nativism in Steelton, see ibid., 13 Oct. 1894, p. 1; ibid., 9 July 1894, p. 3; ibid., 8 Jan. 1893, p. 1.

32. *Reporter*, 21 Mar. 1891, p. 4; ibid., 9 Jan. 1886, p. 4.

33. *Reporter*, 20 July 1889, p. 1; ibid., 27 July 1889, p. 1.

34. *Reporter*, 20 July 1889, p. 1; ibid., 24 Aug. 1889, p. 1.

35. *Reporter*, 18 Nov., 1887, p. 4.

36. *Reporter*, 19 Nov. 1887, p. 4.

37. *Reporter*, 7 Jan. 1888, p. 4; ibid., 23 Aug. 1888, p. 4; ibid., 24 Jan. 1891, p. 4; ibid., 20 Jan. 1894, p. 4; ibid., 27 Jan. 1894, p. 4.

38. *Reporter*, 30 Sept. 1893, p. 1; ibid., 11 Nov. 1893, p. 4; ibid., 2 Dec. 1893, p. 1; ibid., 4 Jan. 1894, p. 5; ibid., 9 Dec. 1893, p. 4; ibid., 16 Sept. 1893, p. 4; ibid., 23 Dec. 1893, p. 4.

39. *Reporter*, 20 Dec. 1893, p. 4; ibid., 13 Jan. 1894, p. 4; ibid., 20 Jan. 1894, p. 4; ibid., 3 Feb. 1894, p. 4.

40. *Annual Report of Pennsylvania Steel Company*, 1903 (Harrisburg, 1901). See also the *Annual Report* for 1911; *Reports of the Immigration Commission, Iron and Steel*, I, 596–97.

41. *Reports of the Immigration Commission, Iron and Steel*, I, 596–97. See also *Harrisburg Call*, 15 Feb. 1897, p. 3; ibid., 20 Feb. 1897, p. 2. In Homestead, Slavs were also first to be laid off during the winter of 1907. See Byington, *Homestead* p. 135.

42. *Reports of the Immigration Commission, Iron and Steel,* I, 598–99; *Reporter,* 30 Apr. 1909, p. 1; *Harrisburg Patriot,* 2 May 1916, p. 2.

43. *Reporter,* 31 Jan. 1908, p. 4: ibid., 7 Feb. 1908; p. 4; *Reports of the Immigration Commission, Iron and Steel,* I, 599.

44. *Reports of the Immigration Commission, Iron and Steel,* I, 599–600; *Reporter,* 30 Apr. 1909, p. 1; ibid., 1 May 1908, p. 1; ibid., 30 Apr. 1909, p. 1.

45. *Reports of the Immigration Commission, Iron and Steel,* I, 600.

46. *Reporter,* 24 May 1909, p. 1.

47. *Reporter,* 17 Jan. 1902, p. 4; ibid., 28 Sept. 1906, p. 4.

48. *Reporter,* 2 Mar. 1895, p. 1.

49. *Telegraph,* 23 Sept. 1898, p. 5; H. M. J. Klein and F. S. Klein, *The State Young Men's Christian Association of Pennsylvania, 1869–1969* (Harrisburg, 1969), pp. 39, 42.

50. *Reporter,* 2 July 1903, p. 1; ibid., 18 May 1906, p. 1; ibid., 5 Oct. 1906, p. 4; ibid., 23 Nov. 1906, p. 4; ibid., 7 Dec. 1906, p. 1; ibid., 16 Nov. 1906, p. 1; ibid., 8 Feb. 1907, p. 1.

51. *Reporter,* 14 Dec. 1906, p. 1; ibid., 21 Dec. 1906.

52. *Reporter,* 15 Oct. 1909, p. 1.

53. *Reporter,* 12 Nov. 1909, p. 1; ibid., 31 Dec. 1909, p. 4.

54. *Reporter,* 21 Jan. 1910, p. 1; ibid., 18 Mar. 1910, p. 1; ibid., 11 Mar. 1910, p. 1; ibid., 21 Jan. 1910, p. 1; ibid., 1 Apr. 1910, p. 1; ibid., 8 Apr. 1910, p. 1.

55. *Reporter,* 8 July 1910, p. 1.

56. *Telegraph,* 22 Aug. 1914, p. 9; ibid., 20 Nov. 1914, p. 13; *Reporter,* 4 Feb. 1910, p. 1; ibid., 27 May 1910, p. 1; ibid., 27 May 1910, p. 1; ibid., 16 Dec. 1910, p. 1.

57. *Reports of the Immigration Commission, Iron and Steel,* I, 713.

58. Brody, *Steelworkers in America,* p. 124. See also Raymond E. Wolfinger, "The Development and Persistence of Ethnic Voting," in *American Ethnic Politics,* ed. Lawrence Fuchs (New York: Harper & Row, 1968), pp. 164, 184. Wolfinger argues that American politics promoted the persistence of ethnic identity since it fostered group cohesiveness as a source of political power.

59. *Harrisburg Patriot,* 29 Jan. 1914, p. 10; ibid., 3 Nov. 1913, p. 8; interview with Steve Suknaic, 6 Oct. 1971.

60. Interview with Meter Dragovich, 27 Oct. 1971; *Reports of Immigration Commission, Iron and Steel,* I, 726, 728.

61. *Reporter,* 8 June 1900, p. 4.

62. Interview with M. Harvey Taylor, 27 Sept. 1971; *Reporter,* 14 Feb. 1902, p. 4.

63. *Reporter,* 28 July 1905, p. 4; ibid., 21 June 1907, p. 1.

64. *Reporter,* 12 Sept. 1902, p. 4; ibid., 26 Sept. 1902, p. 1.

65. Interviews with John Verbos, 12 July 1971; and M. Harvey Taylor, 27 Sept. 1971. Verbos claimed that Nelley was established in the saloon business by Dauphin County Republicans, but Taylor refutes this.

66. *Reporter,* 2 Feb. 1906, p. 4; *Telegraph,* 15 Sept. 1914, p. 7.

67. Interviews with John Verbos, 12 July 1971; and Meter Dragovich, 27 Oct. 1971.

68. *Reporter*, 16 Sept. 1910, p. 1.

69. Interviews with Anna Lopert, 17 Aug. 1971; Thomas Benkovic, 11 July 1971; Mary Jurina, 30 June 1971; Jerome Kucan, 30 June 1971; and Elcora McClane and Charlene Conyers, 14 Aug. 1971.

70. Interviews with Jerome Kucan, 30 June 1971; Thomas Benkovic, 11 July 1971; Charles Bojanic, 13 Aug. 1971; and Steve Suknaic, 6 Oct. 1971. Local campaign literature was always printed in English and Slavic. See "Jedna Pecena Kosos," and M. J. Horvath to T. J. Nelley, 16 Sept. 1929, both in possession of John Verbos. Election statistics are drawn from the *Pennsylvania Mannual* (Harrisburg, 1933), p. 479.

71. *Press*, 26 Mar. 1898, p. 1; ibid., 19 Dec. 1903, p. 1; *Reporter*, 18 Sept. 1886, p. 4; *Press*, 26 Dec. 1903, p. 1; ibid., 16 Jan. 1904, p. 1; ibid., 24 Sept. 1904, p. 1.

72. *Press*, 16 Jan. 1904, p. 1.

73. *Reporter*, 13 Feb. 1904, pp. 1–2; ibid., 27 May 1904, p. 1; 9 Feb. 1906, p. 1.

74. *Reporter*, 27 Feb. 1904, p. 1; ibid., 10 Apr. 1897, p. 4.

75. *Press*, 24 June 1905, p. 1; ibid., 5 Oct. 1907, p. 1.

76. William E. B. DuBois, *The Philadelphia Negro* (New York: B. Blom, 1967), pp. 374–75.

77. *Press*, 22 Aug. 1903, p. 1; ibid., 19 Dec. 1903, p. 1.

78. F. L. Jefferson to Matthew S. Quay, 21 Jan. 1903, William A. Sample to Samuel W. Pennypacker, 21 Jan. 1903, and P. S. Blackwell to Sammuel W. Pennypacker, 23 Jan. 1903, Pennypacker Papers, Box 12.

79. Boies Penrose to Samuel W. Pennypacker, 27 Mar. 1903, Pennypacker Papers, Box 12.

80. *Press*, 25 July 1903, p. 1; ibid., 30 Apr. 1904, p. 1.

81. *Press*, 26 Sept. 1903, p. 1; ibid., 21 Nov. 1903, p. 1. The Pennsylvania Department of Welfare found that as late as 1925 only 13 percent of the blacks in Harrisburg and Steelton owned their own homes. See the *Negro Survey of Pennsylvania*, p. 43.

82. *Press*, 10 Aug. 1907, p. 1.

83. *Reporter*, 27 Nov. 1886, p. 4. J. V. W. Reynders, superintendent of Pennsylvania Steel, objected to the granting of new liquor licenses in Steelton in 1914 as detrimental to the firm's employees. *Harrisburg Patriot*, 21 Feb. 1914, pp. 1, 13.

84. *Reporter*, 22 Feb., 1907, p. 1; *Reports of the Immigration Commission, Iron and Steel*, I, 694.

85. *Reporter*, 22 Feb. 1907, p. 1.

86. Ibid.

87. *Reporter*, 1 Mar. 1907, p. 1.

88. *Patriot*, 6 Aug. 1913, p. 8; *Reporter*, 10 Oct. 1902, p. 4; interview with Elcora McClane and Charlene Conyers, 14 Aug. 1971.

89. *Reporter,* 4 Aug., 1905, p. 1; ibid., 9 Feb. 1906, p. 1; interview with Meter Dragovich, 29 Nov. 1971.

CHAPTER 6: THE NEWCOMERS TURN INWARD

1. A traveler from Croatia in 1905 noted that among Croats in Pittsburgh the main topic of discussion was the administration of the National Croatian Society, an internal matter. See Ante Tresic-Pavcic, *Od Atlantika do Pacifika-Život Hrvata u Sjevernoj Americi* (Zagreb, 1907), pp. 10–33.

2. *Reports of the Immigration Commission, Iron and Steel,* I, 581, 719–25.

3. *Zacetek Slovenske Naselbine v Steeltonu,* p. 5.

4. Ibid., pp. 19–20; *Pozdrav in Castitke,* pp. 19–21; Verbos, "St. Lawrence Story," p. 4; *Spomen-Knijiga 25 Godišnjica Hrvatsko-Radičko Podporno Društvo, St. Lovo, 1895–1920* (Steelton, 1920), pp. 6–9.

5. Interview with Charles Bojanic, 13 Aug. 1971; *Fiftieth Anniversary of the St. Nicholas Serbian Orthodox Church* (Steelton, 24 May 1953). For views of immigrant docility see Peter Roberts, *The New Immigration* (New York: Macmillan, 1912), p. 189, and Oscar Handlin, *The Uprooted* (Boston: Little, Brown, 1951), pp. 109–110. Cf. Smith, "Lay Initiative," pp. 220–40.

6. *Consecration of Iconostas and Fortieth Anniversary of Circle of Serbian Church* (Steelton, 1943), pp. 32–36; interview with Charles Bojanic, 13 Aug. 1971.

7. *Reporter,* 28 Aug. 1903, p. 1; ibid., 30 Oct. 1903, p. 1; interviews with Meter Dragovich, 27 Oct. 1971, and 29 Nov. 1971; and Charles Bojanic, 13 Aug. 1971.

8. *Fiftieth Anniversary of the St. Nicholas Serbian Orthodox Church,* pp. 1–10; interview with Meter Dragovich, 27 Oct. 1971.

9. *Reporter,* 1 Sept. 1911, p. 4; ibid., 13 Sept. 1912, p. 4; ibid., 16 June 1913, p. 5.

10. *Reporter,* 10 Jan. 1908, p. 4.

11. *Patriot,* 7 Jan. 1913, p. 2; ibid., 7 Jan. 1914, p. 10; *Reporter,* 5 Jan. 1906, p. 1; ibid., 11 Jan. 1907, p. 4; interview with Meter Dragovich, 27 Oct. 1971.

12. *Reporter,* 3 Oct. 1902, p. 1; ibid., 25 Sept. 1903, p. 4; ibid., 21 July 1905, p. 1; ibid., 17 Nov. 1905, p. 4; ibid., 10 Jan. 1908, p. 4; ibid., 24 Dec. 1908, p. 1.

13. *Reporter,* 1 Jan. 1909, p. 4.

14. *Reporter,* 13 Dec. 1901, p. 1; ibid., 20 Mar. 1903, p. 1; ibid., 24 July 1903, p. 1; ibid., 20 Sept. 1907, p. 4; *Golden Jubilee of St. Ann's Italian Catholic Church* (Steelton, 1953), pp. 7–9.

15. *Reporter,* 4 Oct. 1901, p. 4; ibid., 13 Feb. 1903, p. 4; ibid., 18 Sept. 1903, p. 4; ibid., 15 Oct. 1909, p. 4.

16. *Reporter,* 22 Jan. 1904, p. 1; ibid., 19 Feb., 1904, p. 1; ibid., 9 June 1911, p. 4.

17. *Consecration, Holy Annunciation Church; Reporter,* 19 Nov. 1909, p. 4; ibid., 11 Mar. 1910, p. 4; ibid., 25 Mar. 1910, p. 1; *Reports of the Immigration Commission, Iron and Steel,* I, 709–10.

18. *Reporter,* 24 Nov. 1911, p. 4; Nakoff, *A History of the Macedonian-Bulgarian Church,* p. 15.

19. *Reporter,* 28 May 1909, p. 4; ibid., 26 May 1911, p. 4; ibid., 26 Jan. 1912, p. 4; *Patriot,* 18 Jan. 1913, p. 9; ibid., 2 Jan. 1914, p. 2; *Telegraph,* 19 Jan. 1918, p. 1; interview with Kero Risteff, 31 Aug. 1971.

20. *Reports of the Immigration Commission, Iron and Steel,* I, 592.

21. *Reporter,* 9 Feb. 1889, p. 1; ibid., 28 May 1909, p. 1; ibid., 15 Oct. 1892, p. 4; ibid., 22 Apr. 1893, p. 4; *Press,* 9 Mar. 1907, p. 1; ibid., 29 May 1907, p. 1; ibid., 26 May 1908, p. 1; *Harrisburg Call,* 13 Aug. 1886, pp. 1–3; *Negro Survey in Pennsylvania,* p. 35; Wright, *The Negro in Pennsylvania,* p. 229; *AME Monumental Church, Programme of Dedication* (Steelton, 21 Apr. 1907); AME Church, *Historical Record* (Steelton, 1905). For a discussion of the importance of Negro churches see Jon Butler, "Communities and Congregations: The Black Church in St. Paul, 1860–1900," *Journal of Negro History* 56 (1971), 118–34.

22. *Reporter,* 20 July 1895, p. 4; ibid., 3 Aug. 1895, p. 4.

23. *Reporter,* 28 Jan. 1888, p. 4; ibid., 19 Sept. 1891, p. 4; ibid., 8 Aug. 1902, p. 4; ibid., 23 July 1892, p. 4; ibid., 23 June 1894, p. 4; ibid., 2 Nov. 1895, p. 4; *Press,* 15 Aug. 1903, p. 1; ibid., 11 June 1910, p. 1; Mark T. Milnor, "Veterans Organizations of the United States with Special References to Dauphin County, Pennsylvania," *Dauphin County Historical Review* 5 (1956), 23–28.

24. *Reporter,* 3 June 1893, p. 4; ibid., 2 June 1894, p. 4.

25. *Reporter,* 29 June 1895, p. 4; *Item,* 26 Aug. 1881, p. 5; ibid., 11 Nov. 1881, p. 5; *Patriot,* 24 May 1913, p. 9; *Press,* 15 June 1907, p. 1; interview with Elcora McClane and Charlene Conyers, 14 Aug. 1971. Mrs. McClane and Mrs. Conyers are daughters of Charles Howard.

26. *Reporter,* 9 Aug. 1890, p. 4; ibid., 6 Sept. 1890, p. 4.

27. *Reporter,* 6 Sept. 1890, p. 4; *Press,* 16 July 1890, p. 4.

28. *Reporter,* 20 May 1904, p. 2; interview with Elcora McClane and Charlene Conyers, 14 Aug. 1971.
Interesting accounts of the annual Douglass Association affairs appeared in the *Press,* 10 June 1911, p. 1; *Reporter,* 2 June 1905, p. 1; ibid., 5 June 1908, p. 4.

29. *Press,* 4 Feb. 1905, p. 1; ibid., 11 Feb. 1905, p. 1.

30. Matthew Anderson to Samuel W. Pennypacker, 12 Apr. 1905, Pennypacker Papers, R. G. 171, Box 38; *Press,* 4 July 1908; *Patriot,* 14 Feb. 1905, pp. 1, 4. Blacks also attended the Avery College Trade School near Pittsburgh, where both black and white students were sent from juvenile court, and a Negro industrial school near Downingtown which was intended to be similar to Tuskeegee Institute in Alabama. The Downington school later became Cheyney State College.

31. *Telegraph,* 11 July 1918, p. 4; ibid., 22 Feb. 1919, p. 15; ibid., 7 Mar. 1919, p. 7; ibid., 13 Mar. 1919, p. 3; ibid., 15 Mar. 1919, p. 10.

32. Interviews with Thomas Benkovic, 11 July 1971; and Steve Suknaic, 28 June 1971.

33. *Zajedničar*, Nov. 1908, pp. 22–24; Handlin, *The Uprooted*, p. 186. Polish peasants, for instance, were confused about their national identity. See Franciszek Bujak, *Zmiaca-Wies Powiatu Limanowskiego: Stosunki Gospodarcze i Spoliczne* (Krakow, 1903); Vladimir C. Nahirny and Joshua A. Fishman, "American Immigrant Groups: Ethnic Identification and the Problem of Generations," *Sociological Review* 13 (1965), 314; Golab, "The Polish Communities of Philadelphia," pp. 233–34. Golab found Philadelphia's Poles always identifying themselves by the village of their birth. Slovak settlers in Pennsylvania's anthracite area also formed their early fraternal lodges around European village or regional groupings. See taped interview with John Sirotnik, 19 July 1973, Scranton Oral History Project, Pennsylvania Historical and Museum Commission. Manuela Dobos has called South Slav nationalism in the late nineteenth century the "politics of other classes" and demonstrated that Croatian peasants were indifferent toward nationalist sentiment. See "The Croatian Peasant Uprising of 1883" (Ph.D. diss., Columbia University, 1974), pp. 331–34.

34. *Zacetek Slovenske Naselbine v Steeltonu*, pp. 8–10; Milan Vranes, "Odsjek 13u Steeltonu Odrazao Sevcano Otvorenje Svog Novog Doma," *Zajedničar*, 23 Apr. 1969; *Narodni List*, 18 Aug. 1900, p. 1; *Spomen-Knjiga, 25 Godišnjica*, pp. 6–7.

35. Interviews with John Verbos, 12 July 1971; Mary Jurina, 30 June 1971; and Thomas Benkovic, 11 July 1971. Benkovic was a former president of the St. Lawrence Lodge. See also *Spomen Knijizica Četrdeset Godišnjice*, pp. 2–6.

36. John Verbos, "St. Lawrence Story," p. 4; *Reporter*, 26 Sept. 1902, p. 4; Vranes, "Odsjek 13u Steeltonu," p. 2. Several members of the St. Lawrence Society disliked the site chosen for the new hall and withdrew to form another lodge of the National Croatian Society in 1901. The best account of the St. Lawrence Society is *Spomen-Knjiga, 25 Godišnjica*, pp. 8–10, which includes a list of early members. Early accounts of Steelton's Croatian settlers can be found in *Narodni List*, 13 June 1901, p. 1; ibid., 15 June 1901, 1901, p. 1. These articles were part of a series on Croatian colonies in Pennsylvania written by Janko Kovacevic which ran for nearly nine months during 1901.

37. A census of Croatians was taken in 1902 by a Croat publisher. See Josip Marohnic, *Popis Hrvata U America* (Allegheny, Pa.: Marohnica, 1900), pp. 99–102. Marohnic estimated that Pennsylvania had about forty thousand Croatians in 1902 and even singled out Steelton Croats for the pride they displayed in their national origin by continually "decorating" their hall.

38. See, for example, *Reporter*, 23 Mar. 1900, p. 1; ibid., 18 Jan. 1901, p. 3; ibid., 10 Jan. 1902, p. 4.

39. Interview with Thomas Benkovic, 11 July 1971; *Spomen Knijizca Četrdeset Godišnjice*, pp. 2–6; Verbos, "St. Lawrence Story," p. 4. See also "Hrvatska Zupa v Steeltonu, Pennsylvania," *Naša Nada* (1932), pp. 92–97. Copies of *Naša Nada* are available at the Immigration History Research Center, University of Minnesota.

40. *Reporter*, 2 July 1898, p. 4; ibid., 5 Oct. 1900, p. 1; ibid., 13 Sept. 1901, p. 4.

41. *Reporter*, 2 July 1903, p. 1.

42. *Reporter*, 28 Aug. 1903, p. 1.

43. *Reporter*, 23 July 1909, p. 4; interview with Thomas Benkovic, 11 July 1971. The library is mentioned in *Zajedničar*, 29 Aug. 1934, III, 7.

44. *Zajedničar*, 30 Mar. 1911, pp. 2, 7. See also *Reporter*, 5 Nov. 1909, p. 4; ibid., 31 Mar. 1912, p. 4.

45. *Reporter*, 30 Dec. 1910, p. 4; ibid., 3 Nov. 1911, p. 4; ibid., 1 Dec. 1911, p. 4; ibid., 26 Jan. 1912, p. 4.

46. *Reporter*, 26 Apr. 1912, p. 4; ibid., 3 May 1912, p. 4.

47. *Spomen Knjizica Četrdeset Godišnjice*, pp. 6–8; interview with Jerome Kucan, 30 June 1971; "Hrvatska Zupa v Steeltonu," p. 94.

48. Interviews with John Verbos, 12 July 1971; Mary Jurina, 30 June 1971; and Thomas Benkovic, 11 July 1971.

49. *Spomen Knizica Četrdeset Godišnjice*, pp. 7–8; *Diamond Jubilee of St. Mary's Croatian Church*; interview with Jerome Kucan, 30 June 1971; Verbos, "St. Lawrence Story," p. 4; *Reporter*, 25 Apr. 1896, p. 1. Bozic was also a frequent contributor of literary pieces to *Narodni List*. See, e.g., 30 Sept. 1899, p. 3.

50. *Spomen Knjizica Četrdeset Godišnjice*, pp. 8–9; Prpic, *Croatian Immigrants in America*, pp. 128–29; Gazi, *Croatian Immigration to Allegheny County*, pp. 2–4. On Gorshe, see *Reporter*, 21 Mar. 1902, p. 4. See also *Narodni List*, 29 Mar. 1899, p. 1; ibid., 20 Jan. 1900, p. 1.

51. Ironically the most accurate accounts of the founding of the school are in the *Reporter*, 7 Aug. 1903, p. 4; ibid., 11 Sept. 1903, p. 1; ibid., 25 Sept. 1903, p. 1; ibid., 11 Mar. 1904, p. 1. The quotation is from the interview with Thomas Benkovic, 11 July 1971.

52. *Spomen Knijizica Četrdeset Godišnjice*, p. 5; *Diamond Jubilee of St. Mary's Croatian Church*; *Pozdrav in Castitke*, p. 24; interview with Thomas Benkovic, 11 July 1971.

53. *Reporter*, 26 Mar. 1909, p. 1; *Pozdrav in Castitke*, p. 24; *Consecration of Iconostas and Fortieth Anniversary of Circle of Serbian Sisters* (Steelton: St. Nicholas Serbian Church, 12 Oct. 1969); *Spomen Knijizica Četrdeset Godišnjice*, p. 9.

54. *Patriot*, 14 July 1913, p. 8. See also *750 Years of the Serbian Church*, p. 31.

55. *Patriot*, 26 Feb. 1914, p. 5; ibid., 1 Apr. 1914, p. 1.

56. Interview with Meter Dragovich, 29 Nov. 1971.

57. Interview with George Dimoff, 29 Oct. 1971.

58. *Reporter*, 23 Oct. 1905, p. 1; ibid., 5 Mar. 1905, p. 4.

59. *Reporter*, 18 Oct. 1912, p. 4; *Zajedničar*, 12 June 1912, p. 5.

60. *Patriot*, 4 July 1913, p. 5.

61. *Patriot*, 22 Jan. 1913, p. 7; ibid., 19 Feb. 1913, p. 6; ibid., 3 Mar. 1915, p. 5.

62. *Zajedničar*, 15 July 1914, p. 2; *Telegraph*, 10 July 1914, pp. 1, 11.

63. *Novi Hrvat*, 9 July 1914, pp. 1, 3.

64. *Telegraph*, 10 July 1914, pp. 1, 11. The *Diamond Jubilee of St. Mary's Croatian Church*, p. 4, stated that Zuvic was asked to come to Steelton because of his outspoken advocacy of Croatian independence.

65. *Zajedničar,* 12 Aug. 1914, p. 1; *Telegraph,* 29 July 1914, p. 8.

66. *Patriot,* 24 July 1913, p. 5; *Telegraph,* 1 Aug. 1914, p. 3; ibid., 6 Aug. 1914, p. 3; ibid., 13 Aug. 1914, p. 10.

67. *Zajedničar,* 12 Aug. 1914, p. 1; *Telegraph,* 3 Aug. 1914, p. 7; ibid., 4 Aug. 1914, p. 9. The *Telegraph* also published a list of all volunteers who left for Serbia.

68. *Telegraph,* 5 Aug. 1914, p. 7; ibid., 13 Aug. 1914, p. 7; interview with Meter Dragovich, 29 Nov. 1971. See also *Spomen-Knjiga 25 Godišnijica,* p. 11.

69. *Telegraph,* 28 Aug. 1914, p. 11. The corporate viewpoint is expressed in "Chandler Bros. Stock Prospectus," Pennsylvania Steel Company materials, Bethlehem Steel Company Library, Bethlehem.

70. *Spomen Knjizica Četrdeset Godišnjice,* p. 8.

71. Ibid.; interview with Meter Dragovich, 27 Oct. 1971.

72. *Telegraph,* 10 Aug. 1914, p. 9.

73. *Telegraph,* 16 Feb. 1918, p. 7.

74. *Telegraph,* 3 June 1918, p. 8; ibid., 4 June 1918, p. 6; ibid., 23 April 1918, p. 16.

75. *Telegraph,* 1 Jan. 1918, p. 7; ibid., 4 Feb. 1918, p. 8; ibid., 21 Feb. 1918, p. 10; ibid., 29 Apr. 1918, p. 16; ibid., 10 July 1918, p. 12; ibid., 3 Sept. 1918, p. 12; ibid., 2 Oct. 1918, p. 6.

76. *Zajedničar,* 8 Oct. 1918, p. 6; *Telegraph,* 1 Oct. 1918, p. 16; ibid., 2 Apr. 1918, p. 11; ibid., 5 July 1919, p. 18.

77. *Zajedničar,* 10 July 1918, p. 3; *Telegraph,* 3 July 1918, pp. 1, 9.

78. *Zajedničar,* 17 Apr. 1918, p. 1.

79. *Zajedničar,* 27 Feb. 1918, p. 2. Actually the letter the Steelton Croats wrote was rejected for publication in Frank Zotti's Croatian paper, *Narodni List.* Zotti's offices in New York were raided by the United States Department of Justice in August 1918. See *Narodni List,* 27 Sept. 1919, p. 2.

80. Interviews with Lewis Zuvic and Gustav Belsak, 25 Aug. 1972. Very few Croats and Serbs ever joined Socialist organizations. The first Croatian Socialist club in America was started in Allegheny City, Pennsylvania, in 1903. This club joined other Croats, Serbs, Bulgarians, and Slovenes in establishing the Jugoslav Socialist Federation in 1910. The federation published newspapers such as *Proletarec* for the Slovenes, *Radnicka Straza* for the Croats, and *Narodni Glas* for the Serbs. By 1924, however, the federation's membership totaled only 1,500 and never exceeded 2,000. Over 80 percent of its membership was Slovene, moreover, and ethnic differences continually drained its strength. In Pennsylvania the active South Slav socialists were almost all in small mining towns such as Strabane or Forest City. Steel towns were extremely weak in socialist activity. *Proletarec,* for instance, had 800 subscribers at one time or another in Pennsylvania between 1915 and 1940 (mostly in the early 1930s). The membership lists, however, contained no Steelton Slovenes. Pittsburgh had less than twenty Slovene Socialists. Strabane, Yukon, and Forest City, small mining towns, had about one-fourth the entire readership of *Proletarec* in the state. See Jugoslo-

vanska Socialistična Zneza Papers, Box 176, Immigration History Research Center, University of Minnesota; *Radnicka Straza*, 15 July 1910, p. 1; *Majski Glas* 15 (1935), p. 50.

81. *Telegraph*, 5 July 1918, p. 5; ibid., 21 Jan. 1919, p. 8. Blacks had been included in a parade of steelworkers in Harrisburg in 1885.

CHAPTER 7: CONTINUITY AND CHANGE

1. *Fourteenth Census, 1920*, p. 872; *Fifteenth Census, 1930*, p. 692.
2. *Patriot*, 6 Jan. 1930, p. 13.
3. *Patriot*, 16 Jan. 1930, p. 7; ibid., 7 Jan. 1931, p. 6; ibid., 7 Jan. 1933, p. 3.
4. *Patriot*, 24 Oct. 1923, p. 10.
5. *Zacetek Slovenske Naselbine v Steeltonu*, p. 5.
6. *Consecration, Holy Annunciation Church*, pp. 2–3.
7. *Thirtieth Anniversary of the St. Nicholas Serbian Orthodox Church* (Steelton, 1933), pp. 4–7.
8. *50th Anniversary of the Serbian Church* (Steelton, 1952), p. 7; *Patriot*, 24 Oct. 1923, p. 10; ibid., 21 Jan. 1930, p. 4; 9 Jan. 1930, p. 2; ibid., 30 Nov. 1933, p. 3; ibid., 7 June 1934, p. 7; ibid., 27 Feb. 1934, p. 3; ibid., 24 Apr. 1934, p. 5; ibid., 26 Nov. 1932, p. 6; *Hrvatski List*, 20 Aug. 1932, p. 3; ibid., 29 Aug. 1936, p. 4; *American Srobran*, 17 Mar. 1934, p. 3.
9. Interview with Jerome Kucan, 30 June 1971.
10. Lists of high school graduates were published annually in the local press. *Patriot*, 17 May 1920, p. 2; ibid., 27 May 1920, p. 9; ibid., 11 June 1924, p. 18; ibid., 14 June 1926, p. 8; ibid., 17 June 1926, p. 27; ibid., 16 June 1927, p. 2. On the construction of a new Croatian school see *Diamond Jubilee Souvenir Book* (Steelton, 1958), p. 10. In 1930 a new Catholic high school was built in Harrisburg, and several Croats, Italians, and Slovenes began to attend, although Orthodox Serbs and Bulgarians did not. The first Croat college graduate in Steelton is reported in *Hrvatski List*, 30 June 1927, p. 3.
11. Interviews with Anonymous, 14 May 1976; and Louis and Catherine Lescanec, 17 June 1975.
12. *Patriot*, 18 Dec. 1933, p. 7; ibid., 16 Dec. 1933, p. 6; ibid., 30 Dec. 1933, p. 4; ibid., 24 Apr. 1934, p. 5.
13. Commonwealth of Pennsylvania v. George Minoff, transcript, 1948, Dauphin County Court House, pp. 254–84.
14. Interview with George Dimoff, 29 Oct. 1971. Harmony between the factions again was to be short-lived. In April 1948 at a church meeting, George Minoff shot and killed Koche Atzeff and Boris Minoff. The incident was a culmination of the persistent factionalism that had ravaged the congregation. In 1948 the Bulgarians were searching for a new pastor. Upon learning of the availability of a priest in Bulgaria, they sent the necessary funds to Sofia to bring him to Steelton. However, they received no reply. When a second request was sent, the priest in Bulgaria replied that he had difficulty in coming because

someone in the Steelton congregation had written "slanderous remarks and untruths" to the Synod which were "interferring with my departure." See Commonwealth of Pennsylvania v. George Minoff, pp. 254–84.

15. See the discussion of occupational mobility in chapter 4.

16. Colakovic, *Yugoslav Migrations to America*, pp. 152–54.

17. The intergenerational occupational mobility of blacks between 1920 and 1939 was measured by identifying blacks in Dauphin County Marriage License Dockets and then tracing them through *Boyd's Director of Harrisburg and Steelton*. Of the 216 blacks, 67 percent did not change their status, while 24 percent moved up and 9 percent declined.

18. Interview with Thomas Benkovic, 11 July 1971.

19. Interview with Walter Lang, 7 Sept. 1973.

20. Horvath describes the campaign in *Zajedničar*, 11 July 1934, p. 7.

21. Ibid. The few Slavs gaining political offices after 1930 were identified in *Patriot*, 9 Nov. 1932, p. 10; ibid., 5 Dec. 1933, p. 17; 8 Dec. 1933, p. 2. Borough officials were listed each year in *Boyd's Directory of Harrisburg and Steelton*.

22. *Patriot*, 29 Nov. 1933, p. 2; ibid., 9 Nov. 1932, p. 10; ibid., 7 Nov. 1933, p. 1; ibid., 6 Nov. 1933, p. 4.

23. *Patriot*, 14 Nov. 1933, p. 1; ibid., 4 Feb. 1934, p. 12; *Zajedničar*, 11 July 1934, p. 7.

24. Interview with Walter B. Lang, 7 Sept. 1973.

25. *Patriot*, 7 Jan. 1930, p. 2; ibid., 10 Jan. 1930, p. 1; ibid., 27 Jan. 1930, pp. 1–2. Among the officers of the Kiwanis was Thomas Nelley. The Civic Club was headed by Mrs. G. P. Vanier, who had been prominent in Americanization programs among "foreign residents," and Mrs. Frank Robbins, wife of the steel mill superintendent. See *Patriot*, 8 Jan., 1930, p. 3.

26. Robert Brooks, *As Steel Goes* (New Haven: Yale University Press, 1940), pp. 146–47.

27. "In the Matter of Bethlehem Steel . . . and the Steel Workers Organizing Committee," *Decisions of the National Labor Relations Board*, 14 (1939), 567.

28. Ibid., pp. 569–71.

29. Ibid., pp. 572–75.

30. Interview with Joseph DiSanto, 19 April 1974. Only six men appeared at a CIO meeting in Steelton after thousands of announcements for the meeting were circulated. See John Sabol to Clint Golden, 20 Oct. 1937, in the George P. Medrick Papers, Labor Archives, Penn State University.

31. Interview with Walter B. Lang, 7 Sept. 1973.

32. "In the matter of Bethlehem Steel," pp. 630–31. Meter Dragovich recalls being part of a group which was assigned to burn the records of the plan at Steelton after the CIO was established. Interview, 29 Nov. 1971.

33. See Pennsylvania Department of Internal Affairs, *Sixth Industrial Directory* (Harrisburg, 1928), p. 235; *Eighth Industrial Directory* (Harrisburg, 1936), p. 233; *Seventh Industrial Directory* (Harrisburg, 1931), p. 237. See also *Patriot*, 26 Oct. 1923; United States Courts of Appeals, *Transcript of Record, Bethlehem Steel*

Company vs. National Labor Relations Board, 11 vols. (Washington, D.C., 1939), I, 10016.

34. *Patriot,* 26 Apr. 1934, p. 12; Commonwealth of Pennsylvania, "Inventory of Unemployed Persons," 3 vols. (Harrisburg, 31 Dec. 1974), manuscript in the Pennsylvania State Library, Harrisburg.

35. *Patriot,* 3 Nov. 1933, p. 24; ibid., 13 Dec. 1932, p. 14; ibid., 14 Feb. 1934, p. 12.

36. *Patriot,* 30 Nov. 1932, p. 4; ibid., 13 Dec. 1932, p. 14; ibid., 4 Dec. 1933, p. 1. The Dauphin County Poor Relief Board had two investigators in Steelton, one for the white poor and one for the "colored" poor. See Department of Welfare Records, R. G. 23, Dauphin County File, Pennsylvania Historical and Museum Commission, Harrisburg.

37. *Patriot,* 4 Dec. 1933, p. 1; ibid., 5 Dec. 1933, p. 17; ibid., 11 Dec. 1933, p. 7.

38. Interviews with John Verbos, 12 July 1971; Steve Suknaic, 6 Oct. 1971; Meter Dragovich, 29 Nov. 1971; and Anonymous, 14 May 1976.

39. *Zajedničar,* 3 May 1933, p. 8; ibid., 8 Mar. 1933, p. 6; ibid., 30 Mar. 1932, p. 9; "Hrvatski Doseljenic u Steeltonu" [Croatian Immigrants in Steelton], *Zajedničar,* 29 Aug. 1934, II, 2.

40. Interviews with Meter Dragovich, 29 Nov. 1971; and Walter Lang, 7 Sept. 1973.

41. *Boyd's Directory of Harrisburg and Steelton,* 1940, p. 729.

42. *No Country for Old Men,* p. 597.

43. *Patriot,* 25 Mar. 1941, p. 1; *Pennsylvania Labor News,* USWA Local 1688, 15 Apr. 1960, p. 1. The identities of the early union leaders were well known by all men interviewed in the study. Dragas and Daniels were singled out most often for their outspoken advocacy of the union. See interviews with Dave Moore, 26 Apr., 1974; Joseph DiSanto, 19 Apr. 1974; Meter Dragovich, 24 Apr. 1974; Hugh Carcella, 23 Apr. 1974. Greater outward support for unions by second generation Slavs than by their immigrant parents was also noted among automobile plant workers by Peter Friedlander, *The Emergence of a UAW Local, 1936–1939* (Pittsburgh: University of Pittsburgh Press, 1975), pp. 37, 97.

44. Interviews with Dave Moore, 26 Apr. 1974; Meter Dragovich, 24 April 1974; John Verbos, 24 Apr. 1974; Joseph DiSanto, 19 Apr. 1974; and Hugh Carcella, 23 Apr. 1974. An interview with Carcella is also on tape at the United Steelworkers of America Oral History Project, Labor Archives, Pennsylvania State University. Brody has argued that the depression experience broke down the system of labor control in corporate industry. It exploded the hopes raised by welfare capitalism during the 1920s and generated a profound sense of betrayal among industrial workers against the corporation. See "Labor and the Great Depression: The Interpretative Prospects," *Labor History* 13 (1972), 242. DiSanto's feeling that the company was responsible for the depression substantiates Brody's point to a degree. The varying outlooks of the second immigrant generation and the rising protest of second-generation Slavs like Verbos and

Horvath, however, suggest that some discontent with social relationships emerged before the entire burden of the depression could be felt. DiSanto was the son of Italian immig;rants and began his occupational career in Steelton in the mill's brick department.

45. *Hrvatski List,* 7 July 1936, p. 3.

46. Interview with Dave Moore, 26 Apr. 1974. The concept of the transition from an ethnic to a class identification and the intermediate step of an "eth-class" was developed by Milton Gordon, *Assimilation in American Life* (New York: Oxford University Press, 1964).

47. *Agreement Between Bethlehem Steel and United Steelworkers of America,* 13 Aug. 1942, copy in files of USWA Local 1688, Harrisburg; interview with Joseph DiSanto, 19 Apr. 1974.

48. Interview with Dave Moore, 26 Apr. 1974. Moore worked on several registration drives. Voting patterns are revealed in *Smull's Legislative Handbook for Pennsylvania* (Harrisburg, 1942, 1946, 1950).

49. *1970 Census,* p. 206. See chapter 1 for population figures from 1920 to 1940.

50. *Local Planning Study of Steelton Borough* (Harrisburg, 1959), p. 10.

51. U.S. Department of Commerce, Bureau of the Census, *Census of Housing, 1960, Part I* (Washington, D.C.: G.P.O., 1963), pp. 7, 96; *Eighteenth Census, 1960,* pp. 410, 415. The only towns in Pennsylvania with lower family income were immigrant coal towns.

52. *Local Planning Study of Steelton Borough,* pp. 1, 10.

CHAPTER 8: CONCLUSION

1. Herbert Gutman, "Class, Status, and Community Power in Nineteenth-Century American Industrial Cities: Patterson, New Jersey: A Case Study," in *Work, Culture, and Society in Industrializing America,* ed. Herbert Gutman (New York: Alfred Knopf, 1976), pp. 234–60.

2. See Maurice R. Stein, *The Eclipse of Community* (Princeton: Princeton University Press, 1960), p. 106. This interpretation is consistent with Robert and Helen Lynd, *Middletown in Transition* (New York: Harcourt, Brace, 1937), pp. 490–91, who argued that the depression was not the sole source of change but that industrialization before 1930 had already informed individuals of the necessity of altering traditional patterns.

3. For a discussion of the rise of rigid social structure produced by industrialization and the role of group consciousness see R. E. Pahl, "The Rural-Urban Continuum," *Readings in Urban Sociology,* ed. R. E. Pahl (London, 1968), pp. 278–79.

4. Handlin, *The Uprooted,* presents a model of industrialization as a destructive force which resulted in immigrant loneliness and familial breakdown.

5. See Rudolph J. Vecoli, "Contadini in Chicago: A Critique of the Uprooted," *Journal of American History* 51 (1964), 404–17; Herbert Gutman,

"Work, Culture, and Society in Industrializing America, 1819–1918," *American Historical Review* 77 (1973), 531–88; David Montgomery, "Immigrant Workers and Scientific Management," in *Immigrants in Industry: Proceedings of the Conference at the Eleutherian Mills,* ed. R. Erlich (Charlottesville, Va.: University of Virginia Press, 1976); Tamara K. Hareven, "The Laborers of Manchester, New Hampshire, 1912–1922," *Labor History* 16 (1975), 2459–65; Virginia Yans McLaughlin, "Patterns of Work and Family Organizations: Buffalo's Italians," *Journal of Interdisciplinary History* 2 (1971), 305–06; Smith, "Lay Initiative," pp. 216, 222–46.

6. For a discussion of how industrialization could evoke feelings of both traditionalism as well as change, see Alan Dawley and Paul Faler, "Working-Class Culture and Politics in the Industrial Revolution: Sources of Loyalism and Rebellion," *Journal of Social History* 9 (1976), 466–80.

7. See Robert K. Berkhoffer, "The New or the Old Social History," *Reviews in American History* 1 (1973), 25.

8. Michael Frisch, *Town Into City: Springfield, Massachusetts and the Meaning of Community, 1840–1880* (Cambridge, Mass.: Harvard University Press, 1972), pp. 48–49.

9. William Kornblum, *Blue Collar Community* (Chicago: University of Chicago Press, 1974), pp. 35, 187.

10. During the 1920s an investigator in another Pennsylvania steel town, Braddock, found Slovaks reluctant to move. When Slovaks were forced to seek work in Detroit and Cleveland during a depression in 1921 and 1922, they quickly returned when the Braddock mills began to hire again. On the other hand, investigators found that British and Americans in Braddock invariably talked of the day when they could save enough money to move elsewhere. See Gwendolyn Shand, *The Sociological Aspects of an Industrial Community* (Pittsburgh, 1923), pp. 202–03.

11. See Warner and Srole, *The Social System of American Ethnic Groups,* pp. 2–3.

12. Thernstrom, *The Other Bostonians,* pp. 182–86.

Bibliographical Essay

UNPUBLISHED SOURCES

This study of Steelton was based on a variety of sources. Unpublished manuscript collections contained significant information on certain questions. The political activities of black leaders, for instance, were detailed in the Samuel W. Pennypacker correspondence. The Croatian collection at the Immigration History Research Center of the University of Minnesota offered unique items such as *Naša Nada,* a Croatian journal. The most important manuscript materials include the Pennsylvania Steel Company Collection at the Bethlehem Steel Company Library, Bethlehem, Pennsylvania; the small group of papers concerning the Pennsylvania Steel Company at the Eleutherian Mills Historical Library, Greenville, Delaware; the Samuel M. Felton Papers at the Historical Society of Pennsylvania; the George P. Medrick Papers, Labor Archives, Penn State University; the Samuel W. Pennypacker Papers at the Pennsylvania Historical and Museum Commission; and the Croatian and Slovene collections at the Immigration History Research Center.

Local unpublished documents and vital statistics were also rich in details on steelworkers. Volumes of the Annual Enumeration of All Persons, Property and Things for Steelton, 1900–1925, are at the Dauphin County Court House and contain special surveys of immigrants for tax purposes in 1903 and 1905. These documents indicate which citizens owned property, the amount of property held, and which individuals rented. Marriage License Dockets for Dauphin County from 1890 to 1940 (on microfilm at the Pennsylvania Historical and Museum Commission) identify applicants for marriage licenses by race, place of birth, occupation, and residence; the names, birthplaces, and occupations of the parents of applicants were also recorded. Such information was essential for identifying the bulk of immigrant children. Other unpublished sources used are listed below.

Commonwealth of Pennsylvania v. George Minoff, Transcript. Dauphin County Court House, 1948.

Drawbaugh, E. Allen. "Early History of Steelton." Manuscript in author's possession.

Golab, Carolyn. "The Polish Communities of Philadelphia, 1870–1920: Immigrant Distribution and Adaptation in Urban America." Ph.D. dissertation, University of Pennsylvania, 1971.

"Jedna Pecena Kosos, 1933." Mimeographed document in possession of John Verbos of Steelton.

Jutronic, Djnja. "Serbo-Croatian and American English in Contact: A Sociolinguistic Study of the Serbo-Croatian Community in Steelton, Pennsylvania." Ph.D. dissertation, Pennsylvania State University, 1971.

Naturalization Service: Position and Record, 1910–1917. Prothonotary's Office, Dauphin County Court House.

Passenger Lists of Vessels Arriving at Philadelphia, 1883–1943. Microfilm Series T–840. Federal Archives and Records Center, Philadelphia.

St. Mary's Croatian Church, Steelton. Records of Internment, 1898–1930.

St. Nicholas Serbian Orthodox Church, Steelton. Records of Interment, 1905–1925.

ORAL INTERVIEWS

Among the primary sources for the study are seventy-seven interviews; twenty-one of them were taped and constitute the recorded oral history. The tapes and the remaining survey schedules are on file at the Pennsylvania Historical and Museum Commission, Harrisburg. Most persons interviewed were either immigrants or their children, and all lived through the events which were discussed. Tom Benkovic, Lewis Zuvic, and Gustav Belsak emigrated from Croatia. Benkovic was the earliest to arrive, in 1902. Louis Lescanéc migrated from Slovenia. Several other respondents were born abroad but had always claimed American birth and asked that that their "secret" be kept, a fact which suggests something of what it meant to be an immigrant. Joseph DiSanto was a steelworker and son of Italian immigrant parents. Hugh Carcella was born in Italy. Dave Moore was raised on a farm in South Carolina and was active in organizing other blacks. Elcora McClane and Charlene Conyers were daughters of a local black educator. M. Harvey Taylor was a powerful political figure, and Walter B. Lang was a former superintendent at the steel plant. The following are the taped interviews cited in the text.

Anonymous, Steelton, 14 May 1976.
John Badovinac, Pittsburgh, 4 Jan. 1972.
Gustav Belsak, Steelton, 25 Aug. 1972.
Thomas Benkovic, Steelton, 11 July 1971.
Charles Bojanic, 13 Aug. 1971.
Margaret Dailey, Steelton, 27 Aug. 1971.
George Dimoff, Steelton, 29 Oct. 1971.
Meter Dragovich, Harrisburg, 27 Oct. 1971; 29 Nov. 1971.
Mary Jurina, Steelton, 30 June 1971.

Hope Kormuschoff, Harrisburg, 19 Sept. 1971.
Jerome Kucan, Steelton, 30 June 1971.
Walter B. Lang, Harrisburg, 7 Sept. 1973.
Louis and Catherine Lescanec, Bressler, 17 June 1976.
Anna Lopert, Steelton, 17 Aug. 1971.
Elcora McClane and Charlene Conyers, Steelton, 14 Aug. 1971.
Kero Risteff, Harrisburg, 31 Aug. 1971.
Steve Suknaic, Harrisburg, 6 Oct. 1971.
M. Harvey Taylor, Harrisburg, 14 Feb. 1971.
Martin Tezak, John Tezak, and Mary Krasovic, Steelton, 25 Mar. 1976.
John Verbos, Steelton, 12 July 1971.
Lewis Zuvic, Steelton, 25 Aug. 1972.

NEWSPAPERS

The development of social relations in the steel town was most clearly revealed through the local press and immigrant and black newspapers. The *Steelton Reporter*, consulted from 1884 to 1913, was the chief journal in the community and consistently supported the views of the steel firm. The only newspaper to criticize the dominance of the company was the *Harrisburg Call*, which was published from 1885 until 1897. Immigrant papers were of obvious value, especially *Zajedničar*, 1908–1936, at the Croatian Fraternal Union in Pittsburgh. Other relevant newspapers include the following:

Harrisburg Telegraph. 1891–1918.
Harrisburg Patriot. 1890–1938.
Iron Age. 1891, 1916, 1918, 1919.
Iron Moulders Monthly Journal. 1891.
Jugoslavia. 1921–22.
Lebanon Daily News. 1906.
Narodni List. 1898–1919.
Narodne Noviny. 1919.
Radnik. 1925.
Steelton Item. 1881–83.
Steelton Press. 1903–12.
Zanje. 1920–21.

CENSUS REPORTS

Federal census material were also invaluable in identifying and tracing individuals and community population changes. Unpublished census manuscripts, of course, allow the researcher to identify individuals and their place of birth. The 1890 manuscripts were destroyed and were not available for use. The manuscripts for the Tenth Census, 1880, were consulted on microfilm at the

Pennsylvania State Archives. The manuscripts for the Twelfth Census, 1900, were finally opened for research in January, 1974 and are available on microfilm only at the National Archives and its regional branches. Published aggregate census reports have been issued regularly. Those most useful for this study were:

Tenth Census
> Manuscript schedules of the tenth census, 1880. Microfilm, Pennsylvania State Archives.

Eleventh Census
> U.S. Department of the Interior, Census Office. *Report of the Population of the United States at the Eleventh Census, 1890, Part I.* Washington, D.C.: G.P.O., 1895.

Twelfth Census
> Manuscript schedules of the twelfth census, 1900. National Archives, Philadelphia.

Thirteenth Census
> U.S. Department of Commerce and Labor, Bureau of the Census. *Thirteenth Census of the United States, 1910, Abstract of the Census with Supplement for Pennsylvania.* Washington, D.C.: G.P.O., 1913.

Fourteenth Census
> U.S. Department of Commerce, Bureau of the Census. *Fourteenth Census of the United States, 1920, III: Population.* Washington, D.C.: G.P.O., 1922.

Fifteenth Census
> U.S. Department of Commerce, Bureau of the Census. *Fifteenth Census of the United States, 1930, Population, Part IV.* Washington, D.C.: G.P.O., 1932.

Sixteenth Census
> U.S. Department of Commerce, Bureau of the Census. *Sixteenth Census of the United States, 1940, Population II: Characteristics of the Population.* Washington, D.C.: G.P.O., 1943.

Eighteenth Census
> U.S. Department of Commerce, Bureau of the Census. *Eighteenth Census of the United States, 1960, Characteristics of the Population.* Washington, D.C.: G.P.O., 1962.

Nineteenth Census
> U.S. Department of Commerce, Bureau of the Census. *1970 Census of the Population, Characteristics of the Population, Part 40.* Washington, D.C.: G.P.O., 1973.

PUBLIC DOCUMENTS

Documents issued by federal and state agencies not only offered relevant statistical data on employment and population but also often focused on labor conditions. They included the *Annual Report of the Secretary of Internal Affairs*, published by the Commonwealth of Pennsylvania. These volumes for the period between 1888 and 1912 were consulted frequently. After 1912 the reports were published by the newly created Department of Labor and Industry. The *First Annual Report of the Commissioner of Labor and Industry* (Harrisburg, 1913) was the most extensive survey of immigration ever done by the state. The details of the company union plan of Bethlehem Steel after 1918 are spelled out in the *Decisions of the National Labor Relations Board* 14 (Washington, D.C., 1939). The U.S. Immigration Commission, *Reports of the United States Immigration Commission: Immigrants in Industries, Part 2: Iron and Steel*, 2 vols., S. Doc. 633, 61st Cong., 2nd sess., serial 5669 (1911), included Steelton as one of its survey towns and left a report of several hundred pages on Steelton's immigrants which proved invaluable. Other documents which were relied upon heavily are cited below:

Commonwealth of Pennsylvania. *Inventory of Unemployed Persons.* 3 vols. Harrisburg, 1934.
———. *Legislative Record.* Harrisburg, 1895.
———. *Legislative Record.* Harrisburg, 1897.
Pennsylvania Department of Internal Affairs. *Sixth Industrial Directory.* Harrisburg, 1928.
———. *Seventh Industrial Directory.* Harrisburg, 1931.
———. *Eighth Industrial Directory.* Harrisburg, 1936.
———. *Ninth Industrial Directory.* Harrisburg, 1938.
Pennsylvania Department of Welfare. *Negro Survey of Pennsylvania.* Harrisburg, 1927.
U.S. Congress. Senate. Committee on Education and Labor. Hearings. *Investigation of the Strike in Steel Industries.* 66th Cong., 1st. sess. 1919.
U.S. Congress. Senate. *Report on Conditions of Employment in the Iron and Steel Industry in the United States.* s. 4 vols. Doc. 110, 62nd Cong., 1st sess., serial 6098. 1913.
U.S. Department of Labor. *Negro Migration 1916–1917.* Washington, D.C., 1919.

BOOKS

Published accounts were quite useful. The annual reports of the Pennsylvania Steel Company, 1890–1915, were available at the Bethlehem Steel Company Library. *Boyd's Directory of Harrisburg and Steelton* provided data for the study of occupational and geographical mobility between 1888 and 1925. *Polks Directory* covered the period after 1930. Vital to the study of the Croatians in Steelton was *Spomen Knijizica Četrdeset Godišnjice, 1898–1938, Hrvatske Rimokatolicke Župe Uznesenja Bl. Dj. Marije* (Steelton, 1938) which was written by immigrants themselves. The activities of the largest Croatian fraternal society in Steelton and a list of its members can be found in *Spomen-Knijiga 25 Godišnjica Hrvatsko-Radničko Podporno Društvo, St. Lovo, 1895–1920* (Steelton, 1920).

Adamic, Louis. *Dynamite, The Story of Class Violence in America.* New York, 1931.
––––––. *From Many Lands.* New York: Harper, 1949.
Albert, George. *History of Westmoreland County, Pennsylvania.* Philadelphia, 1882.
AME Church. *Historical Record.* Steelton, 1905.
Balch, Emily G. *Our Slavic Fellow Citizens.* New York: Charities Publication Committee 1910.
Barton, Josef John. *Peasants and Strangers: Italians, Rumanians, and Slovaks in an American City, 1890–1950.* Cambridge, Mass.: Harvard University Press, 1975.
Binning, Arthur C. *Pennsylvania's Iron and Steel Industry.* Gettysburg. 1954.
Brody, David. *Labor in Crisis: The Steel Strike of 1919.* Philadelphia: Lippincott, 1965.
––––––. *Steelworkers in America.* Cambridge, Mass.: Harvard University Press, 1960.
Brooks, Robert. *As Steel Goes.* New Haven: Yale University Press, 1940.
Buder, Stanley. *Pullman, An Experiment in Industrial Order and Community Planning, 1880–1930.* New York: Oxford University Press, 1967.
Bujak, Franciszek. *Zmiaca-Wies Powiatu Limanowskiego: Stosunki Gospodarcze i Spoliczne.* Krakow, 1903.
Byington, Margaret. *Homestead: The Households of a Mill Town.* New York: Russell Sage Foundation, 1910.
Colakovic, Branko M. *Yugoslav Migrations to America.* San Francisco: R and E Associates, 1973.
Cole, Donald B. *Immigrant City: Lawrence, Massachusetts, 1845–1921.* Chapel Hill: University of North Carolina Press, 1963.
Consecration of Iconostas and Fortieth Anniversary of Circle of Serbian Church. Steelton, 1943.
Consecration and Sixtieth Anniversary, Holy Annunciation Macedonian-Bulgarian Orthodox Church. Steelton, 1970.
Cotter, Arundel. *The Story of Bethlehem Steel.* New York: Moody, 1916.
Davis, Horace B. *Labor and Steel.* New York: International Publishers, 1933.
Diamond Jubilee of St. Mary's Croatian Church. Steelton, 1958.
Dollar, Charles M., and Jensen, Richard. *Historian's Guide to Statistics.* New York: Holt, Rinehart, and Winston, 1971.
DuBois, William E. B. *The Philadelphia Negro.* New York: B. Blom, 1967.
Egle, W. H., *et al. Commemorative Biographical Encyclopedia of Dauphin County Containing Sketches of Prominent and Representative Citizens and Many of the Early Scotch-Irish Settlers.* Chambersburg, Pa., 1896.
Egle, William H. *History of the Counties of Dauphin and Lebanon.* Philadelphia, 1883.

Erickson, Charlotte. *American Industry and the European Immigrant, 1860–1885.* Cambridge, Mass.: Harvard University Press, 1957.

Espenshade, A. Howry. *Pennsylvania Place Names.* State College, Pa.: Pennsylvania State College, 1925.

Eyster, Warren. *No County for Old Men.* New York: Random House, 1955.

Fiftieth Anniversary, Holy Annunciation Macedonian-Bulgarian Church. Steelton, 1959.

Fiftieth Anniversary of the St. Nicholas Serbian Orthodox Church. Steelton, 24 May 1953.

Fiftieth Anniversary of West Side School. Steelton, 1940.

Foster, William Z. *The Great Steel Strike and Its Lessons.* New York: International Publishers, 1920.

Frazier, E. Franklin. *The Negro Church in America.* New York: Schocken Books, 1964.

Gazi, Stjepan. *Croatian Immigration to Allegheny County, 1882–1914.* Pittsburgh: Croatian Fraternal Union, 1956.

Godcharles, Frederic A. *Chronicles of Central Pennsylvania.* 4 vols. New York: Lewis, 1944.

Golden Jubilee of St. Ann's Italian Catholic Church. Steelton, 1953.

Golden Jubilee of St. James Church. Steelton, 1929.

Govorchin, Gerald G. *Americans from Yugoslavia.* Gainesville, Fla.: Florida State University Press, 1961.

Handlin, Oscar. *The Uprooted.* Boston: Little, Brown, 1951.

Higham, John. *Strangers in the Land.* New York: Atheneum, 1971.

History of St. Peter's. Steelton, 1959.

Holbrook, Stewart H. *Iron Brew: A Century of American Ore and Steel.* New York: Macmillan, 1939.

Interchurch World Movement. *Report on the Steel Strike of 1919.* New York: Harcourt, Brace, and Howe, 1920.

Klein, H. M. J., and Klein, F. S. *The State Young Men's Christian Association of Pennsylvania, 1869–1969.* Harrisburg, 1969.

Laverty, George L. *History of Medicine in Dauphin County, Pennsylvania.* Harrisburg, 1967.

Marohnic, Josip. *Popis Hrvata U America.* Allegheny, Pa.: Marohnic, 1900.

Nakoff, David. *A History of the Macedonian-Bulgarian Church of Steelton, Pennsylvania.* Steelton, 1939.

Neidle, Cecyle. *The New Americans.* New York: Twayne, 1967.

Nevins, Allan. *Abram S. Hewitt.* New York: Harper, 1935.

Olds, Marshall. *An Analysis of the Interchurch World Movement Report on the Steel Strike.* New York: G. P. Putnam, 1923.

Pennsylvania Manual. Harrisburg, 1933.

Pozdrav in Castitke, 1909–1945. Steelton: St. Peter's Church, 1945.

Prpic, George J. *The Croatian Immigrants in America.* New York: Philosophical Library, 1971.

Roberts, Peter. *The New Immigration*. New York: Macmillan, 1912.
St. Ann's School Dedication. Steelton, 1961.
St. John the Evangelist Church. *Dedication Booklet*. Steelton, 1953.
Schroeder, Gertrude. *The Growth of Major Steel Companies*. Baltimore, 1953.
750 Years of the Serbian Church, 1219–1969. Cleveland, 1969.
Shand, Gwendolyn. *Sociological Aspects of An Industrial Community*. Pittsburgh, 1923.
Souvenir Booklet, Hygenic Hose Company. Steelton, 1910.
Souvenir Booklet of St. James Church. Steelton, 1900.
Stevens, S. K. *Pennsylvania, Titan of Industry*. 3 vols. New York: Lewis, 1948.
Temin, Peter. *Iron and Steel in Nineteenth-Century America:* Cambridge, Mass.: Harvard University Press, 1964.
Thernstrom, Stephan. *Poverty and Progress: Social Mobility in a Nineteenth-Century City*. Cambridge, Mass.: Harvard University Press, 1964.
———. *The Other Bostonians: Poverty and Progress in the American Metropolis, 1880–1970*. Cambridge, Mass.: Harvard University Press, 1973.
30th Anniversary of the Founding of St. Peter's Church. Steelton, 1939.
Warne, Frank J. *The Slav Invasion and the Mine Workers*. Philadelphia: J. B. Lippincott, 1904.
Warner, W. Lloyd, and Srole, Leo. *The Social Systems of American Ethnic Groups*. New Haven: Yale University Press, 1945.
Wright, Richard. *The Negro in Pennsylvania*. New York: Arno Press, 1969.
Zacetek Slovenske Naselbine v Steeltonu, Pennsylvania. Steelton, 1939.
Zaciatky Ceskej Slovenskej Emigracie Do U.S.A. Bratislava, 1971.

ARTICLES

Appel, John J. "American Negro and Immigrant Experience: Similarities and Differences." *American Quarterly* 18 (1966), 95–103.
Butler, Jon. "Communities and Congregations: The Black Church in St. Paul, 1860–1900." *Journal of Negro History* 56 (1971), 118–34.
"Employment of Negroes in Pennsylvania Industries." *Monthly Labor Review* 12 (1921).
Griffen, Clyde. "Making It in America: Social Mobility in Mid-Nineteenth Century Poughkeepsie." *New York History* 51 (1970), 479–99.
———. "Occupational Mobility in Nineteenth-Century America: Problems and Possibilities." *Journal of Social History* 5 (1972), 310–30.
Gutman, Herbert. "The Worker's Search for Power: Labor in the Gilded Age." In *The Gilded Age*, ed. H. Wayne Morgan. Syracuse, N.Y.: Syracuse University Press, 1963.
Higgs, Robert. "Race, Skills, and Earnings: American Immigrants in 1909." *Journal of Economic History* 31 (1971), 420–28.
Hoffman, David. "The Meaning of the Kolo Club 'Marian' in the Steelton, Pennsylvania Croatian Community." *Keystone Folklore Quarterly*, Fall 1971, pp. 115–31.

"Hrvatska Zupa v Steeltonu, Pennsylvania." *Naša Nada,* 1932, pp. 92–97.

"Iz Povijesti Hrvi Zupe U Steeltonu, Pennsylvania." *Naša Nada,* 1928, pp. 169–78.

Johnson, Charles. "Substitution of Negro Labor for European Migrant Labor." *Proceedings of the National Conference for Social Work,* 1926, pp. 317–27.

Kent, W. H. "History of the 100 Years of the Harrisburg and Dauphin County Y.M.C.A." *Dauphin County Historical Review* 4 (1955), 4–16.

Kirk, Gordon W., and Kirk, Carolyn Tyirin. "Migration, Mobility, and the Transformation of the Occupational Structure in an Immigrant Community: Holland, Michigan, 1850–1880." *Journal of Social History* 7 (1974), 142–64.

Kirk, R. G. "Hrvatski Harlequin." *Saturday Evening Post,* 6 August 1927, pp. 12–13.

Knights, Peter R. "A Method for Estimating Census Under-Enumeration." *Historical Methods Newsletter* 3 (December 1969), 5–8.

Larkin, Emmett. "The Devotional Revolution in Ireland, 1850–1875." *American Historical Review* 77 (1972), 625–52.

Milnor, Mark T. "Veterans Organizations of the United States with Special Reference to Dauphin County, Pennsylvania." *Dauphin County Historical Review* 5 (1956), 23–28.

Modell, John, and Hareven, Tamara K. "Urbanization and the Malleable Household: An Examination of Boarding and Lodging in American Families." *Journal of Marriage and the Family* 35 (1973), 467–79.

Mulacek, Ivan. "Nase Iseljavanje v Stevlikah." *Cas* 7 (Ljubljana, Slovenia, 1913), 26–29.

Nahirny, Vladimir C., and Fishman, Joshua A. "American Immigrant Groups: Ethnic Identification and the Problem of Generations." *Sociological Review* 13 (1965), 311–26.

Pavich, Chedomir. "Serbs and Serbian Organizations." *American Srobran,* 19 June 1918, pp. 1–2.

Robinson, Jesse. "The Amalgamated Association of Iron and Steel and Tin Workers." *Johns Hopkins University Studies in Historical and Political Science* 38 (1920).

Roucek, Joseph S. "The Yugoslav Immigrants in America." *American Journal of Sociology* 40 (1935), 602–11.

Roucek, Joseph S., and Brown, Francis J. "The Problem of Negro and European Immigrant Minorities: Some Comparisons and Contrasts." *Journal of Negro Education* 3 (1939), 229–312.

Scott, Joan W. "The Glassworkers of Caramaux, 1850–1900." In *Nineteenth Century Cities,* ed. Stephan Thernstrom and Richard Sennett, pp. 3–48. New Haven: Yale University Press, 1969.

Sherman, Richard B. "Johnstown vs. the Negro: Southern Migrants and the Exodus of 1923." *Pennsylvania History* 30 (1963), 454–64.

Smith, Timothy L. "Lay Initiative in the Religious Life of American Immigrants, 1880–1940." In *Anonymous Americans*, ed. Tamara K. Hareven. Englewood Cliffs, N.J.: Prentice Hall, 1971.

———. "Religious Denominations as Ethnic Communities: A Regional Case Study." *Church History* 35 (1966), 207–27.

Thernstrom, Stephan. "Immigrants and WASPS: Ethnic Differences in Occupational Mobility in Boston, 1890–1940." In *Nineteenth Century Cities*, ed. Stephan Thernstrom and Richard Sennett. New Haven: Yale University Press, 1969.

Umek, Emma. "Prispevki K Zgdovini I Zseljevanja Is Kranjske v Ameriko v Letih, 1910–1913" [Contributions to the History of Emigration from Carniola to America, 1910–1913]. *Slovenski Izseljenski Koledar* 14 (1967), 199–207.

Verbos, John. "The St. Lawrence Story." *Zajedničar*, 8 Apr. 1970, p. 4; 15 Apr. 1970, p. 4.

Vranes, Milan. "Odsjek 13u Steeltonu Odrazao Sevcano Otvorenje Svog Novog Doma." *Zajedničar*, 23 Apr. 1969, p. 2.

Wolfinger, Raymond E. "The Development and Persistence of Ethnic Voting." In *American Ethnic Politics*, ed. Lawrence Fuchs. New York, Harper & Row, 1968.

Worthman, Paul. "Working-Class Mobility in Birmingham, Alabama, 1880–1914." In *Anonymous Americans*, ed. Tamara K. Hareven. Englewood Cliffs, N.J.: Prentice-Hall, 1971.

Index

Accidents, 38
Accommodation to industrial society, 152
Amalgamated Association of Iron and Steel Workers, 40, 41
AME Church, 94, 95, 107
American Federation of Labor, 45, 46, 47–49
Americanization, 89–92
American Protective Association, 81
Ancient Order of Hibernians, 7
Anti-Saloon League, 99
Azbe, Francis, 113, 116

Benevolent Association, 86
Benkovic, Thomas, 25, 29, 114, 136
Bent, Luther, 6, 7, 8, 11, 12, 173n27
Bent, Quincy, 140, 172n27
Bethlehem Steel Corporation, 35, 45–49, 122, 138, 140–141, 143. *See also* Pennsylvania Steel Company; Strike
Blacks, 5, 15; residential segregation of, 6; recruitment of, 24; household composition of, 31, 33; in work force, 36, 42, 147; and AFL, 48; persistence rate of, 58–59; occupational distribution of, 65–66, 67–68, 135–36; occupational mobility of, 72–73; school for, 95, 108–10; in political office, 97; as property owners, 98, 187n81; religious organizations, 107; ethnic organizations, 108; in union, 145–47

Blackwell, Peter, 95–98, 109, 140
Boarders, 32
Boardinghouses, 25, 26–27, 78–79, 81, 90
Bolshevism, 46
Bozic, Joseph D., 115
Brandenberg, 27, 28
Bulgarians, 15, 20, 24; in work force, 37; in depression of 1907–08, 55, 88; school for, 89–90; ethnic customs of, 104, 106, 128; ethnic organizations of, 106–07; political activity of, 107, 117–18, 130–31; marriage partners of, 131; rival factions of, 193n14

Campbell, Harry, 7, 8
Career immobility, 68
Centennial of Dauphin County, 13
Chain migration, 26–28
Charity Committee, 91
Churches, 6, 8, 9, 102, 103–08, 112, 114–17, 121
Cigar factory, 22, 143
CIO, 141, 145
Citizenship papers, 127
Citizens' Railway Company, 10, 11
Civic Club, 91, 140
Civil Works Administration, 143
Colored Young Men's Christian Association, 90
Committee on Steelton Charities, 89
Community leaders, 8, 9

209